VYING FOR VICTORY

VYING FOR VICTORY

The 1923 General Election in the Irish Free State

edited by

Elaine Callinan, Mel Farrell and Thomas Tormey

UNIVERSITY COLLEGE DUBLIN PRESS
PREAS CHOLÁISTE OLLSCOILE BHAILE ÁTHA CLIATH
2023

First published 2023
by University College Dublin Press
UCD Humanities Institute, Room H103,
Belfield,
Dublin 4

www.ucdpress.ie

Text and notes © the editors, 2023

ISBN 978-19-1-08207-04

All rights reserved. No part of this publication may be reproduced, stored in a retrieval system, or transmitted in any form or by any means, electronic, photocopying, recording or otherwise without the prior permission of the publisher.

CIP data available from the British Library

The right of the editors to be identified as the editors of this work has been asserted by them

Typeset in Dublin by Gough Typesetting Limited
Text design by Lyn Davies
Printed in England on acid-free paper by
CPI Antony Rowe, Chippenham, Wiltshire.

Contents

	Dedication	vii
	Acknowledgements	ix
	List of Figures and Tables	xi
	List of Abbreviations	xiii
	Editor and Contributors	xv
1	Introduction *Mel Farrell*	1
2	'Safety first': Cumann na nGaedheal's election campaign in August 1923 *Mel Farrell*	11
3	'Nothing but a bullet will stop me': Éamon de Valera and the 1923 General Election *David McCullagh*	27
4	Searching for the normal: The Farmers' and Labour Parties in the 1923 Election *Jason Knirck*	38
5	Political propaganda in the 1923 General Election: methods and themes *Elaine Callinan*	50
6	'The only hope was to work the Treaty': Local newspaper coverage of the 1923 General Election in Kerry *Owen O'Shea*	63
7	'Return them to power with sufficient strength to complete their work': the Roman Catholic Church and the 1923 General Election *Daithí Ó Corráin*	77
8	'Without distinction of sex': The roles of women in the 1923 General Election *Claire McGing*	87
9	The AARIR and the 1923 General Election in the United States *Regina Donlon*	99
10	Ireland and the 'end of the European crisis,' 1923–24 *Gearóid Barry*	110
11	From revolution to democracy: Analysing the 1923 General Election *Elaine Callinan*	121
	Appendix 1: Election Results by Constituency	132
	Appendix 2: Election Results by Provinces	136
	Appendix 3: 1923 Election Results by Constituency, based on First Preferences	141
	Notes	145
	Select Bibliography	169
	Index	171

This collection is dedicated to all those who put themselves forward for election and played their part in consolidating democracy in the aftermath of the Civil War

Acknowledgements

The idea for this book was first discussed in February 2022 and a plan formed to draw together a range of perspectives on the important 1923 General Election. The aim was to mark the August centenary and offer new insights on a key moment in the Irish State's democratic development. We knew this was an ambitious target, but we were determined to meet it.

To accomplish this goal takes help and we are extremely grateful to each contributor for the timely manner in which they responded to our deadlines and various queries. We are delighted with the breadth and depth of topics covered in this volume and wish to acknowledge that the book would not have been possible without the contribution of the authors of each chapter.

We are indebted to Noelle Moran for her support and enthusiasm. She believed in this project from the beginning and showed great patience with us editors when deadlines were inevitably stretched. We extend our gratitude to all the team at UCD Press. We thank the two peer-reviewers for their constructive comments which have served to strengthen the book.

On behalf of all the authors, we wish to thank the various institutions and repositories at which research was carried out, and we are grateful to the National Library of Ireland for all images included in the text.

The editors would like to thank our families, friends and colleagues who have supported and advised us throughout the process of finalising this book.

Elaine Callinan and Mel Farrell would like to specifically thank Carlow College, St Patrick's for its generous financial support towards this book.

Elaine Callinan, Mel Farrell and Thomas Tormey
July 2023

List of Figures and Tables

Figures

Figure 1	Crowd in attendance at a Cumann na nGaedheal election rally in St. Stephen's Green, Dublin, 1923, NLI, Hugh Kennedy papers, KEN6, courtesy of the National Library of Ireland.
Figure 2	'Miss McSwiney's friends are concentrating on explosives, gas and fire: vote for Cumann na nGaedheal candidates', Cumann na nGaedheal campaign leaflet for the 1923 election, NLI, Pamphlet volume D144 (Item 53), courtesy of the National Library of Ireland.
Figure 3	'A Peculiar "Leader"', Cumann na nGaedheal campaign leaflet for the general election of 1923 for the Kerry constituency, NLI, Pamphlet volume D144 (Item 54), courtesy of the National Library of Ireland.
Figure 4	'"Arguments" Against the Treaty', NLI, EPH B158, Courtesy of the National Library of Ireland
Figure 5	Keeping Ireland Down Poster, NLI, EPH C200, Image courtesy of the National Library of Ireland
Figure 6	Election Results by Constituency, based on First Preferences
Figure 7	Leinster First Preference Voting Results based on Constituency Voting Percentages
Figure 8	Munster First Preference Voting Results based on Constituency Voting Percentages
Figure 9	Connacht First Preference Voting Results based on Constituency Voting Preferences
Figure 10	Ulster (in Irish Free State) First Preference Voting Results based on Constituency Voting Preferences

Tables

Table 1	Total number of seats by party

List of Abbreviations

AARIR	American Association for the Recognition of the Irish Republic
BN	*Belfast Newsletter*
BNF	Bibliothèque Nationale de France
CC	*Clare Champion*
CCCA	Cork City & County Archives
CE	*Cork Examiner*
CPA	Cork Progressive Association
DEM	*Dublin Evening Mail*
EH	*Evening Herald*
FJ	*Freeman's Journal*
FOIF	Friends of Irish Freedom
IFU	Irish Farmers' Union
II	*Irish Independent*
IPP	Irish Parliamentary Party
IRA	Irish Republican Army
IT	*Irish Times*
KDA	Killaloe Diocesan Archives
LL	*Longford Leader*
NAI	National Archives of Ireland
NLI	National Library of Ireland
NLT	*Nationalist and Leinster Times*
NUI	National University of Ireland
TD	Teachta Dála
UCDA	University College Dublin Archives
UMich	University of Michigan Library
WE	*Westmeath Examiner*

Editors and Contributors

Gearóid Barry is a lecturer in modern European history at NUI Galway, specialising in the First and Second World Wars and the interwar peace movement. His book *The Disarmament of Hatred: Marc Sangnier, French Catholicism and the Legacy of the First World War, 1914–1945* (2012) won the Scott Bills Memorial Prize from the Peace History Society (USA) in 2015. Co-editor of *Nations, and Colonial Peripheries in World War One* (2016) and *1916 in Global Context* (2018), he has most recently co-edited with Róisín Healy, *Family Histories of World War II: Survivors and Descendants* (2021). He has also contributed thematic articles for '1914–1918-online: The International Encyclopaedia of the First World War', and to journals such as the *Journal of Contemporary History* (2015).

Elaine Callinan obtained an MPhil and PhD from Trinity College Dublin. She is currently a lecturer in modern Irish History at Carlow College, St Patrick's on undergraduate and postgraduate programmes. Her book *Electioneering and Propaganda in Ireland 1917–1920: Votes, Violence and Victory* was published by Four Courts Press in 2020. She has peer reviewed Irish history publications and also published in a number of public history forums. She has chapters in edited collections such as *Southern Irish Loyalism 1912–1949*, edited by Conor Morrissey and Brian Hughes (2020) and *The Irish Regional Press 1892–2018: Revival, Revolution and Republic* (2018), edited by James O'Donnell and Mark O'Brien.

Regina Donlon, PhD is a lecturer in nineteenth-century Irish history at Carlow College, St Patrick's. She was awarded a prestigious Irish Research Council Post-Doctoral Research Fellowship in the Moore Institute at NUI Galway for a project entitled 'The Tuke Irish in Minnesota: Transnational analysis of assisted emigration to the American Midwest, 1880–1930'. She has peer reviewed and published journal articles, and published the book *German and Irish Immigrants in the Midwestern United States, 1850–1900* with Palgrave Macmillan in 2018.

Mel Farrell is currently a lecturer in history at Carlow College, St Patrick's having previously lectured in Dublin City University, Maynooth University and University College Dublin. His book, *Party Politics in a New Democracy: The Irish Free State, 1922–37*, was published by Palgrave Macmillan in 2017. He was a co-editor, with Ciara Meehan and Jason Knirck, of *A Formative Decade: Ireland in the 1920s* published by Irish Academic Press in 2015 and was a contributor to *The Treaty: Debating and Establishing the Irish State*, edited by Mícheál Ó Fathartaigh and Liam Weeks (2018). He has also published five peer-reviewed journal articles in *Éire-Ireland*, *New Hibernia Review* and *Parliamentary History*.

Jason Knirck is a professor of Irish and British history at Central Washington University. His work focuses on the political culture of the Irish revolution and its aftermath, including such topics as gender, empire, state-building, and democracy. His newest book, entitled *Democracy and Dissent*, analyses the tension between Sinn Féin's ostensible commitment to multiparty democracy and its desire to create a postcolonial state dominated by a united national movement.

David McCullagh is a journalist with Ireland's public service broadcaster, RTÉ. He was a political correspondent for twelve years, a presenter of current affairs programme *Prime Time* for seven years and is currently a presenter of the *Six One News*. He is also the author of five books: *A Makeshift Majority: A History of the First Inter-Party Government*; *The Reluctant Taoiseach: A Biography of John A. Costello;* a two-volume biography of Éamon de Valera, *Rise: 1882–1932* and *Rule: 1932–1975*; and, most recently, a book for children, *The Great Irish Politics Book*.

Claire McGing is a member of the senior management team at the Institute of Art, Design and Technology (IADT), Dún Laoghaire, where she has strategic oversight of equality, diversity and inclusion. A social scientist, she has published extensively on gender politics and electoral politics in Ireland. Recent publications include 'The Seanad election: Voting in unprecedented times' in *How Ireland Voted 2020* (2021) and 'Women's political representation in Dáil Éireann in revolutionary and post-revolutionary Ireland' in *Women and the Irish Revolution* (2020). She has also authored several reports for policy makers. Claire was formerly a John and Pat Hume Scholar and Irish Research Council Scholar at Maynooth University.

Daithí Ó Corráin is a lecturer in history in the School of History & Geography at Dublin City University and is chair of the MA in History Programme Board. A former Government of Ireland Research Scholar in the Humanities and Social Sciences, he completed his PhD at Trinity College Dublin in 2004. Daithí's broad research interests are nineteenth and twentieth-century Irish political, cultural and religious history. At present he specialises in the history of the Irish Revolution 1912–23 and in the history of Irish Catholicism. He is co-author of the acclaimed *The Dead of the Irish Revolution* (2020), and co-editor of the landmark *Irish Revolution* series published by Four Courts Press.

Owen O'Shea is the author of several books on history and politics in his native Kerry, *Ballymacandy: The Story of a Kerry Ambush* (2021) and he is the author of *No Middle Path: The Civil War in Kerry* (Merrion Press, 2022). He co-authored/edited books on Kerry and the 1916 Rising and a political history of Kerry over the last century. Owen is an Irish Research Council-funded PhD student at University College Dublin, researching electioneering and politics in Kerry in the decade after the Civil War.

Thomas Tormey holds a PhD from Trinity College Dublin and is an expert in the Decade of Centenaries. He has worked as Historian-in-Residence for Louth County Council and currently tutors at University College Dublin.

Chapter 1

Introduction

Mel Farrell

On 27 August 1923 voters cast their ballots in the first general election fought since the establishment of the Irish Free State, and the adoption of its Constitution on 6 December 1922. Twelve weeks earlier, on 24 May, the guns fell silent as the eleven-month civil war that was fought over the terms of the Anglo-Irish Treaty came to an end with anti-treaty IRA Chief-of-Staff Frank Aiken's 'dump arms' order.[1] That conflict had overshadowed the birth of the new state and the reality of a partitioned Ireland. It concluded without a negotiated settlement ensuring there was no consensus about the Free State's existence, its constitutional arrangement, how to address partition or the relationship with Britain and the empire. For many, political loyalties were cemented by the events of 1922.[2]

Significantly, those who were defeated in the Civil War participated in the 1923 General Election thus giving the electorate an opportunity to cast their judgement on that conflict and developments since the Treaty was ratified in 1922. The two main parties contesting the election represented the two factions of the old Sinn Féin Party split apart by the Treaty. Four months before the election, Cumann na nGaedheal was launched as a new pro-treaty party by attendees to a convention in the Mansion House on 27 April. In June, Cumann na nGaedheal's opponents, on the insistence of their leader Éamon de Valera, succeeded in taking over the husk of the old Sinn Féin and repurposing it as an anti-treaty party.[3] On the hustings there were ample reminders of the excesses of both sides during the Civil War that flowed from the treaty split. The first anniversaries of the deaths of lost pro-treaty leaders Arthur Griffith and Michael Collins fell mid campaign, on 12 and 22 August respectively.[4] Coming within three months of the ceasefire, the election can, therefore, be viewed both as the climax of the revolutionary era in Ireland, and the beginning of 'civil war politics', offering as it did a shared space in electoral competition between the civil war combatants.

This first dedicated study of the 1923 General Election offers a unique insight into a key moment in the Irish Free State's democratic development as it embarked on independence and built a state from the rubble of revolution and civil war. It examines the immediate post-civil war vision presented by Irish political parties and the ways in which they sought to influence voters through various forms of propaganda. It also explores the attitude of powerful institutions like the Catholic Church and its efforts to sway voters in the election. The results, obtained across 30 constituencies, could be taken as a vote of confidence in the Free State project and the government in place since the transition from British rule. The outcome was of singular importance in the context of a new state that was desperately short of finance, grappling with the legacy of fratricidal conflict, and trying to establish its international credentials. The achievement, so soon after the 'dump arms' order, of a relatively peaceful election in August 1923 has been under-appreciated in studies of this period. This book is a timely addition to Irish revolutionary historiography and adds to our knowledge of this pivotal election. It investigates the range of parties that contested the election and examines the propaganda battles that waged between all sides. It outlines the influence of newspapers in this period and the impact of the widening of the franchise to encompass all adults without distinction of sex. It also explores American perspectives on the election and contextualises the Irish experience of 1923 with reference to wider European developments.

The General Election

Before the election was even announced potential candidates scrambled for information as to the exact polling date. In the summer of 1923, political organisations and movements rushed to create cohesive parties to be ready to appeal to ordinary men and women for their votes. It was an open secret that an election would take place once the new electoral register, necessary due to the state's introduction of universal adult suffrage, was completed.[5] In the Dáil, Independent TD Darrell Figgis questioned ministers, including the President of the Executive Council, W. T. Cosgrave, about the likely date of the election. Cosgrave, as a veteran of the independence movement who had fought in the Easter Rising and served as Minister for Local Government in the Dáil cabinet during the War of Independence, was the natural choice to become pro-treaty leader after the deaths of Collins and Griffith in August 1922.[6] Responding to Figgis, Cosgrave remained tight lipped on the likely date of the election.[7] In frustration, Figgis wrote to the *Irish Independent* on 19 July to allege that local Cumann na nGaedheal activists in his constituency appeared to know the date of the election whereas he, an elected member of the Dáil, did not:

> In the Dail [*sic*] to-day I asked the Minister two questions with a view to ascertaining the date of the forthcoming General Election. The reason I did so was that I had been warned by a local manager of the official Ministerial Party in Co. Dublin that preparations were being rushed through for the holding of the election at a very early date. He added that he had been desired to hold himself in readiness for such an election. I failed to elicit the information which, it would appear, was in the possession of one of several political parties.[8]

Figgis concluded his letter by stating that prospective candidates in all constituencies should be prepared for the eventuality of an election being 'sprung on the country, during the time of holidays'. On 9 August Cosgrave ended the uncertainty by dissolving the third Dáil. Polling was set for Monday 27 August and declared a public holiday. There was a certain incongruity about the election. The horrors of the Civil War remained fresh in people's memory and the future of the new state remained quite uncertain. Speaking in the Dáil on the day of the dissolution Tom Johnson, the Labour Party leader and *de-facto* leader of the opposition on account of the anti-treatyite policy of abstention, said that:

> Most of us, I suppose, would very much prefer not to have lived through the last twelve months, and I think, perhaps, the less said about the last twelve months the better. If it would be possible to blot out of Ireland's history the last eighteen or twenty months we would be pleased, but it is not possible… I still have hope that we will get through the period of the next year or two without the calamity that at the moment seems to face us.[9]

Labour and the Farmers' Party, a small agrarian party focused on representing agricultural interests, made it clear they would challenge Cumann na nGaedheal at the polls. Sinn Féin, on the other hand, was gripped by indecision as to whether the party should even participate in the election. As the only party that was opposed to the treaty settlement, the stakes were high for Sinn Féin. In 1923 it was, essentially, an 'anti-system' party denying the legitimacy of the new state.[10] If Sinn Féin did participate, and was to fare badly, this would be taken by the pro-treatyites as another vote of confidence in the Free State and would thus represent a major blow for the anti-treatyite cause. Besides, with some 12,000 of the most active republicans still in prison, some in the party believed the election would not be a free or fair contest. A month before polling, Sinn Féin had still not made a definite decision. De Valera believed that abstention was the safest option in the circumstances or that, based on the disappointing results of the June 1922 election in which there was strong backing for the treaty, the party should put forward a maximum of one candidate per constituency. Sinn Féin's organising committee disagreed, insisting that the party contest the general election in full. Having decided to enter the fray, Sinn Féin put forward 85 candidates, thus ensuring that the Free State government was going to face a strong challenge in every constituency.

On the other side of the divide there was also an element of danger for the pro-treatyites. Although the pro-treaty cause had won the backing of voters in June 1922, there had been a civil war since that election and the Free State's conduct in the conflict, not least the controversial policy of executions in which 81 individuals had been executed, was likely to have caused friction with the electorate.[11] Furthermore, as the party of the treaty, Cumann na nGaedheal's fortunes were intertwined with the prospects of the new state so it needed to perform well in order to demonstrate that the public still backed the settlement. The pro-treatyites were also contesting the election with a new party that had a patchy organisational presence in the constituencies. Cumann na nGaedheal organisers worked the constituencies desperately trying to build up an organisation. Government ministers also engineered an ambitious Land Bill as its signature policy even though the new state was facing a mounting financial crisis brought about by the steep cost of the civil war.[12] Unsurprisingly, confidence in the new state was at a very low ebb and Ireland remained deeply unsettled. Much of the country's infrastructure lay in ruins while the fledgling state faced a precarious financial position with spending exceeding revenue by 50 per cent on account of civil war expenditure. As an untested post-conflict state that was yet to prove its credentials, the Free State was essentially priced out of the money markets and was unable to borrow. Financial experts believed that it had to demonstrate resourcefulness and show that the treaty settlement would endure.[13]

In April, the Irish banks agreed to assist the government with a temporary loan until an election could be held. A decisive vote in favour of the treatyites would allow the state to float a national loan prompting *The Economist* to assert that the August election was a 'test of the constructive capacity of the present generation of the Irish people'.[14] This explains Cumann na nGaedheal's 'Safety first' approach to the election and its concerns that a strong performance by the minor parties could hand victory to the anti-treatyites by default thus undermining its efforts to portray the Free State as settled and stable. Faced by Sinn Féin on one flank, and Labour, the Farmers' Party and Independent candidates on the other, Cumann na nGaedheal campaigned as a 'national party' that could reconcile competing interests, defend the new state and provide stable government.

August 1923 was a landmark election in other ways. It is essentially the point marking the true beginning of modern Irish democracy and genuine electoral competition. Prior to 1918, contested elections were a rarity in Irish politics. Two thirds of the Irish Parliamentary Party (IPP) intake at the December 1910 election were elected unopposed,[15] while 25 Sinn Féin candidates were elected without contests in December 1918, an election in which the franchise had trebled in Ireland. In the area designated 'Southern Ireland', there were no contests in the May 1921 General Election held under the Government of Ireland Act (1920). Sinn Féin treated this as an election to the Second Dáil and had 124 candidates returned unopposed alongside four southern unionists who were given a free run on the Dublin University panel. While the 1921 Election was a formality south of Ireland's new political frontier, in the north Sinn Féin and the Nationalist Party, the inheritor of the IPP's northern apparatus, both contested on a message of self-determination and anti-partition.[16] They both failed to win converts from unionism. Twelve nationalists were elected, six of them Sinn Féiners, while the Ulster Unionists took 40 seats.[17] In the so-called 'pact election' in June 1922 the pro- and anti-treaty wings of Sinn Féin initially agreed a deal to fight the election jointly so as to minimise their losses from the other parties contesting and thereby replicate, as closely as possible, their standing in the Second Dáil.[18] A total of eight constituencies were uncontested in 1922 with the pact working to the advantage of the anti-treaty side who won 36 seats to Labour's 17 despite polling a similar percentage of first preferences (21.8 per cent to 21.3 per cent). By contrast, every seat (except Dublin University) was contested in August 1923 by a multiplicity of candidates and different interests resulting in a more representative outcome. A record 376 individuals stood for election thus establishing the subsequent trend of competitive electoral politics in Ireland.

Also, for the first time in an Irish election, all adults aged 21 or over, regardless of social status or gender, had the right to vote in 1923. In most European countries, and in both Canada and the United States, women's political rights became a major issue during, or shortly after, the First World War, with service in that conflict serving as a strong argument for extending political rights. In post-revolutionary Russia the Bolsheviks were at the forefront when it came to women's emancipation while post-war Germany and Austria saw the cause of women's suffrage advanced by the Social Democratic parties. Women won the vote under many of the new constitutions adopted by the newly created 'successor states' of Czechoslovakia, Estonia, Latvia, Lithuania and Poland. Nevertheless, in many other states, universal adult suffrage was not introduced. French and Italian women would have to wait until the end of the Second World War to vote on the same basis as men.[19] In Greece women were granted the vote in 1952 while in Switzerland, the first federal vote in which women were able to participate was the 1971 Election. All of Ireland was still part of the United Kingdom when universal male suffrage was introduced in 1918 at the same time that women over 30 were granted the vote. In 1916 the proclamation had promised government 'representative of the whole people of Ireland and elected by the suffrages of all her men and women' and this, at least, was realised in 1923.[20] The new Irish state's Electoral Act 1923 confirmed that every 'person without distinction of sex who is a citizen of Saorstát Éireann and has attained the age of 21 years and is not subject to any legal incapacity imposed by this Act or otherwise shall be entitled to be registered once as a

Dáil elector'.[21] According to a report in the *Freeman's Journal*, the Free State's adoption of an 'equal franchise' led the Belfast Women's Advisory Council to 'congratulate it' – universal adult suffrage was adopted by the United Kingdom in 1928.[22] The government party made the Irish Free State's adoption of franchise reform a signature campaign issue with one election advertisement reminding electors 'You Can't Ignore Politics because Politics Won't Ignore You' and urging them to 'Show You Are Worthy of the Franchise by Voting for the Cumann na nGaedheal Candidates'.[23]

On the day before the dissolution, the Prevention of Electoral Abuses Bill was also signed and passed into law. This wide-ranging legislation covered the full sweep of corrupt and illegal practices at elections. These included bribery and personation, the failure to publish the name and address of the printer on election materials, the making of false statements concerning a candidate's character or conduct, and interference with either ballot papers or ballot boxes. This legislation also covered the type of premises (such as schools and public houses) that could not be used as a committee room for the purpose of promoting an election candidate and dealt with the appointment of agents, the payment of election expenses and intimidation of candidates.[24] Strict penalties were introduced to deter individuals from engaging in these activities. Personation, voting in the name of another elector whether living, dead or fictitious, or voting more than once, could lead to fines of as much as £100 and imprisonment.[25] Repeat offenders would face heavier fines and up to three years in prison.[26]

August 1923 was the first election in Ireland that could be considered a fully open and competitive contest. In 1922, the divided Sinn Féin movement tried to fight the 'pact election' as a single entity, but by August 1923 it had finally split into two clear parties. It was the 1923 Election that saw the true emergence of Ireland's party system with Cumann na nGaedheal on one side and Sinn Féin on the other. Voters now actually had a clearer choice in August 1923 than they had in June 1922, and it was this election that set the mould of Irish politics in the twentieth century. However, it is important to highlight that many voters stood outside the treaty split and were catered to by parties and candidates who focused on socio-economic issues rather than on the constitutional question. While Cumann na nGaedheal was content to allow the constitutional question to dominate as the main issue in its battle with Sinn Féin, it also had to contend with parties of the left and right who could appeal to voters who may have supported the treaty but opposed the government's policies. A sizeable block of voters, 34 per cent, opted for candidates representing the Farmers' Party, Labour, Independents, and others such as the Businessmen's Party, the Cork Progressive Association, the National Democratic Party, the Dublin Trades Council, the Ratepayers' Association and the Town Tenants'. Minor parties and independents elected to the Fourth Dáil in August 1923 helped to consolidate Irish democracy by serving as an opposition to the Cosgrave government while Sinn Féin continued to abstain in the formative years of the new state.

Historiography

The importance of the August 1923 General Election, in transitioning from revolution to democracy, has been neglected in Irish history. Scholarly attention has focused on two distinct areas – the revolutionary period, 1912–23, and state building under successive governments, 1923–37. A few examples include David Fitzpatrick's *Politics and Irish Life*, Roy Foster's *Vivid Faces*, Michael Laffan's, *The Resurrection of Ireland*, Charles Townshend's *Easter 1916* and *The Republic*, Peter Hart's *The IRA and its Enemies*, and Gavin Foster's *The Irish Civil War and Society*. There are many biographies of key men and women associated with the revolutionary period, and histories of unionism, Home Rule and Sinn Féin. These include works such as Martin O'Donoghue's *The Legacy of the Irish Parliamentary Party*, Anne Dolan and William Murphy's *Michael Collins*, David McCullagh's *De Valera Rise* and *Rule*, Daithí Ó Corráin and Gerard Hanley's *Cathal Brugha*, Margaret Ward's *Unmanageable Revolutionaries*, Linda Connolly's *Women and The Irish Revolution*, and Brian Hughes and Conor Morrissey's *Southern Irish Loyalism*. More recently there have been a number of new local studies of the revolutionary period as part of the *Irish Revolution* series edited by Marian Lyons and Daithí Ó Corráin. The debate surrounding the ratification of the treaty and the establishment of the Free State is the focus of two books edited by Mícheál Ó Fathartaigh and Liam Weeks, *The Treaty: Debating and Establishing the Irish State* and *Birth of a State: The Anglo-Irish Treaty*.[27]

Although the Free State period, by contrast, has received less attention there is a growing body of work dealing with state-building and the politics of the 1920s and 1930s for instance Kevin Hora's *Propaganda and Nation Building* and Ciara Meehan's study, *The Cosgrave Party* which offers the first full history of the Cumann na nGaedheal Party, 1923–33. Meehan's work focuses on the breadth of the party's achievements and its innovative approaches to electioneering mainly in the late 1920s and 1930s. Donal P. Corcoran's *Freedom to Achieve Freedom* is a study of state building rather than electoral politics, although it does reference the relevance of the 1923 Election in relation to the raising of a national loan. Jason Knirck's *Afterimage of the Revolution* reconnects Cumann na nGaedheal, and the Free State itself, to the aims of the revolutionary generation suggesting that 'the language of the revolution continued to exert a dominant influence'. Knirck was also co-editor with Mel Farrell and Ciara Meehan, of the volume *A Formative Decade: Ireland in the 1920s*. While this volume offered new perspectives on 1920s Ireland, no single chapter explored the August 1923 Election.[28]

Political scholars have also been attracted to the early years of the Free State. For instance, Michael Gallagher, in his seminal article on 'The Pact General Election of 1922' and his *Irish Elections, 1922–44: Results and Analysis*, dealt with the state's early electoral contests. Works by Tom Garvin in *1922: The Birth of Irish Democracy*, and Joseph Curran in *The Birth of The Irish Free State, 1921–23* reflect a tendency to base the Free State's legitimacy on the outcome of the June 1922 Election rather than the August 1923 Election.[29] Bill Kissane in his *The Politics of the Irish Civil War* and *Explaining Irish Democracy* offers a more nuanced approach to the anti-treatyites than either Garvin or Curran. John M. Regan's *The Irish Counter-Revolution* also took a different approach to Garvin and Curran, calling into question the pro-treatyite commitment to democracy. While Regan does explore the 1923 Election, the scope of his book is much broader and is organised around his central argument that the Cumann na nGaedheal administration became actively counter-revolutionary and adopted a more conservative character that was more in keeping with the ethos of the old Home Rule Party. Separately, Regan has critically assessed the pro-treatyite mandate from the June 1922 Election, on which the Free State's self-proclaimed legitimacy rested. He has argued that the 1922 Election proved little on account of the background threat of British coercion should the treaty be violated and Collins's subsequent abandonment of his pact with de Valera on the eve of polling.[30] Looking more broadly at the Free State, authors such as Mary Kotsonouris and Terence Brown characterised the Free State as a disappointment, poor and stifling.[31]

In terms of electoral politics in this period Elaine Callinan's *Electioneering and Propaganda in Ireland, 1917–21: Votes, Violence and Victory* offered a detailed analysis of the electoral politics in the closing years of Ireland under the Union, covering the momentous 1918 General Election through to the local government elections of the early 1920s. Mel Farrell's *Party Politics in a New Democracy: The Irish Free State, 1922–37*, offered a wide-ranging treatment of political competition in the first 15 years of Irish independence. As such, both works reflect the wider pattern in the historiography which has seen more prominence given to the elections of 1918, 1922 and 1932 rather than the 1923 Election.[32] This volume addresses a clear void between works that focus on the revolutionary period and those that concern the Free State. As will become clear from the chapters that follow, democracy was precarious in 1923 and this election would determine whether it had a future in the new Ireland.

It is clear that the literature on 1920s Ireland is growing and this book hopes to make a significant contribution by offering the first comprehensive overview of the Irish state's inaugural general election. It takes as its premise that the election is an important milestone within the Decade of Centenaries given that it marked a clear and decisive shift from revolution to democratic politics. Election campaigns, and their consequences, can be turning points in history and the 1923 Election is one such instant. It was the moment where southern nationalism transitioned from revolutionary action to keen electoral competition. It set the new state, born in the blood and turmoil of civil war, on a new course that saw it emerge as a remarkably stable democracy in the late 1920s and early 1930, at a time when dictatorships of the left and right were on the rise in Europe.

However, the outcome of the Free State's first general election raises a number of questions and these are dealt with by the contributors to this volume. Why, in the first general election in which women voted on the same basis as men, were so few women (five) elected to the Dáil? Defeated in the Civil War three months before the election, the anti-treatyites polled a credible 27 per cent of the vote showing that more than a quarter of all voters were ambivalent if not completely opposed to the newly established state. While the pro-treaty party, now organised as Cumann na nGaedheal, won 39 per cent of the first preference vote this meant candidates representing other interests had secured 34 per cent, so what did this mean? While it is true that most voters, some 73 per cent, remained broadly supportive of the treaty and voted for parties that had either explicitly endorsed the settlement or had at least agreed to work within the framework of the Free State there was the potential among this 34 per cent for a future anti-treaty advance should socio-economic conditions worsen.

This book offers a unique insight into the new state as it emerged from the shadow of the Civil War and faced its first general election. In the chapters that follow, the contributors to the volume examine how political leaders looked to process and move forward from the Civil War, and they explore how ordinary Irish voters were influenced by political parties, newspapers and powerful institutions like the Catholic Church. They cover topics ranging from the two main parties, Cumann na nGaedheal and Sinn Féin, to questions about the influence of the Church and why it remained so difficult for women to be elected to Dáil Éireann despite the introduction of universal adult suffrage. The volume addresses how the Irish diaspora, so active during the revolutionary period, reacted to post-treaty politics and sought to influence voters in August 1923.

Mel Farrell opens with an examination of the Cumann na nGaedheal Party's 'Safety first' election pitch. As we have seen, the stakes were high for the pro-treaty party in August 1923. Free State ministers dealt with a series of crises in the summer of 1923 with the fate of their government, and ultimately the treaty settlement itself, resting on the performance of a new political party founded four months before polling day. Although organisers worked to build the new party structure in June and July its organisational presence was patchy with the push to form branches continuing into August 1923. Ten days out from polling day the party was still ratifying candidates and hiring organisers. While Cumann na nGaedheal was unable to replicate the enthusiasm of its parent party, the August 1923 Election proved a high watermark with the Party registering 39 per cent of first preference votes and 63 of the 153 Dáil seats contested. Farrell challenges the idea that Cumann na nGaedheal's performance was disappointing arguing that in the 100 years since the election, Fine Gael as the successor party to Cumann na nGaedheal, only ever matched its 39 per cent of the national vote on one occasion, November 1982.

In his chapter, David McCullagh argues that the 1923 Election was perhaps the most important Éamon de Valera ever fought, given that it paved the way for his dominance of Irish politics over the next half century. In mid-1923 de Valera's career was truly in the balance. He found himself out manoeuvred on the treaty question and had become an increasingly marginal figure during the Civil War as more militant figures directed the anti-treaty campaign.[33] The Sinn Féin organising committee's insistence that the party should contest the elections 'to the full limit of our hopes' arguably revitalised de Valera's career. The party's highly credible result showed that democracy was the way forward and that de Valera had a future in Irish politics.

As Jason Knirck explains in chapter four, the smaller parties in the Free State thought this would finally be an election held under circumstances favorable to them. Ireland's constitutional question had dominated elections in the revolutionary era leading Labour to stand aside in the 1918 Election. In June 1922 Labour and the Farmers' Party contested some constituencies even though the Sinn Féin pact was in operation with the election dominated by the treaty question and the threat of civil war. The Labour and Farmers' parties thought that the August 1923 Election would herald the death of Sinn Féin's nationalist hegemony in Irish politics. They had high hopes that free state politics would begin to look like the politics of other European states that were divided along left–right lines with parties differing from each other largely over social and economic issues.

Elaine Callinan's chapter explores how the various parties used propaganda to try and persuade voters to vote for them through canvassing, debates, speeches and such campaign materials as newspaper advertisements and posters. She compares the propaganda used by the parties in 1923 under such themes as economic – the bread-and-butter issues of life (pensions, taxation and employment); social and cultural (equality issues, Irish language, and education); law and order; and historical factors (the revolution and subsequent civil war). Her analysis demonstrates the contradictory views and ideologies that were put before the voters during the election, and she examines the extent to which they may have changed the mindset of ordinary voters.

Newspapers exercised great influence as the principal conduit of news and information in the early 1920s. Historians make extensive use of newspaper sources, but few have examined how the newspapers actually influenced political discourse and electoral outcomes and this is addressed in Owen O'Shea's chapter. Using Kerry, where the Civil War was 'more brutal, violent and protracted than any other county' as a case study, he shows how newspapers approached the election and looked to influence the outcome. Cumann na nGaedheal received positive coverage from the Kerry newspapers while the anti-treatyites attracted derision and minimal coverage.

Another powerful player in this election was the Catholic Church. In his chapter, Daithí Ó Corráin shows that the Catholic hierarchy 'stood shoulder to shoulder with Cumann na nGaedheal' in the 1923 Election with many members of the clergy going on record to strongly back the party's campaign for re-election. In 1923, priests appeared on many Cumann na nGaedheal platforms. However, such active intervention by the clergy was not replicated in subsequent elections. The hierarchy and clergy warned against voting for the anti-treatyites and cautioned against returning a large number of non-government TDs to the Dáil. Ó Corráin shows that the hierarchy's stance in the election was rooted in its endorsement of the treaty, deference to the legally constituted government, repudiation of republican violence and support for order and social stability.

Claire McGing's chapter examines the role of women voters and candidates in the 1923 General Election and its impact on gender politics in the early years of the Irish Free State. While the election was a pivotal one for women in terms of the right to vote, the fight on the part of the Irish Free State to marginalise republicanism was interlinked with the removal of active women in political life and at odds with the liberal-democratic ethos of the Irish Free State Constitution. The routes for women to enter politics became narrower and the connection between women politicians and dead nationalist heroes, dating to the revolutionary period, was copper fastened. Of the five women TDs elected in August1923, Margaret Collins O'Driscoll, a sister of the late Michael Collins and a Cumann na nGaedheal candidate in Dublin North, was the only one to take her seat and became the sole female voice in the fourth Dáil.

Regina Donlon's chapter deals with the role of the Irish diaspora in the 1923 Irish Free State General Election. She depicts an American Association for the Recognition of the Irish Republic (AARIR) that was in decline as 1923 began and was in danger of becoming irrelevant in a post-treaty context. She argues that 'the 1923 General Election simply represented one final opportunity for the diaspora to interpose on a society it no longer fully understood'. In 1923 Ireland did not exist in a vacuum and Gearóid Barry's chapter positions the election in its wider European context. Europe in 1923 existed in the shadow of the Russian Revolution of 1917, the complicated process of demobilisation after the First World War and the 'wars after the War'. Violent transfers of power characterised Europe, 1918–23, so the Free State was not unique in this regard. When added together, the various conflicts in the five immediate post-war years 'cost an estimated four million lives in Europe'. Barry concludes that the willingness of both sides in the Irish Civil War to 'share the electoral space' so soon after the end of the conflict pointed to a democratic future whereas the fate of democracy looked rather more fragile in many other parts of Europe.

The August 1923 Election in the Irish Free State brought the curtain down on the revolutionary period and marked a moment in time when the violence of revolution and civil war gave way to electoral competition between democratic parties looking to govern a new Irish state. In August 1923, politics in the new state moved decisively from bullets to ballots. The election reflects a nuanced and complex political situation among the voting population, and it gives voice and insight into the mindset of ordinary voters in Irish society. The results were of central importance in building confidence in the new Irish state and securing its future as a stable democracy. It was the August 1923 Election that confirmed public support for the Free State and set the mould for politics in the newly independent state, with two big parties divided on the constitutional issue, a number of smaller parties representing different interests, a fragmented left and the emergence of successful independent candidates. Yet this pivotal election has received remarkably scant attention. In the year of its centenary, this volume aims to address this void and re-focus attention on its significance in the history of the Irish state.

Chapter 2

'Safety first': Cumann na nGaedheal's Election campaign in August 1923

Mel Farrell

> The motto for this election is 'Safety first'. Strengthen those who have brought peace to the nation, consolidate your gains by your votes, mark your preferences in the order of ability to maintain sacred life, liberty, and security. Continue your preferences in that order. Attend the polls at whatever sacrifice on this 27th August to register your contribution towards stability of government in Saorstát Éireann.[1]

So wrote W. T. Cosgrave, President of the Executive Council and leader of the Cumann na nGaedheal Party, when asked to provide the *Irish Times* with a final message to the electors ahead of the new state's first general election. It was a succinct summary of his party's message throughout the campaign. Cumann na nGaedheal was a unique party. Its leaders had existed in government for over a year before the party's official launch on 27 April 1923. After the deaths of Michael Collins and Arthur Griffith in August 1922, Cosgrave and his ministers had overseen the foundation of the state and took responsibility for the 'war for its survival'.[2] During that conflict, supporters of the Anglo-Irish Treaty worked to build up a new party that would defend the settlement and uphold the new state. Consequently, the new party would bear the deep scars of that conflict.

The decision to formally establish a distinct pro-treaty political party was taken on 29 August 1922, one week after the death of Collins, by the treatyite General and Election Committee formed to oversee the campaign for the June 1922 election.[3] In October and November a number of potential party names were proposed with An Cumann Náisiúnta (the clear frontrunner), United Irishmen, Páirtí Náisiúnta and Cumann na tSaorstát, among them.[4] On 7 December 1922, a small number of treaty supporters were invited to a conference in 5 Parnell Square. Attendees to this gathering resolved to name the party 'Cumann na nGaedheal' as a tribute to Griffith. This meeting was overshadowed by one of the more shocking incidents of the Civil War. Two pro-treaty TDs, Seán Hales and Pádraic Ó Máille, were attacked by anti-treaty gunmen. Hales was shot dead while Ó Máille was left seriously wounded. On the following morning, without any pretence to legality, the Free State executed IRA prisoners Joe McKelvey, Liam Mellows, Rory O'Connor and Richard Barrett as a reprisal. As a consequence, a formal public launch of Cumann na nGaedheal was deferred indefinitely. By the Spring of 1923 conditions had stabilised to the extent that Cumann na nGaedheal's public launch was arranged for 27 April in the Mansion House. This gave it four months in which to set up branches ahead of the general election.

In the summer of 1923 Cumann na nGaedheal ministers faced more pressing issues than matters of party organisation. After the Civil War ended, the dire financial position of the new state came into sharper focus. Unsurprisingly, confidence in the new state was at a low ebb with fratricidal conflict dominating its foundation and spending exceeding revenue by 50 per cent. Ministers turned to the Irish banks. The banks kept things afloat with a temporary loan until the August when it was hoped that a solid election for Cumann na nGaedheal would demonstrate public support for the state and allow the floating of a national loan. This led *The Economist* to assert that the election was a 'test of the constructive capacity of the present generation of the Irish people'.[5] Despite these constraints, the Party was also under pressure to deliver tangible improvements for voters. For example, as the Land Purchase and Arrears Conference in April 1923 made clear, 'the people meant to have the land cheaply' and if Cumann na nGaedheal did not deliver, 'they would put in a government the next time who would'.[6] On the international arena, Cumann na nGaedheal ministers pushed for an expansive reading of the Free State's rights under the treaty settlement, formally applying to join the League of Nations in April 1923. However, the Civil War had hardened the Party's attitudes in terms of domestic politics with support for the Treaty converted into something 'of an article of faith'.[7]

As it prepared for the election, Cumann na nGaedheal faced the task of balancing the realities of a post-civil war state, seeking to establish its international credibility, with the aspirations of voters who hoped independence would improve their lives. Its ambitions in this regard were curtailed by the harsh realities of financial scarcity in 1923 leaving promised peace and stability as Cumann na nGaedheal's one trump card.

Although upholding the treaty settlement came to define Cumann na nGaedheal's mission, the Party presented itself as successor to the revolutionary tradition, claiming a 'direct political lineage' to the Sinn Féin movement.[8] However, operating in a post-civil war context, with nationalism divided and political loyalties cemented by the treaty divide, Cumann na nGaedheal could not hope to replicate the electoral success of revolutionary Sinn Féin.[9] Shaped by the crises it was born into, Cumann na nGaedheal never matched the levels of support or organisational reach of its parent party.[10] Therefore, to maximise its vote in the August 1923 Election, Cumann na nGaedheal needed to make inroads with what were euphemistically referred to as the 'new elements', the middle and professional classes who were so critical to getting the treaty accepted in 1922. This meant cultivating new support beyond the pro-treaty Sinn Féin base with voters anxious to avert a return to violence and uncertainty.[11] These voters, often ex-adherents of the Home Rule Party and southern unionism, desired stability, the restoration of law-and-order, and balanced budgets. It was in this context that Cumann na nGaedheal offered its cautious 'safety first', message that was so closely linked to the Cosgrave government's agenda. In the election, Cumann na nGaedheal asked for votes on the basis that a strong performance by the Cosgrave government was required to bed down the new state's institutions and show the world, and potential investors,[12] that the government still had the support of the people.

Of this, there were no guarantees. A great deal had changed since the June 1922 Election when the unpopularity of the anti-treaty position was much in evidence.[13] Although there was still broad acceptance of the treaty settlement, the manner of the Free State's victory in the Civil War, and the process of state-building itself, had caused friction with many voters.[14] Moreover, in a climate of voter apathy and post-civil war pessimism, merely getting 'out' the pro-treaty vote would itself prove a challenge. In order to campaign, canvass, select candidates and 'get out the vote' Cumann na nGaedheal would first need to build an organisation in the constituencies.

Building an Organisation

Séamus Dolan, Secretary of the Standing Committee and a TD for the Leitrim-Roscommon North constituency that was abolished ahead of the August 1923 Election, was actively involved in the party's efforts to build an organisational structure. On 3 May he issued a circular letter urging treaty supporters to form Cumann na nGaedheal branches in the constituencies. He promised that the committee would assist by supplying copies of the party's constitution, membership cards and suitable literature. Within weeks, the party launched an organising fund over the names of party president Eoin MacNeill, party vice president Jennie Wyse Power, George Nesbitt and Batt O'Connor (both 'money men' in the War of Independence). The response was underwhelming when contrasted with the treaty election fund raised in 1922.[15] In February 1923 the party's provisional executive was keen to stress that membership was open to all who agreed with its programme.[16] With this in mind, Dolan suggested that meetings be advertised in a way that made clear that 'all interests' were welcome. This was particularly evident in the South-East counties of Waterford and Wicklow where Redmondite sentiment remained strong, and the Redmond dynasty would ultimately endure until 1952.[17] Waterford would prove an especially problematic constituency for Cumann na nGaedheal given the scale of the farm labourers' strikes in the county during 1922–3.[18]

In Dublin, Cumann na nGaedheal had begun to organise in January 1923.[19] R. J. Purcell, a veteran Sinn Féin organiser, was hired to push the party's organisational drive in the capital. Purcell was pro-active in establishing branches and attending their meetings as the organisation developed in Dublin. While reports from Mayo and Cavan were favourable a sense of apathy prevailed outside Dublin with the public slow to show an interest in joining the party.[20] A steady stream of organisers were appointed and despatched to stir support and organise Cumann na nGaedheal in the constituencies. In their instructions, organisers were asked to enlist the support of influential people in towns and cities to help organise new *cumainn*. Once the organisers had worked to build branches in urban areas, it was hoped that these new members would go on to establish the party's structures in the outlying districts. Each organiser was issued a set of instructions which detailed what was expected of them:

> Instructions to Organisers
> 1. Organiser to work the towns in his district, enlist the support of influential people and ask them to organise *cumainn* in outlying parish areas.
> 2. Affiliate *cumainn* immediately.
> 3. Will be judged on the number he can affiliate.
> 4. To send chief organiser weekly report with a programme of work for the coming week.[21]

Cumann na nGaedheal's rapidly growing network of paid organisers was led by a chief organiser named P. J. Ryan who had been responsible for Leinster during the 1922 Election.[22] In appointing organisers, preference was given to men with a military background in the War of Independence and Civil War.[23] After resigning from the army on 16 June 1923 Henry Coyle was appointed as the party's organiser for North Mayo. On 18 July Coyle delivered a 'heartily received' address at a Cumann na nGaedheal rally that he himself had organised in Belmullet. The positive reception to Coyle's oration, and the party's desire to field candidates with a national record, would result in the organiser being added to the party's election ticket in Mayo North.[24] In June and July 1923 Ryan oversaw the appointment of new organisers and submitted weekly progress reports to the Standing Committee. These reports brought mixed news. While there was a positive reception in urban areas, this was balanced out by the disappointing reaction the party was receiving in rural districts. Numerous reports blamed this on apathy. In an attempt to drive activity and publicity in the constituencies, the Standing Committee asked that every branch send reports of their meetings to headquarters and the local press.[25]

As instructed, Cumann na nGaedheal organisers concentrated on forming strong branches in the larger towns. Organisers adopted familiar tactics, including the old Sinn Féin movement's aversion to class politics. When a branch was formed in Naas County Kildare, party organisers presented the organisation as a national movement that was not organised along class lines. Cumann na nGaedheal, it was claimed, was 'above all party [and class] interests' and those intending to join the branch could also belong to farmer and labour organisations as long as they 'put their country before their immediate class interests'.[26] Cumann na nGaedheal's organising effort also reflected the reality of a nationalism that was now divided. Kevin O'Higgins, Vice President of the Executive Council, visited Westmeath to help launch the new Mullingar town Cumann na nGaedheal branch. In his speech, O'Higgins summarised the events of the previous few years before declaring that his main objection to the anti-treaty party was their attempt to dictate their views to the majority. A local priest, Fr Macken, was elected president of the branch.[27] In Ballina County Mayo a local branch was formed ahead of a public meeting to promote the party.[28]

Ryan's report of 29 June provides a unique insight into the efforts of Cumann na nGaedheal to manufacture an organisation ahead of the election. To combat apathy, Ryan instructed organisers to arrange as many public meetings as possible and sent out posters and such materials as might help attract people into Cumann na nGaedheal. He also informed the Standing Committee of the recent appointment of yet more organisers – Seán Scanlon in Clare, William Breen in County Dublin, Michael O'Hara in Longford-Westmeath and Michael McGrath in Wexford.[29] Every constituency was assigned an organiser and some of the larger ones ended up with two. By polling day, some 40 paid organisers were hired to work for Cumann na nGaedheal. Ryan's report of 6 July revealed that some of the party's structures were inhibiting the drive to organise Cumann na nGaedheal across the Free State. He suggested that some meetings arranged for the purpose of forming new *cumainn* had been abandoned by organisers on the grounds that only seven or eight people were present.[30] Party rules stipulated that a minimum of twelve members were required to establish a new Cumann na nGaedheal branch. This issue was raised again during a meeting of the party's National Executive on 9 July. Ryan urged organisers to form temporary election committees in those districts where it had not been possible to form a full branch. The party's desire to have one local branch per ward or parish was reaffirmed and it was decided to break up some of the larger branches into smaller committees.[31]

Although the third Dáil was not dissolved until 9 August, the evidence suggests that this meeting of the Cumann na nGaedheal National Executive had put the party on an election footing. It resolved to launch an election fund on 23 July and to merge the new fund with the organising fund set up after the party's launch. It was agreed that the party would also take on the assets, and liabilities of the 1922 pro-treaty Election Committee with £643 from the treaty fund transferred to Cumann na nGaedheal's election account.[32] Party headquarters would be liable for nomination fees and expenses incurred in each constituency less ten per cent.[33] A report of this meeting, circulated to the press, was rather optimistic in declaring that 'apathy is disappearing' and 'before long the organisation will have gripped the public mind as firmly as did the Sinn Fein [sic] organisation'.[34] By referencing Sinn Féin, and setting out to organise as a non-class, national party with a presence in every ward and parish in the Free State, the party's executive was clearly looking to emulate the success of the past national movements – Sinn Féin and Home Rule.[35] In so doing, the party was setting up for a disappointment. Cumann na nGaedheal was operating in a very different environment to its predecessors and there is little evidence that party workers and organisers had adjusted to that new context. Irish nationalism was now divided along treaty lines with the old Sinn Féin membership split into two factions. It would be impossible to match the organisational reach of its parent party without cultivating members from outside the revolutionary fold and these were catered to by the Farmers' Party and Labour. Added to that, the party's leaders were the first members of an Irish government that was expected to deliver on the expectations of voters who had waited for the coming of independence. In 1923 Cumann na nGaedheal workers and organisers could not re-create the passions of 1918.

In his progress report of 20 July, Ryan indicated that 31 new Cumann na nGaedheal branches had been affiliated in the previous week.[36] While new branches were being formed, the work of building a new national organisation was still moving slowly. Given the proximity of the election, the party's attention switched from the task of building the organisation to that of electioneering. As Ryan had instructed, election committees began to appear in those districts where branches could not be established and these were expected to carry out election work.[37] Michael O'Hara, the organiser in Longford-Westmeath, oversaw the setting up of a branch in Edgeworthstown and formed election committees in Ballinalee and Clonbroney.[38]

Candidate Selection

Candidate selection was also on the agenda for the 9 July meeting of the National Executive. It was decided to have dates for selection conventions arranged by the National Executive with the Standing Committee given powers to make special arrangement for candidate selection in constituencies where there were few or no *cumainn*.[39] As the election came into focus, the party's structures were sparse, especially in rural constituencies. This explains the urgency of organisers to get committees up and running in those areas where full branches could not be formed. Although the government party's organisation should have had a better sense of the likely date of the election,[40] no Cumann na nGaedheal selection convention had yet taken place by 27 July.

New branches were still being formed in late July and early August just as the Standing Committee was finalising the dates of constituency selection conventions. Having such a patchy organisational structure was not ideal and the Standing Committee tried to address it by suggesting that affiliated *cumainn* in unorganised constituencies should 'invite representatives from areas as yet unorganised, to a meeting for the selection of candidates'.[41] This plan was open to interpretation and in some cases was found to be impractical.[42] Unsurprisingly, practice varied from constituency to constituency. Nowhere was this more pronounced than in Clare. Although an Ennis branch was set up in March 1923, there was little evidence of any Cumann na nGaedheal organisation through the rest of the constituency.[43] On 28 July the party placed a note in the *Clare Champion*. For 'want of organisation', it invited treaty supporters to a 30 July convention in the courthouse, Ennis, to select the party's candidates for the upcoming election. Invited to the Clare convention were:

1. All priests in the county
2. All county, district and urban councillors
3. All officers of Sinn Féin Executive east and west
4. All former officers of Sinn Féin *Cumainn*
5. All pre-truce Volunteers not attached to the National Army
6. Representative farmers, businessmen and workers.[44]

This list of prospective delegates bore a 'striking resemblance' to the manner in which the Home Rule Party had attempted to ensure that its selection conventions were representative of nationalist opinion.[45] As was the case prior to independence, the clergy were held in high esteem as leaders and their presence on a platform enhanced the credibility of a party or candidate.[46] Daithí Ó Corráin's chapter shows the extent to which the Catholic hierarchy and clergy backed Cumann na nGaedheal, and the county's priests were incredibly active in the party's election campaign in Clare. Local political representatives, pre-truce members of Sinn Féin and the Volunteers and representative farmers, businessmen and workers completed the list of prospective delegates. The official report of the convention went on to say that the meeting included 'a majority of the men who have borne the brunt of the struggle for independence for many years past'.[47] Reports suggested that 150 people attended the convention. Séamus Hughes, chairing, outlined the aims and programme of the new party. Five candidates were selected including minister for education Eoin MacNeill, who was not in attendance, and had already been put forward for the National University panel.[48] Having selected the Cumann na nGaedheal candidates the convention then moved to establish a constituency committee. This was chaired by Fr Charles Culligan, Kilkee, with Canon William O'Kennedy, Ennis, appointed as Director of Elections.

However, the existence of a stronger branch structure was no guarantee of efficiency. A new branch in Carlow met on 4 August for the purpose of appointing delegates for the Carlow-Kilkenny selection convention due to take place on the next day. Subsequently there was a race to organise branches in 'Bagenalstown, Tullow, Hacketts-town, Rathvilly and Borris'.[49] Similarly, the first business before the new Kenmare branch in county Kerry was the ratification of delegates to attend the selection convention in Tralee on 7 August. The selected delegates were asked to endorse a member of the branch, J. Keating and the outgoing Kerry-Limerick TDs James Crowley, Fionán Lynch and Piaras Béaslaí.[50] On the day of the Kerry convention, Keating was unsuccessful. After 'protracted deliberation' some 'seventy-four delegates representative of all parts of the county' selected, Lynch, Crowley, Professor John Marcus O'Sullivan and Thomas Dennehy, a local councillor.[51]

In constituencies where the organisation was more extensive, candidate selection was relatively straightforward. In Kildare, a three-seat constituency, a convention took place in Naas on 2 August on a night when Ireland was battered by a series of violent thunderstorms. Despite the storms, delegates from 'every part of the county' participated in the Kildare convention. George Wolfe, Thomas Lawler and Simon Malone were selected.[52] In the eight-seat Dublin North constituency, where Cumann na nGaedheal had established a strong branch network in the spring of 1923, there was surprise when outgoing Minister for Industry and Commerce, Joseph McGrath, announced that he would not go forward as a candidate.[53] Each branch in the constituency was invited to send two delegates to the selection convention at 5 Parnell Square, on 1 August.[54] On 3 August, the candidates put forward by the convention were ratified by party headquarters, with Richard Mulcahy and Collins's sister Margaret Collins O'Driscoll among seven candidates in the eight-seat constituency.[55] The presence of 'big name' candidates would boost the party's vote in constituencies like Dublin North. By contrast, the decision of General Seán MacEoin, who had topped the poll with over 10,000 first preferences in June 1922, not to stand in Longford-Westmeath, and instead concentrate on his career in the army proved a major blow for the party.

Cumann na nGaedheal's Cork city convention took place on 5 August. In Cork, the party's activists showed much greater restraint than they did in other constituencies selecting two candidates. Postmaster General J. J. Walsh, a veteran of revolutionary politics, was nominated alongside Mary Collins Powell, another sister of Michael Collins.[56] There were reasons for this restraint. Cork Cumann na nGaedheal had decided to cooperate with the city's business interests as represented by the Cork Progressive Association, 'a highly organised group of over 400 local businessmen and disgruntled citizens' that was formed in 1923. While the Progressives' grievance was with Cork Corporation, the group were disliked by many within Cumann na nGaedheal members on account of their former associations with Home Rule and southern unionism. In his diary, Liam de Róiste wrote that he had 'naturally' disliked being asked to 'join with the business organisations and conservatives for election purposes' given that their candidate, Richard Beamish, had been a prominent Cork unionist.[57] Despite these issues, the pact held until polling day.

As the newspapers became increasingly intrigued at the large number of candidates in the field, Cumann na nGaedheal continued to show a somewhat reckless approach to selection. In mid-August Cumann na nGaedheal was still ratifying candidates and hiring organisers. There was something particularly casual in the manner of Professor Alfred O'Rahilly's invitation, ten days before polling, to stand as a second Cumann na nGaedheal candidate in Cork after Powell withdrew from the race.[58] On 17 August, a day before the closing date for nominations in the election, Cosgrave wrote an open letter to Joseph McGrath, urging him to reconsider his decision to retire from national politics. Cosgrave prevailed on his minister to 'stand in Mayo – for peace against chaos. You have a war record to be proud of, and with this record which I would be proud to have to my credit, stand for Ireland in this crisis'.[59] McGrath consented and at the eleventh hour; P. J. McAndrew, one of the four candidates chosen by the Mayo North selection convention, withdrew in favour of the minister.[60]

Campaigning

Cumann na nGaedheal placed the treaty at the centre of its election campaign and set out its stall as a non-class 'national party'. Speakers in the constituencies endeavoured to demonstrate that Cumann na nGaedheal alone could deliver peace, stability and ordered government. The party was keen to draw a distinction between the anarchy of the Civil War and the promise that peace and stability would be secured by the continuation of the Cosgrave government. It suited the party to fight the election on this ground and to mobilise the pro-treaty vote by portraying Sinn Féin as a threat to the state. Nationally, Cumann na nGaedheal laid emphasis on the record of the Cosgrave government. The party highlighted the enactment of the Free State's constitution, the passage of universal adult suffrage ahead of the 1923 Election, the formation of new government departments, the efforts to restore of law-and-order, and the potential of the 1923 Land Act to complete land purchase.[61] The Land Bill passed into law on 9 August, the same day that the Dáil was dissolved. As Terence Dooley has observed it made 'good political sense' to have the bill enacted before the election.[62]

Cumann na nGaedheal constituency committees were responsible for running the election locally. Canvassers were provided with electoral registers to guide their work. *The Freeman's Journal* noted that there had been an 'energetic canvass' by Cumann na nGaedheal in the three Dublin constituencies.[63] In Clare, where party activism seems to have been stirred by the success of the selection convention, an election headquarters for the county was established in the Queens Hotel Ennis and a busy programme of election meetings was arranged by the committee. Cumann na nGaedheal's campaign opened in Clare on 5 August, with a public meeting in Kilkee addressed by all five candidates. MacNeill said he was only standing as a candidate on the invitation of the people of Clare.[64]

Constituency committees also arranged outdoor public meetings where the party's message could be put directly to the electorate.[65] These usually took place in locations with good natural acoustics – street corners and town squares in urban centres or at crossroads in more rural districts. Locations where crowds were already assembled, such as church gates or during organised fairs and markets, were also favoured. Occasionally, major events attracted many competing parties and candidates. In one example, the fair at Borris, county Carlow on 15 August witnessed public demonstrations by Cumann na nGaedheal, Labour, the Farmers' Party and Sinn Féin (in that order).[66] Attendances at these public demonstrations were taken as an indication of a party or candidate's level of support in the area. Voters unable to attend in person were reached via the extensive coverage these rallies were given in the local newspapers. In his 1933 study of free state politics, American political scientist Warner Moss noted that the local newspapers were 'gossipy' with the sheer attention to detail of reporters significantly widening a politician's audience.[67] As is clear from Owen O'Shea's chapter, the pro-treatyites, now organised as Cumann na nGaedheal, still enjoyed considerable support in the national and local newspapers.[68]

'Safety first': Cumann na nGaedheal's Election campaign in August 1923

Crowd in attendance at a Cumann na nGaedheal election rally in St. Stephen's Green, Dublin, 1923, NLI, Hugh Kennedy papers, KEN6, courtesy of the National Library of Ireland.

In the capital, Cumann na nGaedheal's campaign opened with a large rally at College Green on 12 August. This was chaired by Jennie Wyse Power, one of the more prominent pro-treaty women activists, and addressed by its candidates in the three Dublin constituencies. Irish-American leader, Judge Daniel F. Cohalan, who was holidaying in Ireland, appeared on the platform to endorse the Cumann na nGaedheal candidates. Cohalan, whose relationship with de Valera had broken down while the latter was in the United States, subsequently campaigned with Cosgrave in several constituencies. According to the *Irish Independent* an 'overflow meeting' had to be arranged on Dame Street to cater for the large crowd attending. The rally was subject to interruptions and at times became a bad-tempered affair. O'Higgins stated that Ireland 'was a bigger thing than a Republic or a Free State' while Desmond FitzGerald defended the government's actions in the Civil War. Responding to interruptions, FitzGerald said that 'Griffith and Collins lived and worked to show that not by shouting "Up the Republic" could they get a republic'.[69] Cosgrave used this address to rally the party's supporters. Cosgrave, who 'enjoyed forcing republican hecklers to admit' they had never fired a shot,[70] entered a bitter back-and-forth with Maud Gonne-MacBride who was heckling during his address. He asked another heckler 'Where did you fight?' and stated that he and his colleagues would never 'draw a gun against the will of the people'. He and his colleagues had only ever fought 'to free our country and drew them for the flag there (pointing to the tricolour)'.[71] Cumann na nGaedheal reaped positive headlines from Cohalan's attendance at the rally. In an interview with the *Irish Independent*, Cohalan praised Cosgrave's government and claimed that Americans were shocked that 'the Irish divided amongst themselves' over the treaty. Echoing the party's election message, Cohalan said it was essential that the Free State government establish order so that 'lovers of liberty throughout the world' would understand that the Irish people had 'regained their self-control'.[72]

Across the Free State, the party was on message. Voters were constantly told that Cumann na nGaedheal stood for order and Sinn Féin stood for anarchy. Peace and stability were within grasp and would be secured if voters endorsed Cumann na nGaedheal candidates. In Sligo, Cosgrave described the Civil War as the 'most dangerous phase of our national existence' and claimed that the 'danger is almost past'. To progress, voters needed to elect 'representatives of the people who will do their duty by the people, for the people and by the people's wishes'.[73] A Cumann na nGaedheal election meeting in Waterford heard that voters faced a choice between 'ordered government and Irregularism'. One of its candidates in Waterford, Vincent White, defined 'the real issue in the present elections' as whether the people were still 'in favour of the treaty?'.[74] In Longford-Westmeath, a colourful rally in Mullingar, complete with a motor lorry decorated with tricolour flags serving as a platform from which Cumann na nGaedheal speakers could address the crowd, heard local candidate P. W. Shaw declare that voters would have to choose between ordered government and anarchy.[75] In north Longford Frank McGuinness urged voters to support the government that had 'risked their lives and property' during the Civil War and had made the country 'safe for the farmers, the business men and all others'. Failing to return the present government would 'react disastrously on the well-being of the country in the present generation'.[76]

References from Cumann na nGaedheal platforms to the treaty and 'ordered government' suggest that the party was confident that the anti-treaty position remained unpopular with voters. Framing the electoral contest in such stark terms allowed the party to campaign on a broad platform that avoided the more difficult socio-economic questions it faced in a post-civil war context. With Sinn Féin focusing on the oath, prisoners and the abstract ideal of the republic,[77] Cumann na nGaedheal could claim that de Valera had nothing to offer those voters who were concerned with bread-and-butter issues. Campaigning in his own Carlow-Kilkenny constituency, Cosgrave claimed that his opponents had 'very little knowledge of real nation-building' and were not capable of restoring business and commercial life.

Elsewhere, local Cumann na nGaedheal candidates saw no conflict between their ardent nationalism and advocacy of the treaty. Seán Gibbons, a Cumann na nGaedheal candidate in Carlow-Kilkenny, claimed that he 'stood for the complete independence of Ireland' and would 'never attach himself to any party that would make for the subversion of that sacred principle'.[78] In Clare one of the Cumann na nGaedheal candidates, Michael Hehir, was introduced as having been Michael Brennan's right-hand man during the War of Independence. William Sears, a Cumann na nGaedheal candidate in Mayo South, asserted that the British had been 'driven out of Ireland'.[79] This, combined with the effort to ensure that candidates with a military record went forward for Cumann na nGaedheal, shows that the treatyites felt the need to shore up their nationalist flank against Sinn Féin.

With the party also seeking support from those voters anxious for a return to stability, Cumann na nGaedheal was, essentially, in an electoral battle on two fronts.[80] While Sinn Féin was the only party standing on an anti-treaty platform, Cumann na nGaedheal did not enjoy a monopoly on pro-treaty support. It faced strong electoral competition from Labour, the Farmers' Party and Independent candidates.[81] In Clare, MacNeill identified the Farmers' Party as the 'only rock in the road' and capable of detaching 'a lot of votes' from Cumann na nGaedheal. He thought the 'same may be said of the Labour Party' who were strong among farm workers in the county.[82] The party was particularly vulnerable in those constituencies where a former home ruler was standing. In Waterford, a constituency identified as problematic for Cumann na nGaedheal, William Archer Redmond stood as an independent constitutionalist in the tradition of his father, John Redmond, and Charles Stewart Parnell. Redmond broadly accepted the treaty but campaigned on the need for economic development. He was also able to appeal to voters who were concerned about the new state's finances.[83]

With the Boundary Commission coming into focus, partition, largely absent from the Dáil treaty debates and the June 1922 election, was now becoming a political issue. Reporting on Cumann na nGaedheal's 5 August campaigning in counties Cavan, Clare, Meath and Westmeath, the *Irish Times* noted that 'three points were dealt with by nearly all the speakers – the country's need of stability and security; the financial adjustments with Britain; and the boundary problem'.[84] In Monaghan Blythe suggested that the 'six counties could never be brought in by force' but only through 'their own free will'. He argued that there 'must be prosperity, and security' in the Free State before they would 'come in'. At Ballyragget, County Kilkenny, a heckler challenged Cosgrave on the issue of partition. Cosgrave replied that 'de Valera was the first to agree to that particular clause of the treaty'.[85]

A stark reminder of what had been lost over the previous twelve months came mid-campaign as the first anniversaries of Griffith and Collins were marked by extensive mourning. Both of the pro-treatyites' lost leaders were given widespread coverage in the local and national newspapers. Thomas Lawler, one of the party's candidates in Kildare, connected himself to Collins by making clear he had first entered national politics 'at the urgent personal request of the late General Michael Collins' in the June 1922 election.[86] The anniversaries may also have served as a reminder to the party faithful of the vacuum in charisma that was a consequence of their deaths given the effectiveness of Griffith and Collins on the hustings and on the canvass.[87] Now the party presented Cosgrave as the leader who had stepped into the breach to continue the work of the two lost leaders. In Monaghan, Cosgrave was introduced by A. H. Boylan as 'the man who saved the country from a great disaster'. If 'William Cosgrave had not stepped in to face the danger when Michael Collins was shot, the country would long since have been in a worse state than Russia'.[88] In Waterford, Senator Patrick Kenny told a Cumann na nGaedheal audience that they were 'there to loyally honour the treaty and the signatures of their glorious dead' and had 'not departed from their Republican principles'.[89] Addressing the same rally, Mulcahy said the Cosgrave government had the 'proud privilege' of taking up the work as 'Griffith and Collins laid it down'.[90]

On the hustings Cosgrave was not averse to dealing directly with the genesis of the treaty settlement and the subsequent civil war. During his speech in Monaghan, Cosgrave responded to a republican interrupter 'if they [anti-treatyites] were worth a damn they would have beaten us twelve months ago. They had more men, better armed men and better disciplined men and we produced an Army that knocked the devil out of them'. When challenged in Galway on the civil war, Cosgrave stated that he was happy to submit to the electorate for a verdict on everything that had been done.[91] On 19 August, while electioneering in Clare, the constituency of the anti-treaty leader, Cosgrave was introduced to the much publicised (see cover) Cumann na nGaedheal rally in Ennis as the person who had 'saved the country' and was the 'deliverer of our people, the protector of our rights, and the liberator of our country'.[92] Addressing the rally Cosgrave referenced de Valera's arrest days earlier, noting that he was 'fairly safe' and unlike 'many other people' was not dead. Cosgrave also attacked de Valera for not attending the treaty negotiations in 1921 and recalled how he and others had urged de Valera to go to London. The 'spokesman of the country refused to take his responsibilities' and, Cosgrave concluded, this meant de Valera was 'not worthy to be head of the nation'.[93] Cosgrave's use of four air corps aeroplanes to get from the Ennis Cumann na nGaedheal meeting to a rally in Carlow caused something of a storm in the *Irish Times* given that their use for a political rather than state function was an inappropriate use of government property.[94]

As the election drew closer Cumann na nGaedheal seemed confident that it could secure a large majority. With some 40 paid organisers in the field the party was able to make-up for any deficiencies in organisation that remained. In addition, three provincial organisers were appointed to provide a link between constituency organisers and Ryan who remained Chief Organiser. Prior to polling day, the Standing Committee arranged for the 2,000-word Cosgrave manifesto, 'To the people of Ireland', to appear as a front-page paid advertisement in the *Irish Independent*, the *Irish Times*, the *Freeman's Journal* and the *Cork Examiner*. Divided into two parts, 'Record of Work Done' and 'Future Programme' this was Cosgrave's direct appeal to his 'Fellow-citizens of Saorstát Éireann'. In each newspaper, the message ended by imploring readers to 'support Cumann na nGaedheal candidates'. Cosgrave signed off on the address using the Irish form of his name, Liam T. MacCosgair, and in the version that appeared in the *Freeman's Journal*, the words Cumann na nGaedheal were printed in Gaelic type.[95] The committee also printed 100,000 copies of the same text in large poster form for distribution.[96] Ciara Meehan has shown that Cumann na nGaedheal used elaborately designed election literature and posters from the September 1927 election onwards. In the early 1920s, the pro-treatyites used more simple but striking materials as reflected in the examples below. De Valera's character was a frequent target while the party was keen to present a clear distinction between its promise of 'Ordered Government' and the anti-treatyite threat of violence. The '"Arguments" Against The Treaty' leaflet, depicting a revolver, pepper and petrol, was perhaps the most effective of all.[97]

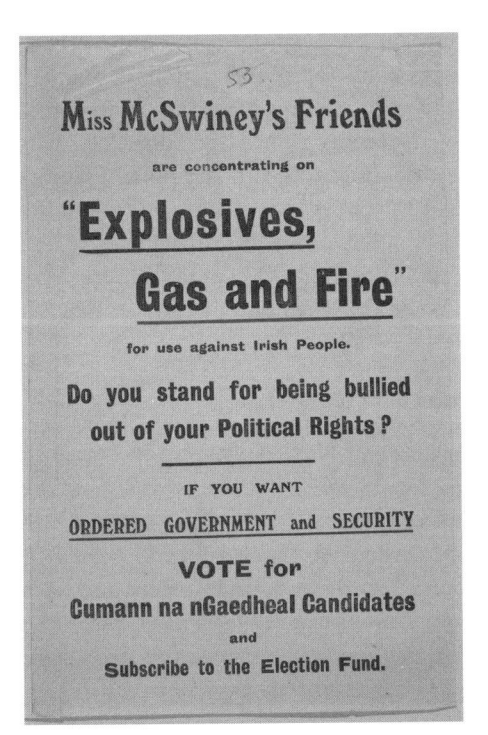

'Miss McSwiney's friends are concentrating on explosives, gas and fire: vote for Cumann na nGaedheal candidates', Cumann na nGaedheal campaign leaflet for the 1923 election, NLI, Pamphlet volume D144 (Item 53), courtesy of the National Library of Ireland.

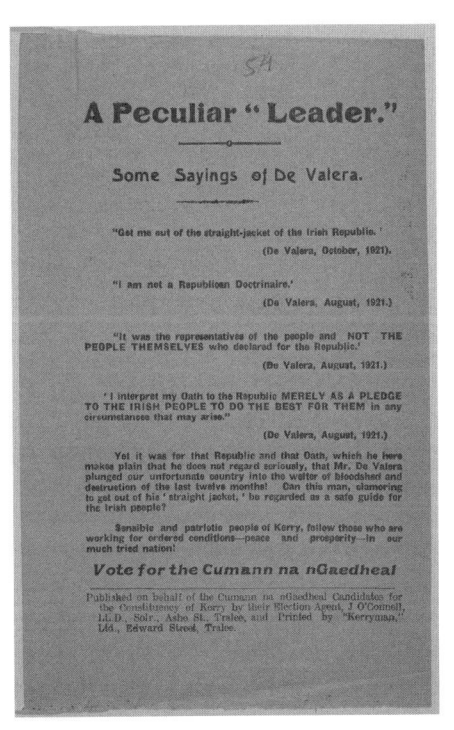

'A Peculiar "Leader"', Cumann na nGaedheal campaign leaflet for the general election of 1923 for the Kerry constituency, NLI, Pamphlet volume D144 (Item 54), courtesy of the National Library of Ireland.

'"Arguments" Against the Treaty', NLI, EPH B158, Courtesy of the National Library of Ireland

Front page advertisements taken out by the party on 23 August appealed directly to women voters who were voting on the same basis as men for the first time.[98] Women, according to the advert, had three options. They could vote 'irregular', abstain from voting or vote Cumann na nGaedheal.[99] On polling day itself, further front-page advertisements warned against apathy and pressed voters to make the effort to go to the polls. Electors were urged to 'Vote for Cosgrave's candidates' as 'not to vote is to help anarchy'.[100] In the *Cork Examiner*, an election day advert showed that the alliance with the Progressives had endured. It asked those electors opting for Beamish and O'Shaughnessy of the Progressives to continue their preferences for O'Rahilly and Walsh of Cumann na nGaedheal. It continued:

> This is a quite peaceable election. There will be no doubt of the issue if you vote. All your Candidates will be Elected. Will you let your country and your city down simply because you are too careless or lazy to spare ten minutes of your time on a National Holiday?[101]

In Cosgrave's Carlow-Kilkenny constituency a caption under a front-page photo of him with the other Cumann na nGaedheal candidates declared that 'these men will not catch rainbows for you, but they will safeguard your liberties, protect your interests and save your country from anarchy and ruin'.[102] There rested Cumann na nGaedheal's case. The count would reveal whether or not the party had done enough to convince the Free State electorate to stick with Cosgrave, the government, and the pro-treaty position.

Result and Aftermath

Cumann na nGaedheal won 39 per cent of the vote and 63 seats, a gain of five on the number won by pro-treaty Sinn Féin in 1922, in a Dáil had just been increased from 128 to 153 seats. This constituted a lead of 19 seats over abstentionist Sinn Féin, down, slightly, from the 22 seat advantage the pro-treatyites had enjoyed over the anti-treatyites in June 1922. Although short of an overall majority, the abstention of Sinn Féin would give Cosgrave a comfortable majority inside the Dáil. Cumann na nGaedheal performed particularly well in the west, in urban centres such as Dublin and in any constituency where it could field a big-name candidate. In Dublin North, Mulcahy won 22,205 first-preference votes giving the party enough of a surplus to win four of the eight seats with the election of Seán McGarry, Margaret Collins O'Driscoll and Francis Cahill, who was swept in on Mulcahy's transfers despite only securing 790 first preferences.[103] In Carlow-Kilkenny, Cosgrave took 17,709 first preferences or 44.1 per cent of the vote, enough to bring in Seán Gibbons who had obtained 615 first preferences. Kevin O'Higgins also secured a big vote, winning 20,821 first preferences in Dublin County.

By contrast, Seán MacEoin's decision to forego a political career in preference for one in the army cost the party dearly in Longford-Westmeath. MacEoin was a big loss to the party in 1923. When MacEoin returned to national politics later in the decade he won 28,445 first preferences in the 1929 Leitrim-Sligo by-election, while, for decades to come, his daring exploits in the War of Independence added colour to Cumann na nGaedheal and later Fine Gael campaigns.[104] His absence more than likely cost the party a seat in 1923. Although the midland constituency increased from a four-seat to a five-seat constituency in 1923, the anti-treatyites almost doubled their vote, in the process of gaining a seat, while Cumann na nGaedheal lost one of the pro-treaty seats won in 1922. In a major twist of fate, Cumann na nGaedheal candidate Frank McGuinness lost his Dáil seat to Paddy McKenna of the Farmers' Party. In 1917, McKenna had lost the home rule seat to McGuinness's brother Joseph in the famous South Longford by-election.[105]

Cumann na nGaedheal also faced a major disappointment in Clare where MacNeill was the only one of the five Cumann na nGaedheal candidates elected. MacNeill was elected with less than half the number of first preferences won by de Valera, and two of his running mates lost their deposits. Cumann na nGaedheal's disappointment in Clare was compounded by the fact that the local constituency committee had run the campaign in a profligate manner leaving it with debts of £630.[106] After the election Harry Guinane, the constituency secretary, agreed that the party should have selected three candidates in Clare and complained that those who wanted to field a full team had 'on a most extravagant and irresponsible manner run the election'. Other figures in the party subsequently blamed the disappointing result in Clare on a negative reaction in the county to the arrest of de Valera by Free State troops on 15 August.[107] However, the constituencies of Cork North and Waterford provided the worst results of all for the government with Cumann na nGaedheal failing to win a seat in either. In Cork North, 'cow country', the Farmers' Party won the most first preferences and shared the constituency's three seats with Labour and Sinn Féin. As expected, William Redmond performed strongly in Waterford, garnering 19.8 per cent of first preferences in the process of taking one of the four seats. Here Sinn Féin's Caitlín Brugha, widow of the late Cathal Brugha, topped the poll with 25.4 per cent of the vote, with the final two seats going to Labour and Farmers' Party candidates.[108] The government party had underperformed throughout the South-East, winning two seats out of twelve in the constituencies of Waterford, Wexford and Wicklow.

Cumann na nGaedheal paid a heavy price for its election win. Its reliance on paid organisers left party headquarters with debts of £4,673.[109] Within days of the election the Standing Committee set about reducing costs. All but two paid organisers were told that their services were no longer required.[110] J. J. Walsh was prepared to ask constituency committees to pay their own liabilities while other senior figures suggested that outstanding nomination fees dating from 1917 to 1921, now controlled by Cumann na nGaedheal members, should be obtained.[111] Cumann Sugradh an Airm, a body providing recreational facilities for soldiers,[112] began renting a room at the party headquarters. This brought in a yearly rent of £52.[113] When the Clare constituency committee asked the Standing Committee for funds to help it clear its significant debts headquarters sent £150 to the Clare constituency and explained that it faced its own financial difficulties.[114]

Conclusion

This election was fought to determine who governed the Free State and it resulted in a continuation of the Cosgrave administration. Most importantly of all, the result was taken as another vote of confidence in the treaty settlement and the Free State itself. *The Economist* welcomed the 'heavy vote for the Constitution and stability' in the election and, in October, the government succeeded in launching the long anticipated National Loan which was oversubscribed by £200,000.[115] This went some way towards establishing the credentials of the Free State and instilling confidence in its future viability.[116]

Cumann na nGaedheal's performance in the August 1923 Election has long been viewed as something of a disappointment by numerous authors, including the present writer.[117] However, in the 90 years since Fine Gael was founded as the successor party to Cumann na nGaedheal it has only managed to secure 39 per cent of the national vote on one occasion, November 1982. In February 2011, when Fine Gael achieved its highest ever seat total, 76 in a 166 seat Dáil, it did so on 36.1 per cent of the national vote. Cumann na nGaedheal's performance in the August 1923 Election remains one of the strongest showings, in any election, by a party in the treatyite tradition. This result was achieved at a time when the party was still in the process of building constituency structures and government ministers grappled with several major crises. Furthermore, the party's share of the vote in 1923 must be considered against the emergence of a competitive multi-party system and the fact that Cumann na nGaedheal did not enjoy a monopoly on the pro-treaty vote. It faced competition from Labour, Farmers' Party and Independent candidates who could offer pro-treaty voters greater choice while working within the framework of the treaty.[118] The widely held perception that Cumann na nGaedheal's performance in 1923 was underwhelming has probably been coloured by the dominance of nationalist parties prior to independence and the electoral dominance Fianna Fáil would demonstrate after 1932.

While the election result helped instill confidence in the new state it had long-term consequences for Cumann na nGaedheal. Its victory came at great financial cost to the party. Upholding the treaty settlement and establishing the new state's credentials was of paramount importance to the founders of Cumann na nGaedheal and the August 1923 Election result, undoubtedly, advanced these two goals. However, electoral competition to the party's right, and its 'safety first' election campaign in August 1923, would further tie Cumann na nGaedheal to the treaty settlement as it existed. The August 1923 Election represents Cumann na nGaedheal's high-water mark because the party failed to move on and offer something fresh in subsequent general elections. While Michael Collins had talked about 'stepping stones to freedom', Cumann na nGaedheal became increasingly identified with caution. While years of governing through adverse conditions undoubtedly took its toll, the party struggled to break free of the post-civil war mindset. Versions of the same campaign theme were rolled out in the next three elections thereby handing the political initiative to de Valera and Fianna Fáil after 1927. Fianna Fáil's flair for organisation and de Valera's success in seizing for himself the cloak of the myth of 1916 was a potent combination that allowed it to eclipse the treatyite party after 1932 and dominate Irish politics in the twentieth century.

CHAPTER 3

'NOTHING BUT A BULLET WILL STOP ME': ÉAMON DE VALERA AND THE 1923 GENERAL ELECTION

David McCullagh

Éamon de Valera did not take elections lightly. Each one was important in its own right, from his first, the 1917 by-election victory in East Clare, to his last, the narrow win over Tom O'Higgins in the 1966 Presidential contest. Each electoral contest in between had its own importance, its own particular circumstances, and its own place in his career. But the 1923 General Election was in a class of its own. It did not just decide his immediate political future – it decided whether he *had* a political future. And that, in the early months of 1923, was very much an open question. To understand the precarious nature of de Valera's political position in the summer of 1923, it is worth reconsidering – from his point of view – the events leading up to the Civil War.

The most salient fact for de Valera was that, since the end of 1921, his political power had been seeping away. First, he failed in his attempts to control from Dublin the plenipotentiaries negotiating the Anglo-Irish Treaty in London. The result was an agreement which failed what he regarded as the acid test – it did not maintain the unity of Sinn Féin (which his own proposal, external association, would have done had it been acceptable to the British). Then, to his surprise, he was outvoted in Cabinet on the question of whether to reject the treaty. This was in part his own fault – he had reduced the size of the cabinet, removing a number of doctrinaire republicans in the expectation that this would make it easier to win acceptance of a deal on the lines he had envisaged. Then, he was defeated in the Dáil in a vote on the treaty, with TDs supporting the agreement by 64 votes to 57. Even worse, after he resigned as president, he more narrowly lost a re-election bid, by 60 votes to 58. The margin was slim, but it was still a defeat.

He set great store by unity; the desire to keep the movement united lay behind his idea of external association and explains the lengths to which he went to promote it long after it was clear it was unacceptable to the British. Its main virtue in his eyes was that it was acceptable to the republican hardliners in cabinet such as Cathal Brugha and Austin Stack. Ironically, it was his quest for unity which now left de Valera – widely seen as a moderate – on the side of the hardliners. The double defeat in the Dáil did not just cost him the office of president, it also deprived him of his status as the leader of a united national movement. This was a particularly traumatic blow for de Valera because up to this point dealing with dissent or internal opposition had not been a major problem for him. He had, thanks to a lot of luck and to his own sharp elbows, emerged successively as the leader of the convicted

1916 prisoners, the unanimous choice as president of Sinn Féin, and the acknowledged leader of Irish nationalism. Now that was gone.

Directly after losing his attempt to regain the Presidency, he articulated this loss of political position, telling the anti-treaty TDs that he wanted to resign and return to teaching; while he was prepared to be the leader of the Irish people, he did not wish to be leader of a party.[1] Not for the last time, his followers prevailed upon him to stay. But the prestige, the power and even the point of his leadership rapidly diminished in the weeks and months to come. De Valera was the political head of a faction which had lost faith in politics; increasingly, the power of decision was seized by more radical figures – those who saw the only solution as a military one.

Ominously, de Valera too lost faith in politics. The most famous expression of this loss of faith was his St Patrick's Day speech in Thurles, in which he warned that if the Volunteers of the future wished to complete the work of achieving independence, they would have to 'wade through Irish blood, through the blood of the soldiers of the Irish Government, and through, perhaps, the blood of some of the members of the Government in order to get Irish freedom'.[2] The point of this rather lurid oratory was that de Valera doubted that there was a political path to undo the terms of the treaty. He believed that the treaty imposed restraints on independence which could not be negotiated or bargained away; they would have to be removed at gunpoint. But of course, if the political path was futile, there was not much call for politicians either.

That was certainly the view of the rising men on the anti-treaty side, men like Rory O'Connor, Liam Mellows and Liam Lynch, who paid less and less attention to de Valera as they reorganised the IRA as a self-governing entity, seized control of buildings in the heart of Dublin, and rejected the authority of the Dáil. De Valera, usually quick to react to any perceived slight on his authority, accepted this meekly. He later admitted that he had been 'foolish' to defend Rory O'Connor's 'unfortunate repudiation of the Dáil' but explained that he had done so 'in order to avoid the appearance of a split'.[3] Once again, the desire to avoid schism reduced his room for manoeuvre and left him even more reliant on hardliners. The only way to reassert his own primacy was to reassert the importance of politics. And he appeared to have done that by agreeing a pact with Michael Collins to present a united Sinn Féin panel in the general election of June 1922.

The Sinn Féin panel in each constituency would be filled by candidates from each side in proportion to their strength in the outgoing Dáil. Afterwards, a coalition government was to be formed in which the anti-treaty side would hold five of the eleven seats. Had the pact worked as de Valera envisaged, it would have ensured a continued role for himself, and would have protected the position of anti-treaty Sinn Féin, while acknowledging that it was in the minority. But the pact did not work as anticipated, for two reasons. Firstly, other interests were free to contest the election, giving the voters in 20 of the 28 constituencies an opportunity to demonstrate exactly what they thought of the anti-treaty position. And, despite the best efforts of Michael Collins, the British government rejected a quasi-Republican constitution for the new Free State, with the result that no opponent of the treaty would be able to serve in government (in the event, of course, they were not invited to).

De Valera's anti-treatyites won 36 seats, compared to 58 for pro-treaty Sinn Féin. Elected also were 34 non-Sinn Féin TDs, all broadly speaking pro-treaty. As de Valera admitted, 'we are hopelessly beaten, and if it weren't for the Pact, it would have been much worse'.[4] De Valera had said 'we', so he must have been aware that many on his own side considered the defeat to be his, and the dismal election results undermined his position with the militants even further. When the shelling of the Four Courts marked the formal start of the Civil War, he signed on as a private in his old unit, the Third Battalion of the Dublin Brigade, his leadership role seemingly at an end.

He had lost power; he had lost status; he had lost influence. His doubts about the point of continued hostilities were ignored, as were his repeated calls for the establishment of some form of republican 'government', as a political focus for the anti-treaty side. He summarised his position, shortly after the death of Michael Collins, at a clandestine meeting with Richard Mulcahy. According to Mulcahy, de Valera said that 'some men are led by faith, others were led by reason – that personally he would tend to be led by reason but as long as there were men of faith like Rory O'Connor, taking the stand that he was taking, that he, de Valera, was a humble soldier following after'.[5] He was certainly a follower rather than a leader, though the extent of his humility may be questioned. In fact, de Valera felt his fall from power during this period keenly, expressing his feelings most famously in February 1923 stating, 'I have been condemned to view the tragedy here for the last year as through a wall of glass, powerless to intervene effectively.'[6] But he was already looking for a way out, for a way to reassert the primacy of politics, and of course his own leadership.

A republican 'government' was finally set up in October 1922, though under strict conditions – the IRA Executive was careful to retain the final say on any peace negotiations, and to promise support to de Valera's body only 'while it functions as the Government of the Republic'.[7] Liam Lynch and his colleagues distrusted politicians; de Valera had regained only a very limited amount of power and influence.

Meanwhile, he was attempting to shore up his position on another front, seeking to gain control of the Sinn Féin party organisation. After the treaty split, he had established his own, republican, party, Cumann na Poblachta, but he was well aware that such an organisation would have limited appeal. However, he faced an uphill struggle to convince his colleagues that Sinn Féin was worth fighting for. The republican members of the party's Standing Committee asked what – apart from getting their hands on party funds – was the point of gaining control.[8] De Valera explained that the Sinn Fein organisation was an existing, all-Ireland body:

> with a constitution exactly suited to Republican purposes and policy… the Free Staters are anxious, in my opinion, to let the organisation die, and the money consideration alone keeps them from killing it outright… We should, for these very reasons, see to it that it does not die…

He wanted republican committees established around the country, which could then infiltrate and take over the Sinn Féin *cumainn*, while also being available to work separately and independently for republican election candidates.[9] If the other side blocked them, they could always work out of the Cumann na Poblachta headquarters in Suffolk Street, but he felt it was worth trying to work under the Sinn Féin banner – 'we can make far more rapid progress through Sinn Féin than through new Republican clubs, and there will be less danger of having organisers arrested.'[10] That letter was written on 31 October 1922 at a point when the Civil War was descending into a bitter spiral of reprisals, executions and assassinations, a time when few could see any way out of the morass. And yet de Valera – on the run, in danger of execution should he be caught, a pariah in the eyes of the Catholic bishops, the newspapers, and the economic establishment – was trying to prepare the ground for a political comeback.

When the two pro-treaty Joint Treasurers of Sinn Féin, Jennie Wyse Power and **Éamonn** Duggan, summoned a meeting of the Sinn Féin Standing Committee for 26 October, de Valera moved to fight them, arranging for substitutes to be nominated for himself and Austin Stack, who could not appear in public, and insisting that he, as sole trustee, should have control of the party's funds.[11] The problem with his strategy of capturing Sinn Féin for the anti-treaty cause was that the party's Ard Comhairle (which elected the Standing Committee) was 'composed mainly of the nominees of the other side… If the majority of the old Ard Comhairle were alright, we would be in a splendid position, but I think they are mostly all wrong.'[12] Therefore, the republican members convened a meeting of the Officer Board (which had equal representation of the two sides, unlike the Standing Committee or the Ard Comhairle). Wyse Power and Duggan insisted that the party could not be controlled by the Officer Board, but that the Ard Comhairle could not meet in the present unsettled state of the country; therefore, no business could be transacted, and the party funds could certainly not be handed over to de Valera, 'as conditions had entirely changed' since he was appointed trustee. The three remaining members of the Officer Board – Dr Kathleen Lynn, Kathleen Clarke (representing Stack) and P. J. Little (representing de Valera) – went ahead anyway, resolving that the old party headquarters in Harcourt Street should be reopened, with stenographer Vera McDonnell appointed acting secretary.[13] But without access to party funds, and with continued raids and harassment by Free State troops, making McDonnell's job impossible, such decisions were without practical effect.[14]

An election would be held at some point, and de Valera wanted to be ready for it. But he also knew that some on the republican side would view participation in electoral politics, particularly under the hated Free State regime, as a betrayal. So, he argued that they must 'deal with the new Castle junta as we did with the old – use their machinery where it suits us. It is very important that all our friends get on the [electoral] Register…'[15] He made a similar point in a few months later – using the Free State political machinery was acceptable in the circumstances, 'we should tie ourselves in a black knot if we tried to be rigidly consistent in everything.'[16]

As early as December, he suggested that 'the time is ripe and suitable' for political organisational work, that the Army must help, and that it was vital to 'make the new Sinn Féin thoroughly Republican and labour if possible.'[17] With civilians reluctant to work for Sinn Féin due to Free State pressure, the IRA was crucial to reorganisation efforts, and organisers were directed to base their efforts on the IRA's Divisional areas, as the work was 'so largely dependent on Army'.[18]

He remained convinced of the need to control Sinn Féin, worrying that if 'the others have a majority, as they are likely to have, they would be able to select their candidates, etc etc in case of an election and we would have no organisation at all'.[19] But many republicans continued to doubt the value of the party. Count Plunkett advised that the Sinn Féin organisation was dead, 'and held in contempt pretty generally… the name does not define or indicate a positive belief in the Republic'.[20] But for de Valera, that was part of the attraction of the old name – it could help to bring back supporters who were not extreme republicans: 'our aim is not to make a close preserve for ourselves, but to win the majority of the people again. I understand the difficulties but we must teach our people to be broad in this matter.'[21]

This desire to create a 'broad church' to maximise electoral support made sense in political terms, but it had very little appeal to hardline republicans who saw themselves as fighting to the death for a noble cause. His arguments made little impact on those like the implacable Mary MacSwiney for whom principle trumped pragmatism. In mid-March 1923, de Valera told MacSwiney that 'a military victory in the proper sense is not possible for us'. He advocated massing 'the public opinion of all who want peace against them [the Free State], and the more moderate our statements are, the better'.[22] He got nowhere with MacSwiney because at this point, de Valera's opinion did not matter. Liam Lynch continued to rule the Republican roost, and Lynch continued to believe, against all the evidence, that the military campaign could and should continue.

And then, on 10 April, Liam Lynch was killed in action, and everything changed. Lynch was replaced as Chief of Staff by Frank Aiken, who was both more realistic about the prospects of military victory and more open to persuasion (or, as some would say, domination) by de Valera. Aiken ordered an end to offensive operations by the IRA on 30 April in the vain hope that this would lead to negotiations with the Free State Government. When it became clear that Cosgrave and his colleagues had no intention of offering anything to their defeated opponents, IRA units were ordered to 'dump arms' on 24 May.

The Civil War was over; the militarists were defeated; and Éamon de Valera seized the opportunity to resume untrammelled leadership. Three issues dominated his thinking in the immediate aftermath of the end of the Civil War: money, publicity, and control. Given attitudes in Ireland – particularly among the wealthy – the only realistic source of finance for the republican cause was in the United States. On 20 June he was complaining to a clerical supporter in New York that a combination of government harassment and lack of funds meant they would be unable to contest the forthcoming general election.[23] But, within two weeks he was rethinking this position – after all, what use was a political leader who could not contest elections? Now he argued that while the priority for available funds remained the care of prisoners, the wounded and the bereaved, it was also true that 'it is only by political means that we can hope for any measure of success in the near future'. Therefore, he needed cash to bankroll an election campaign. And while he was not being over-ambitious, only thinking of contesting one seat in each constituency, he still needed $100,000, 'which I think is the smallest sum on which we could hope to put up anything like a decent fight'.[24] He added that he detested the need 'to send round the hat again' – but send it round he did.[25]

Closely related to the money question was the issue of publicity. He had a long-standing obsession with the press, which had been almost uniformly pro-treaty. He complained at the very start of the Civil War that 'the newspapers are as usual more deadly to our cause than the machine guns'.[26] Now, he told Constance Markievicz their next project must be to get a daily newspaper off the ground. He stated, 'in meeting them in arms we were fighting them on their own chosen ground . . . If we develop properly the line of peaceful political attack, building upon the undoubted desire of the people for complete independence, it is we who are invincible.'[27] There was, he fretted, 'no hope in the future without a paper',[28] and subscriptions were solicited for a fund to establish 'an Irish Daily Republican Press'.[29]

This obsession would stay with him, and the importance of the *Irish Press* to the political success of Fianna Fáil suggests he was right. The existence of the Irish Press allowed de Valera to get his political message across, undiluted, to voters; the absence of such an avenue of communication in the 1920s meant his views were reported through the prism of the pro-Treaty stance of the existing newspapers.

Finally, there was the question of control. Having been side-lined for most of the Civil War, de Valera was determined to wrest control from the IRA Executive. Fortunately for him, Frank Aiken was considerably more pliable than Liam Lynch had been. De Valera referred back to the original decision establishing the republican 'government', which said that questions of peace and war needed to be ratified by the Executive. In other words, other issues did not need IRA sanction, and in the new situation, the politicians should regain their freedom of action. He declared, 'I do not think the combination Army Council and Government should continue in its present form. The Army could be represented on the Ministry by the Chief of Staff, the Adjutant General, and, if necessary, the Assistant Chief of Staff?'[30] And just in case anybody on the military side got ideas, he warned against any resumption of armed conflict.

> I am convinced of this absolutely – that any war started in the immediate future, unless under the pressure of brutal attacks from the other side or the attempt to establish a military tyranny by them, would be only a half-hearted war on our side, would not be successful, and would be disastrous to the cause, and I foresee no circumstances that are likely to arise which would justify the attempt.[31]

The war was over, he was back in the saddle, and he was determined to remain there.

While he had regained control, there were still some reservations about de Valera on the republican side. He was treated with respect within the anti-treaty movement, certainly: with the egalitarianism of revolutionaries, everybody, of whatever rank, was addressed by their Christian name – except him. 'There was one exception. Nobody called Éamon de Valera anything but "Mister" de Valera, "Sir" or, if one was reasonably close to him, "Chief".'[32] But there was suspicion, too. In a prison camp in Gormanstown, County Meath, Frank Gallagher heard a (false) rumour of de Valera's arrest and asked for a Mass to be said for him. Oscar Traynor, the camp commandant, said de Valera was only one of many heads of families to face arrest, while Seán MacEntee thought the Mass would have no effect if the priest was hostile. Gallagher remarked, 'my God said I, he is our President, our Head of State, we have only one President, every nation prays for its head when in danger… Said angrily if they were ashamed of their President I wasn't, and I'd ask the priest.'[33]

De Valera told Mary MacSwiney he was 'sick' of being told he was easily misunderstood, 'those who misunderstand me are either those who find it convenient not to see what I mean, or those who have not the will to interpret what I say except in the distorted field of their own prejudices and preconceptions.'[34] His particular skills were recognised, of course. Aiken once asked him to rewrite the draft minutes of a meeting: 'I don't like troubling you but I must ask you to "touch" them up, as you are well known to be a good "artist".' De Valera thought this 'a very back handed compliment'[35] – which of course it was.

As the election loomed, he continued his efforts to capture the Sinn Féin organisation, enlisting the help of Joseph Connolly, a Belfast businessman and Sinn Féin activist recently returned from serving as Consul General in New York. Connolly had not taken an active part in opposing the treaty, and therefore had more freedom of movement than many who had. De Valera was somewhat grudging in his assessment of his new collaborator, 'I do not know Connolly very well, but I believe him sincere, patriotic, wise and able, if not perhaps inspiring…'[36] But whatever about his failure to inspire, Connolly had a more important quality – he agreed with de Valera. He had written to the republican leader in December, urging him to bring the fighting to an end and to pursue political opposition instead.[37] This was exactly what de Valera wanted to hear, and he now asked Connolly to help him re-establish the party. The Belfast man consented to chair the committee of 'Sinn Féin Reorganised', on the promise that there would be a ceasefire at an early date, allowing republicans to devote all their energies to political work.[38] A week before the ceasefire, de Valera told another confidant that 'it may be necessary soon to change the defence of our national Independence from the plane of arms to that of unarmed effort'. Sectional interests were springing up – farmers, labour, etc. – which would distract from the purely national issue. De Valera stated that, 'it is vital, therefore, that the reorganisation of Sinn Féin as the national organisation should be pushed forwards with all speed.'[39]

The task of reorganisation was a formidable one: from a peak of 1,500 branches only about 60 remained by the beginning of 1923, dropping to only 16 by June of that year.[40] However, de Valera felt that the jailing of so many anti-treatyites provided 'a wonderful opportunity for political discussion and reorganisation' in captivity, though he was careful to stress that those involved in the military campaign should be excluded from the reorganising committee, as they might 'frighten off those we wish to attract into the organisation'.[41] To Molly Childers, widow of Erskine, he wrote, 'the hope for the future lies in again reorganising the main body of nationalist opinion… the formation by the others of Cumann na nGaedheal has left the way for Sinn Féin clear… very many who opposed the method of arms are with us heart and soul as far as our objective is concerned and would be delighted to work through Sinn Féin.'[42] But a preliminary meeting of the reorganising committee demonstrated the difficulty de Valera faced in trying to direct it by remote control. A number of members – particularly Áine Ceannt and Kathleen Lynn – objected to the name 'Sinn Féin'. It was not popular, it would not attract uncompromising republicans, and it could be infiltrated by supporters of the Free State. Alternative names were suggested – Irish Republican Organisation or Irish Independence Organisation.[43] Asked for his opinion, de Valera wrote that they should consider themselves the 'Committee for the reorganisation of Sinn Féin as the Irish Independence Organisation'. Those who felt Sinn Féin was too broad would still have the Cumann na Poblachta Party, but the new Sinn Féin would put forward election candidates, 'their exact platform and programme can be determined later.'[44] But the committee was having none of it, passing a resolution that the new party should be called 'the Irish Republican Political Organisation'.[45] De Valera's supporter Michael Comyn warned him that if the word 'republic' wasn't in the title, 'it is quite probable that an independent republican party would be started.'[46] De Valera wrote a strongly worded letter, stressing the need to gather not just republican opinion, 'but what might be called "Nationalist" or "Independence" opinion in general. If we do not do it, the other side will, and the loss will be immense'. He urged them to accept his recommendation (backed as it was by his government and by the IRA Executive) that Sinn Féin should be reorganised.[47] But this suggestion was rejected by every member of the committee, bar Comyn.[48] Kathleen Lynn said she could see 'nothing but disaster in this idea of camouflaged Republicans contesting elections, the country wants the republic, it is sick of the F. S. and only those who boldly uphold the Republic will have any chance of making headway.'[49] Eventually, though not a member of the Committee, and though he appeared to be in a minority of one, de Valera had his way: the new, or reorganised, party would be called Sinn Féin. As he explained to John Hagan, Rector of the Irish College in Rome and a key supporter of the republican cause, he kept the name because the people 'are too fidgety just now for us to risk anything like a change'.[50]

De Valera took the view that the re-organising committee, 'as a group of ordinary members, are entitled on behalf of the general body to take steps to see that the organisation is preserved.'[51] A quarter of a century later, in the High Court, Mr Justice Kingsmill Moore took a different view; the ad hoc Organising Committee did not have the legal power to call the Ard Fheis which re-established Sinn Féin, and therefore the party which emerged in 1923 was 'not in any legal sense a continuation of the organisation'.[52] This meant that the Sinn Féin Party of 1948 could not get its hands on the funds deposited in court by Jennie Wyse Power and Éamonn Duggan; and that the various successor parties were not legally the same entity as the Sinn Féin of the years 1917–22.

This interesting legal point was, however, of no concern in 1923, when what was at stake was the political survival of opposition to the treaty, and of Éamon de Valera. In continuation of de Valera's 'broad' policy, Joseph Connolly did his best to keep mentions of 'the Republic' to a minimum. He asked de Valera to write to the committee 'saying (if possible) quite frankly that it is not serving our purpose to shriek the Republic on every bill poster'.[53] The agreed aims of the party, as approved by de Valera, did not mention the Republic, but instead stressed the need to oppose every form of foreign interference: 'Ireland is an independent State, and that whilst the form of Government may be changed by the free vote of the people, Ireland's Independence cannot be signed away, or voted away.' In a further effort to give himself the maximum freedom of manoeuvre, he stated that 'questions of method are open, provided there is no formal recognition of the legality of the Free State regime'.[54]

At a meeting on 11 and 12 July, the Army Executive approved the policy of contesting elections, and also the aims and programme of Sinn Féin, recommending that all Volunteers join the organisation.[55] With the Executive's backing in place, de Valera sent a message to all prisons and internment camps, extoling the virtues of the re-established party: 'the words Sinn Féin express both our objective and our means.' He told the prisoners that the future of the cause depended on their spirit: 'the Camps should be converted into miniature Universities – the language, the history, the economics of our country can be taught and studied… But all the intelligence in the world will not be sufficient unless we organise thoroughly. I give Education, Temperance, Organisation as your mottos…'[56]

With some money coming in, a policy programme agreed, and the rudiments of a party organisation in place, the anti-treaty cause was ready to make some kind of showing in the general election. Characteristically, de Valera now dithered about how many candidates Sinn Féin should nominate – or even whether it should contest the election at all. He began by enthusiastically favouring participation, as refusing to stand 'lets the case go by default'.[57] In June, he was predicting the return of 35 Sinn Féin TDs – 'a very substantial nucleus for future political action'[58], but then his optimism seemed to falter. On 25 July, a month before polling, he pointed out to his Sinn Féin colleagues that there were four options: to abstain completely, on the grounds the elections would not be free or fair; to put forward only one candidate per constituency, as he had suggested; to put forward a few candidates in selected places – 'my own case in Clare, on account of the O'Connell precedent as regards the oath, is an example'; or to put forward as many candidates as they could hope to get elected. In the absence of comprehensive information from each constituency on which to base the decision, he thought the first option, abstention, to be 'undoubtedly, the safest ground'.[59]

Luckily for Sinn Féin, the Organising Committee disagreed, insisting that the party should contest the elections 'to the full limit of our hopes' (as well as pointing out that if they were to abstain, the abstention would have to cover everyone – 'even including yourself' – putting paid to his suggestion of making Clare a special case).[60] Within a couple of weeks, de Valera's doubts had been dispelled – if anything, he was becoming overconfident, telling the Sinn Féin Director of Elections that he heard his own constituency of Clare was 'magnificent', and wondering if they could 'put up sufficient candidates in the constituencies so as to secure a majority or near it?'[61] The Clare canvass returns were certainly encouraging, claiming as they did '95 per cent of the electorate… in many areas'.[62]

After Free State Minister for External Affairs Desmond FitzGerald said that he would be 'kept on the run', de Valera issued a defiant statement, 'if the people of Clare select me as their candidate again, I will be with them and nothing but a bullet will stop me.'[63] He told Ruttledge that 'of all the men on our side, I have the best chance, I think', by which he presumably meant the best chance of surviving the conflict. He also recognised that he might be wrong, a prospect he viewed philosophically, 'if anything happens – well, the cause will benefit.'[64] To Molly Childers, who knew more than most about the risks involved, he said 'there is, of course, danger, but I think it is wise nevertheless… I do not err as a rule on the rash side – but I can face the inevitable'.[65] He intended to keep the promise he had made to appear, come what may. 'As regards Clare, and my recent commitment, enemy action will settle that. Either way, the effect will be good', he told the Sinn Féin organising committee.[66]

The danger of a bullet actually stopping him seemed very real. The IRA's Director of Intelligence, Michael Carolan, warned him several times that his life was in danger if he went to Ennis, claiming he had absolutely reliable information that he would be targeted in revenge for the killing of Michael Collins. According to Carolan, senior Free State official Diarmuid O'Hegarty was claiming that de Valera had actually taken part in the ambush in which Collins died.[67] On 12 August, de Valera left for Clare, with every expectation that he could be killed or arrested.[68] His loyal secretary, Kathleen O'Connell, who arrived in Ennis the night before the meeting, found the atmosphere disturbing, 'the air seemed charged with strange rumours. All seemed so panicky. Expecting anything to happen tomorrow.'[69] On his way into Ennis, de Valera received a message from Frank Aiken, warning he was certain to be arrested and advising him to change the time and venue of the meeting. But he considered it 'too late to change'.[70]

The Government was anxious to arrest de Valera before he appeared in public,[71] but he managed to reach the stage before he was recognised.[72] He spoke for several minutes, denying that republicans stood for anarchy and destruction, or for 'brother's hand being raised against brother'; they stood for unity, and believed that 'if the people of this country stood together and were united, it could achieve its independence'.[73] At this point Free

State troops arrived, pushing their way through the crowd with fixed bayonets, and opened fire without orders.[74] The firing led to a stampede among the 3,000 people in the square. At least 20 people were injured, four of whom suffered bullet wounds, despite the soldiers supposedly firing into the air.[75] De Valera was hit in the leg, either by a stray bullet or by splinters. When the troops reached the platform, he made no attempt to escape, but 'went down the steps of the platform to where the soldiers were waiting for him'.[76] As the crowd jeered the arresting troops, he was marched off to the barracks, and later transferred to Arbour Hill Prison in Dublin and was held as a danger to public safety.[77]

Cosgrave announced de Valera's arrest to an election rally in Drogheda, claiming that 'many a grave is in the graveyards of the country tonight because of the formulas, the metaphysics and nonsense he put before the needs of the nation'.[78] P. J. Ruttledge, who de Valera had nominated to take his place if he were arrested or killed, claimed the arrest showed the Government's 'pretence of free speech and a free election is as hollow as their pretence that they represent the people of Ireland'.[79] However, the arrest did the republican election campaign no harm; as some had predicted, it might even have helped. On polling day, the republican share of the vote was 27.6 per cent, up from 21.5 per cent the year before (partly because seven strongly Republican constituencies in the west were contested this time).[80] It was a remarkable performance, given the undoubted unpopularity of the Civil War, the imprisonment of so many republican activists and leaders, and harassment by the Free State authorities (though, of course, it was still a defeat). Although, had they followed de Valera's suggestion of putting up only one candidate per constituency, they would have won just 25 seats; instead, they ended up with 44. As one of the first time Republican TDs noted, it was a huge boost to their confidence, 'the road back was going to be shorter than we dared hope'.[81] By October 1923, Sinn Féin had 729 *cumainn*; by contrast, Cumann na nGaedheal had just 247 by the end of the year.[82]

In Clare, de Valera had faced his first contested election since his 1917 by-election victory. His performance was a triumph, securing 17,762 votes, 45 per cent of the poll, more than two quotas. It was the highest percentage share in the country (though Richard Mulcahy won more votes in Dublin North, with 22,205, a 40 per cent share). De Valera dragged in a running mate, Brian O'Higgins, whose own first preference vote was just 114 votes, or 0.29 per cent. Three other Republican candidates secured 1.22, 0.56, and 0.29 per cent of the poll – clearly, vote management was not a priority.

On the other side of the treaty divide, there was a similar, though not quite as extreme, story, with Eoin MacNeill securing the bulk of the pro-treaty vote, with a 20.78 per cent share, also being elected on the first count. His four running mates were unsuccessful. The final seats were taken by the Farmers' candidate Conor Hogan and Patrick Hogan of Labour. The party shares of the vote were: Sinn Féin 48 per cent, Cumann na nGaedheal 29 per cent, Famers 12 per cent, and Labour 11 per cent.[83] The result must have been a particularly unpleasant shock for MacNeill – two weeks before polling, he told his wife 'we are confident of a big majority'.[84]

Meanwhile, de Valera was languishing in Arbour Hill, unable to enjoy his electoral triumph. His wife, Sinéad, had been kept completely in the dark as to what had happened to him; on 23 August, eight days after his arrest, she wrote to the Adjutant General, demanding to know where he was being held, after a telegram and repeated phone calls had elicited no information.[85] A telegram the following day confirmed he was in Arbour Hill and she was able to hand in letters and clothes, but was told her letters would have to be censored, and that her husband could not write to her.[86] It was entirely natural that Sinéad was worried about her husband's safety. Given the continued, though reduced, violence on the outside (Noel Lemass had been abducted on 3 July and murdered, presumably by Free State forces) it might be argued that de Valera was safer in prison than outside it. Indeed, on at least one occasion Cosgrave claimed this was the reason for his continued imprisonment.[87] However, given what had happened to Liam Mellows and Rory O'Connor, there could be no guarantees of his safety in the custody of the Free State.

The Executive Council had their man; but what were they to do with him? The day after his arrest, they decided 'that a charge should be brought against him with the least possible delay', and Mulcahy was asked to have all the available evidence examined and given to the Attorney General, Hugh Kennedy.[88] And here they came up against a surprising and rather embarrassing problem; there were very few incriminating documents on which a prosecution could be based, particularly as Kennedy insisted only those dated after 6 December 1922, when the Free State Constitution came into force, would be of value. Kennedy 'was not clear as to what charge could be put against him'; having examined the available documents 'there did not seem to be much in them to form the subject of a charge'.[89] In fact, the only 'real evidence' that could be used appeared to be a letter from de Valera to the Honorary Secretaries of Cumann na mBan.[90] Given all that had been said about de Valera's war guilt, a prosecution on this basis might well have appeared ridiculous, and the idea was quietly dropped. Held in solitary confinement, de Valera was philosophical:

> they will seal me in the tomb as well as they can … they will neither be able to provoke me nor make me really unhappy, no matter what they do… If I were out there is little I could do of value – what I can do will be better later – that's my principal consideration.[91]

But while he was locked away, he was still alive – unlike Griffith, Collins, Brugha, Boland, and a host of others. He was still, to many people, a pariah. But the 1923 General Election had demonstrated conclusively that de Valera still had a political future. He had outlined his strategy of attracting a broad swathe of opinion, not just those who had taken up arms in the Civil War, in order to peacefully overturn the terms of the treaty. The disastrous loss of faith in political action, outlined in his 'wading through blood' speech, was at an end. To be sure, the road ahead was a steep one, but it was there, and as he was to prove in the coming years, it could be climbed.

CHAPTER 4

SEARCHING FOR THE NORMAL: THE FARMERS' AND LABOUR PARTIES IN THE 1923 ELECTION

Jason Knirck

Across the 1920s, many residents of countries that had fought in the First World War sought a return to what they perceived as a sense of normality that had been broken by the radical effects of the war. Warren Harding's call for normalcy instead of heroism in 1920, Stanley Baldwin's 'Safety first' slogan in 1929, and even the Nazis' pledge for women's 'emancipation from emancipation' all promised a return to more settled conditions and pre-war values. The 1923 General Election in the Irish Free State also featured candidates, particularly those from non-Sinn Féin parties, calling for and anticipating the arrival of normal conditions, at least in politics. However, in the Free State such references generally indicated a desire to move on from the conditions caused by colonialism, revolution, and civil war, rather than those directly stemming from the First World War.

The normal conditions that the Labour and Farmers' parties wanted to create, though, had never actually existed in Ireland. In the aftermath of the triumph of a long-suppressed nationalist movement that imagined itself as monolithic, there was considerable expectation within Sinn Féin that single-party or non-party politics would remain a distinguishing feature of the new state. This was often couched as hostility to the perceived corruption of the British two-party system and the backroom dealings of the old Irish Party. The smaller parties, in contrast, desired the creation of a political system that mirrored the continental model of left–right politics, a system they believed would elevate parties organised around class instead of Sinn Féin's broad nationalist coalition.

This desire sat uneasily with Sinn Féin's hegemonic nationalism and its oft-stated aspiration for a type of anti-politics that would reject and reshape pre-war norms. Sinn Féin wanted the replacement of the outmoded two-party politics and colonialist tropes that had prevented 'politics' from working for Ireland during the long colonial period. This was conditioned by the observation that Home Rule or Irish reform had rarely been decided on its merits, but instead its support was conditioned by the vagaries of British party politics. The smaller parties imagined a different post-revolutionary landscape, one in which a long, albeit intermittent, anticolonial struggle did not assume an apostolic succession from Wolfe Tone to Charles Stewart Parnell to W. T. Cosgrave or Éamon de Valera. They instead thought that class-based parties would ascend, as had happened in pre-war Europe.

Despite the rather consistent characterisation of Irish nationalism as backward-looking and retrograde, all parties in the election wanted to modernise Ireland while decoupling modernisation from Anglicisation, as they felt that Britain's example – urbanisation, industrial pollution, class conflict, and party politics – was unsuited to Ireland. All parties thought colonialism had slowed Ireland's modernisation but each had different goals now that a form of independence had been won. Sinn Féin wanted to develop the Free State economically behind tariff walls and without an ongoing neocolonial relationship with Britain. Labour hoped to reverse the subordination of the Irish working class by the twin evils of capitalism and colonialism. The Farmers' Party, which often railed against many elements of modernity, also urged the Free State to embrace rural modernisation along Danish lines as a way of both preserving Ireland's rural character and preventing the emulation of urbanised England. The 1923 election was the first chance for the Labour and Farmers' parties to test their ideas with the electorate in somewhat peaceful conditions.

Scholars have generally neglected the role of the smaller parties in the development of Free State democracy. John Coakley argued that 'only a few' minor parties 'have become politically relevant', although he does not include Labour among the minor parties.[1] Labour has received some credit for helping to secure democracy in the Free State, but most of the literature on Labour focused on its electoral futility.[2] Despite Labour's electoral troubles throughout most of the rest of the decade, the prevailing opinion in 1923 was that nationalist hegemony would be broken and the class-based parties such as Labour and the Farmers would take on greater prominence. Patrick Hogan, the Cumann na nGaedheal Minister for Agriculture, told an election audience: 'this was the first normal election since the [1801] Union – in fact, it was the first ordinary election in the history of Ireland.'[3] A letter to the editor in the *Irish Independent* observed, 'the coming election is unique in the history of Ireland. Hitherto elections to Parliament were for the most part in the hands of a class or party; now at least we have one free and democratic.'[4] Both Hogan and the *Independent* noted the number and variety of candidates as particularly healthy signs for Irish democracy.[5] For the first time in decades, an election would be competitive in many constituencies and would not be dominated by a single nationalist political party.

Labour and the Farmers were poised to reap the benefits of Sinn Féin's anticipated decline. Thomas Johnson, the leader of the Labour Party, said in Cork that 'they were coming to the real cleavage that was to divide political parties in the future', by which he meant class politics.[6] An editorial in the Labour newspaper proclaimed, 'the time has come when some new force, some living truth must replace the dying delusions and pitiful falsehoods of bourgeois nationalism.'[7] This optimism stemmed from a Marxist assumption about the inevitable collapse of bourgeois nationalism, a belief that both wings of Sinn Féin had lost credibility because of the Civil War, and an optimism stemming from Labour's electoral performance in 1922. This descent of normality over the country would benefit Labour as it believed itself to be the party most concerned with bread-and-butter issues, instead of the arcane minutia of oaths and Dominion status. A Labour editorial commented,

> That indeed has been the great value of Labour, its sense of realism. ... Labour is showing that realist view of things now, when we are coming into a kind of a peace and actual issues that have no bearing upon past controversies are rising up as the everyday material of political affairs.[8]

The Farmers also thought themselves on the cusp of power. The secretary of the Meath Farmers' Union said in 1923, 'it was only in peace that the union would really come into its own. The possibilities for the farmers through representation in Parliament had been only partially demonstrated.'[9] According to the Farmers' Party's Standing Committee, the Free State 'opened a new chapter in Irish history,' although it quickly became clear that 'all were not satisfied with the new order of things'.[10] The Farmers' Party thought it could expand because of the discontent with nationalism and the centrality of agriculture in Irish life. At a Farmers' meeting in Limerick, the organiser told his listeners that 'they had a political asset in the Farmers' Party that they never had before. Numerically it was small, but it was the nucleus of a larger party which would be in the Dáil when it was re-modelled, as it would be very soon'.[11] The *Independent* noted that many of the oddities of the 1922 election had fallen away and 'nothing but the indifference of the electorate can prevent the results from being a true reflex of popular feeling'.[12]

The smaller parties believed, genuinely, that they could take advantage of these settled conditions to make substantial inroads against nationalist political hegemony. They claimed that such an electoral change would benefit the country as a whole as their advocates believed they had meaningful advantages over the two wings of Sinn Féin. The *Irish Independent* wrote that times had changed and that elections no longer needed to be about vetting revolutionary credentials or choosing prominent Sinn Féiners so as to defy England. Instead, what Ireland needed now was 'prudent and far-seeing lawmakers', which was a different skill set.[13] Seeking people outside of the nationalist party would make parliament more representative. Labour leader Thomas Johnson argued that a further denial of the rights and place of sectional parties would be disastrous for Irish democracy:

> The Government Party was appealing to the people in the same language that the [Collins–De Valera] Pact used a year ago. They said the time was not yet ripe for separate parties. Suppose the people took them at their word, what would the result be? It would be similar to the experiences of the last few months. The Government have had about 80 supporters in the Dáil and hardly once had any member of its Party put up one word of criticism to a Government proposal. No Parliament could carry on under such conditions.[14]

Instead, Labour wanted representation at least according to its demographic strength, ensuring that the voice of the workers would be heard in the Dáil.

The Farmers made similar arguments. They believed agriculture was massively underrepresented in the Dáil, belying Ireland's status as a fundamentally agrarian country. Sir Henry Grattan Bellew put this succinctly: 'they [farmers] constitute the majority and if majorities have the right to rule, the farmers have the right.'[15] They controlled, in their estimation, nearly two-thirds of the voting power in the country and the Dáil should reflect this demographic fact.[16] And, according to the Farmers' Party, farmers were not being sufficiently represented in the Dáil by either Cumann na nGaedheal or Sinn Féin. Adding more Farmers' Party deputies would not only make Dáil Éireann more representative of the society it governed but would bring a different type of deputy into the Dáil without sacrificing the national interest. The chairman of the Galway Farmers' Association said, 'there is no man in the land capable of having a wider outlook, a deeper sympathy with the national progress than a man thoroughly conversant with all that agricultural Ireland stands for.'[17]

The Farmers' Party saw Ireland's prosperity as dependent on agriculture, making the underrepresentation of agricultural interests even more problematic. Farmers' TD John

Rooney said, 'they represented the agricultural industry of the country, which was the staple industry, and the one on which their prosperity must be built, and which would make this country wealthy in ten years. In England it was the industrialists who governed and made England wealthy and it was the farmers who would make Ireland wealthy.'[18] This was a particularly Irish path to modernity, one built on agriculture instead of on industrial capitalism. That prosperity would not come about under the current leadership, which was perceived by the Farmers' Party as being too urban, industrial, bureaucratic, and Dublin-centric. Farmers' Party supporter P. F. Baxter told a crowd that, 'statesmen and soldiers would not build up a nation. The Farmers' candidates were just as good patriots as the others. A half-dozen men in Dublin were managing the affairs of the country.'[19] As Farmers' TD Michael Doyle said in the final run-up to the election, 'agriculture was the chief industry in Ireland and could not be better looked after than by those engaged in it. A man who required a doctor does not go to a blacksmith, and if he required a pair of boots, he would get very bad value from a lawyer.'[20] This was a clear argument for sectional and vocational representation in the new Dáil, contrary to Sinn Féin's wishes.

Similar to the workers and farmers, business and commercial interests also felt absent from the revolutionary Dáil. Despite a growing connection between Cumann na nGaedheal and the business classes as the 1920s went on, initially there was a push in Cork and Dublin to have businessmen themselves run for Dáil seats. William Findlater argued, 'if their legislature was to be established on a democratic basis it must be representative of all sections of the community, and the Dáil would not be representative of all sections if they had not there a strong and compact representation of the trade and commerce of the country.'[21] Business leaders, however willing they were to work with Cumann na nGaedheal, did not feel directly represented by that party. The Cork Progressive Association, which ran two successful business candidates in the 1923 election, contended, 'in recent elections very little consideration was given to the commercial community, and that their interests had not suffered more was a very fortunate thing.'[22] The inclusion of business interests would also bring financial skills to bear on the Free State's problems. A Dublin candidate said, 'if there was a smattering of businessmen amongst the last Dáil they would have a very different Exchequer today.'[23]

Women were another underrepresented group and there was some discussion outside of the major parties of the need for female candidates. A conference of 'representative women' was held in the Mansion House before the election and it 'expressed strong views as to the neglect of women's interests in the Dáil'.[24] They eventually decided to propose several candidates in Dublin, whose platforms would focus on neglected women's issues: 'housing and educational reform, the restoration of the dead meat trade … and the fostering of other suitable Irish industries, by which they aim to provide work for all citizens and abolish the unemployment dole. They will concentrate on business and commercial interests and will be advocates for the better protection of animals.'[25] A female journalist promised to run under the banner of the 'Independent Women's Party', but none of this ended up transpiring and the only female candidates were put forward by Cumann na nGaedheal and Sinn Féin.

Labour, Farmers' Party, and independent candidates claimed that their presence would not only change the composition of the Dáil, but the way in which Irish politics functioned. Nearly all Irish political figures denied that they were politicians and 'politics' was a much-derided term in Irish political culture. For Sinn Féin, politics connoted the corruption of the Irish party and the perceived meaninglessness of the British two-party system. For the smaller parties, though, politics was used to denigrate Sinn Féiners' excessive focus on political issues such as the oath and the status of the state, rather than foregrounding social and economic issues. Labour felt that its role was to highlight such issues and remained frustrated with the continuing relevance of the treaty and what it perceived as the government's unwillingness to tackle the country's growing economic problems. Labour already noted that the treatyite party 'will make much show of being a "no class party" …[but] it will be found that this party's programme when promulgated will not fulfil the requirements of the worker because its foundation will be purely political, instead of social'.[26]

Labour hoped that the more politically settled conditions of 1923 would lead to fewer 'political' issues and more attention to the plight of the workers. The *Voice of Labour* wrote

> 'a strong Labour party will be needed. The new Dáil may last four years. It will be under no necessity to devote so large a share of its time to matters of machinery as was the case with its predecessor, and it will be compelled by the pressure of facts, even if it did not feel bound to do so of its own initiative, to devote itself to the social and economic issues which have been neglected for years.[27]

This was part of an editorial titled 'Labour Confident about Elections' and indicated that the party thought that Sinn Féiners still inhabited a political fantasyland in which abstract issues regarding the Crown mattered to the lives of ordinary people. Labour's William O'Brien confidently predicted during the 1923 campaign that 'the experience of this election would show that the country desired the Dáil to drop academic discussions on political issues and to grapple seriously with housing, unemployment, public health, education, and development of their industrial resources'.[28] Another Labour candidate tellingly said it was 'absurd and unpatriotic to try and make the treaty an issue in the present'.[29] That was precisely what Sinn Féiners were doing, much to Labour's frustration: anti-treatyites were still campaigning against its flaws and treatyites claimed that their election was necessary to preserve the stability it brought.

The Farmers saw themselves as an antidote to politics in much the same way as Labour. Limerick Farmers' candidate Batt Laffan told an audience that the last election had been decided on political issues and had resulted in a Dáil that underrepresented economic actors.[30] A Farmers' candidate in Westmeath said, 'the farmers were not a political party. Their aim was national economy.'[31] At times, this non-political badge was used as a way of explaining that the party did not mandate a particular take on 'political' issues from its members. A potential member was told in 1923 that 'the Farmers' Union was a non-political organisation that welcomed and expected Republican farmers into its ranks'.[32] At times, though, this language was used to indicate that the Farmers intended to focus on economic issues instead of nationalist ones. A Farmers' campaigner in Clare noted 'the Farmers were standing as an economic party and not as a political party, and therefore had never attacked or defended either side'.[33]

As with Labour, this was an attempt to place economic issues at the forefront of Irish political discourse in a way that they had not been during the revolution. The idea, as always, was to elevate class in the face of consistent Sinn Féin attempts to erase it as a political category. Farmers' candidate Patrick McKenna asserted that voters 'should consider their own class first, and then divide their votes on any political party they liked after. The people were sick of party politics'.[34] The Farmers, like Labour, saw themselves as outside of party politics as they defined it, even though they had a political party and were in fact active in politics. But party politics to them connoted sterile conversations about Anglo-Irish relations and nationalist shibboleths, as against the bread-and-butter issues that the smaller parties highlighted. The 1923 election was a chance to capitalise on the electorate's fatigue with such party politics, which was merely 'hot air' of 'a very inferior type'.[35]

The business candidates also railed against the prevalence of 'politics' or 'party politics'. Candidate P. L. Ryan in Tipperary 'desire[d] to say at the outset that I am not a Politician, and in my opinion we have had far too much politics in this country for many years past… I allow my name to go before you as a business man.' As was the case with many independent or business candidates, he assumed that people were tired of lengthy political speeches and vowed 'my observations will be as brief as possible.'[36] As with the Farmers' Party, business or independent candidates wanted to emphasise that practical experience and business acumen, rather than nationalist credentials, should be the litmus test for political office. The *Irish Independent* editorialised frequently in favour of these candidates and emphasised that times had changed from the revolutionary era:

> [business] nominees have been chosen, not because of their political views, but because they are men of ability, of experience, and of success in commerce. That is as it should be, for there is no longer any political issues at stake, and those who seek to raise one will receive little favour from the populace.[37]

This again demonstrates the idea that the 1923 election was a new chapter in Irish political history. The electorate would continue to move away from 'politics', but whereas in 1918 that connoted ending the reign of the Irish Party and its place in the British two-party system, by 1923 the desired shift was one that reduced squabbling over the forms of independence and instead focused on economic development and social ills. The business and farmers candidates in particular equated the running of a country not with theatrical protests against the colonial power, but with running a business. The Cork Progressive Association (CPA) claimed that 'we want our business done on business, not political, lines and for the attainment of this we intend to get business men to do it for us'.[38] Business candidates thought that 'political' fights reduced the chances of successful Irish economic development. None of these political groupings wanted to scrap the treaty, but they wanted to move past the treaty as the single defining issue in Irish politics.

At times, this desire to create a new politics was specifically framed as a way of moving on from the destruction of the Civil War. While historians have frequently cited a silence about the Civil War, this was never true in politics, as politicians talked about it openly for decades. The smaller parties and independents depicted it as a futile obstacle that needed to be put to rest, rather than as the saving of democracy. P. J. Bermingham, a Farmers' candidate in Leix, wondered 'if the Farmers' Party are returned fairly strong to the Dáil they might be the means of [bridging] the gulf that divided the two rival organisations – Free State and Republicans'.[39] Candidate J. J. Fitzsimons somewhat tenuously connected civil war strife to the Farmers' chief political plank: 'there was only one way to forget the tragedies of the past, and that was to reduce expenditure.'[40] The basic idea, however inartfully expressed, was that economic interests could supersede political divisions. A CPA supporter argued that the Progressive programme 'will help to eradicate the divisions of the past by uniting all responsible citizens on an economic basis. The substitution of an economic for a political background will go a long way towards bringing about the new unity which will be so essential for the rebuilding of our country.'[41] This was an explicit inversion of Sinn Féin's revolutionary era calls for unity, which prioritised political positions and attempted to mask economic differences. This unity was rooted in attempts to re-orient class politics, as the Farmers thought they could attract business voters, particularly from rural towns, and Labour believed it could win the votes of agricultural labourers and small farmers.

Labour too claimed an ability to end civil war politics if only given a chance. During the Third Dáil, the Labour Party had worked to 'create an atmosphere for ending the fratricidal strife'.[42] Labour did so by condemning the militarism of both sides and protesting civil war violence in the Dáil. They bore no responsibility for the treaty split and so could play the role of neutral arbiter much better than the parties that had evolved out of Sinn Féin. As Labour leader, Ronald Mortished, noted, 'the Labour Party was the only Party whose hands were clean enough to be able to secure a lasting peace.'[43] The smaller parties could promote peace because they were largely focused on the future, not on the past. Eamonn O'Carroll in North Dublin said that he opposed 'the substitution of stale political cant for statesmanship' and 'futile effeminate gossip about incidents that occurred nearly two years ago and could not be undone at this stage'.[44] O'Carroll's written election address showed both a fondness for upper-case letters and a desire to move beyond the Sinn Féin split: 'Recent events go to show that there is an INSANE TENDENCY on the part of the two of the Parties clamouring for your suffrage to RE-OPEN THE OLD SORES and thus DIVERT THE MINDS OF THE PEOPLE from these pressing domestic questions.'[45] Labour banked heavily on the assumption that the voters were ready to put the nationalist debates of early 1922 behind them and turn to those who took no part in them.

Independent candidates made the same arguments. Former Sinn Féin stalwart turned government critic Darrell Figgis credited Independents for the success of the state and the constitution. This stability was 'mainly due to the Independents who stood in the election last year and whose return by the people broke the [Collins–de Valera] Pact.'[46] He also claimed that economics was being neglected for the sake of worn-out political issues: 'while we waste time arguing about old political issues natural wealth was lying by unused, and a large body of Irish people were unemployed. It was essential to turn the Nation's attention away from the past into the future.'[47] Figgis had always been concerned about Irish economic development and became rapidly disillusioned with the new government's abandonment of a policy of general tariffs. However, he saw the 1923 election as a chance to right the ship: 'an opportunity was now available of finally ending recrimination, conflict, and savage destruction by returning candidates who are not concerned for the spoils of office, who will speak their minds fearlessly and apply themselves to constructive work.'[48] Another independent candidate criticised government ministers who were 'waving old banners and repeating the war cries of the past decade.'[49]

Candidates from smaller parties or independents thought that they were best positioned to change politics for the better because they had platforms focused on economic issues and had not been involved in the torturous treaty settlement. They believed the continuing emphasis on nationalist priorities, in particular the intricacies of the Anglo-Irish relationship, was both deleterious to non-Sinn Féin candidates and harmful to Irish politics in general. Beyond that, though, they also claimed that they could better address even nationalist issues at which Sinn Féin had markedly failed.

The most cited one of these was partition. John Regan has argued that southern nationalists never much cared about the north and demonstrated a willingness to rapidly disengage from the north in exchange for preserving Free State stability.[50] Despite an apparent historical consensus around this assertion, the newspapers demonstrate that partition remained a live issue well into 1923. The *Irish Independent* fairly consistently claimed that two of the major issues facing the country were the postponement of the Boundary Commission and the continuing uncertainty over the Free State's share of the British national debt. The non-Sinn Féin candidates argued that they could handle these ongoing issues better than the government. Labour thought it could end partition by uniting workers north and south.[51] Business candidates in Dublin maintained that Free State prosperity would entice the north. William McCabe said 'it was the intention and interest of all the candidates that there should be no partition of Ireland. He would welcome the Six Counties in there, because they were hard-headed and sound businessmen up there.'[52] As independent candidates were disproportionately Protestant, their election could also demonstrate Free State tolerance. Bryan Cooper made this argument directly: 'if we show that we can govern ourselves peaceably and well and that all classes get a fair chance in the Free State in a comparatively few years we will have Ulster in, and that will be better than any amount of Boundary Commissions.'[53] He later added a reduced tax burden to the list of incentives for Ulster.[54] This was basically an accusation that neither idealistic rhetoric about Ireland being one nation, nor the specific treaty mechanism of the Boundary Commission, had ended partition. As William Findlater told a Businessmen's Party election meeting, business principles, not sentimentality, would bring in the north. Like Sinn Féin's Belfast Boycott, this notion invoked stereotypes of northerners as driven fundamentally by economic interests, rather than emotional connections to the empire.[55] Sinn Féin had failed at one of its own priorities and its continuing dominance would perpetuate such failures.

Finally, the smaller parties believed they brought a needed independent criticism to the Dáil. The abstention of the republicans gave treatyites an artificial majority and contributed to the sense that the Free State Dáil was effectively a one-party assembly, as the revolutionary Dáils had been. The *Voice of Labour* editorialised that the Dáil, 'with the honourable exception of the Labour TDs and three or four others ... is so hide-bound to the Ministry that it will do nothing except what the Ministry tells it.'[56] The paper consistently criticised the unwillingness of ordinary TDs to question the government and called out the resulting machine politics that passed treatyite bills. This echoed Sinn Féin criticism of the British parliament during the revolution, as Irish revolutionaries consistently articulated a desire to have a parliament where backbenchers acted independently without party whips.

Independents, in particular, claimed that their election could lead to a more deliberative and responsible Dáil. Kevin J. Kenny, a business candidate in North Dublin, urged electors to: 'VOTE for the man who is free to work for you. ... I AM NOT TIED TO ANY PARTY. I am free to work for you, to vote on every occasion as you would wish me to vote, to consider your interests all the time.'[57] Bryan Cooper asserted, 'he prefers to be the servant of his constituents than the servant of a party.' Cooper in particular seemed to take particular pride in going it alone, as he told the crowd at his meeting that 'there would be no Chairman because he [a Chairman] was wanted for two reasons, one to keep order, and the other was to introduce the candidate. He was sure order would be kept and was bold enough to think that he needed no introduction to the meeting. There would be no other speakers ... although he could have got them if he wanted them.' The paper laconically noted that this was a meeting 'at which the attendance was not large.'[58]

At another, possibly more well-attended, meeting for Cooper, a speaker said 'the election of independent members would strengthen the Government. They were men who had the courage of their convictions and would stick to them. They would stand by the Government when they were right and oppose them when they were wrong.'[59] In response to criticism of Independent candidates, a letter-writer to the *Independent* claimed 'they would not represent exclusively class interests, nor act as voting-machines'.[60] The former separated them from Labour and the Farmers, while the latter elevated them above Cumann na nGaedheal backbenchers. Independents also claimed to be better qualified because they had been elected for something other than their revolutionary record.[61] A non-party, non-Sinn Féin, voice was seen as of benefit to the government and to Irish democracy writ large.

Lurking behind all of these claims was a desire to move the Free State forward and a suspicion that Sinn Féin was not up to the job. Despite much talk about Irish nationalism being fundamentally backward looking, all sides in Irish politics wanted to modernise the State in the 1920s. They differed, though, on what model for modernisation would be followed. There was general consensus on the desire to avoid following what was perceived as the British model: unregulated industrialisation with its attendant urbanisation and class conflict. Instead, Irish politicians looked elsewhere, usually to smaller nations in Europe, for alternative models. Labour often pointed to Scandinavian countries, which were seen as models of advancement that had not been limited by colonialism. The *Voice of Labour* noted that Irish workers suffered from the twin oppression of capitalism and colonialism, although it stopped short of drawing sympathetic comparisons with non-white colonised peoples: 'the workers of Ireland have been throughout many centuries a slave class within a subject nation, and their oppression has lasted longer and has been more degrading than that of any class of white men or white women on the globe.' The new Dáil, with a significant Labour presence, would start the long postcolonial process of reversing these trends, as 'an active and militant group of Labour representatives in the next Dáil' would 'set to work clearing away the political and economic obstacles which have already been removed from the path of the workers in the more advanced nations, such as Norway, Sweden, and Denmark.'[62]

The Scandinavian countries, particularly Denmark, were often touchstones for the smaller parties' visions of modernity. Denmark was seen by Labour as an alternative to British industrialisation and class conflict, as it was a small country where the economy was seemingly driven by co-operatives and workers had more input into government. An article titled 'Denmark: The Land of Co-Operative Democracy' explained that after the Napoleonic Wars, the Dane

> abandoned dreams of factories and smoke stacks, and bent all her energies upon the tillage of

her land. … She has no 'imperialist vision' and her army to-day might be scattered by a decent fire brigade. But she has greater strength than is born of cannon; she has her people on the soil.

The writer also extolled Denmark's nationalisation of railways and subsidies for steamship travel, concluding that 'the Danes are pioneering in co-operative democracy, and co-operative democracy as a national policy pays'.[63] While Labour looked to Denmark as a place where co-operation and state investment in the economy created prosperity, members of the Farmers' Party saw Denmark as both their chief rival and a model for an agrarian path to modernisation. Denmark was taking an increasing share of the import markets for butter and eggs in England, and Irish farmers thought this was because Danish farmers had modernised and standardised their dairy industry, particularly through the use of co-operative creameries and mechanised cream separators. Many of the Farmers' Union members who testified to the State's commission on agriculture in 1923 referenced superior Danish practices in egg marketing and butter making, while the *Farmer's Gazette* was filled with information about Danish farming. Despite calling generally for lower taxes and rates, as well as less interference from Dublin, Farmers' union members and candidates wanted greater government investment in agricultural education, marketing, and modernisation. IFU member W. H. M. Cobbe admitted,

> I think myself that the whole system of agriculture in this country will have to be revolutionised. We must get different ideas from those in vogue the last two centuries… Denmark might give us a line in that direction, but you cannot get the farmers to do the same as in Denmark and in other countries without Government assistance and Government propaganda.[64]

The smaller parties used the election to lay out their vision of a modernising project that neither mimicked England, nor left workers and farmers behind.

This all pointed to a different version of politics than that preached by the two successor parties of Sinn Féin. The smaller parties thought Ireland needed to move on from a nationalist-dominated political system and instead work within a political divide organised largely around economic or vocational lines. Cumann na nGaedheal and Sinn Féin unsurprisingly disagreed. Sinn Féin continued to litigate the case against the treaty, with one 1923 electoral advertisement still arguing about whether David Lloyd George was bluffing during the treaty negotiations nearly two years prior.[65] Cumann na nGaedheal feared that a divided result could end up empowering republicans and sinking the treaty. Eoin MacNeill admitted, 'his aim was to have the election fought on the national issue pure and simple.' He specifically called out 'the Farmer and the Labour parties' who 'seemed to think that the national crisis had passed and that the time had arrived when the Irish people were secure in their own country and could afford to subordinate national to particular interests'.[66] This was a difficult line for Cumann na nGaedheal to walk, as they wanted voters to credit them with ending the Civil War and restoring stability, while still convincing those same voters that the need for a national party had not passed. Cosgrave told voters in Cavan that 'the people ought to send into their Parliament representatives whose first consideration would be the whole of the country and not particular sections of it'.[67] The worry was that too many abstentionists and too few Cumann na nGaedheal TDs would lead to a weak and unstable state. Seamus Burke, a Cumann na nGaedheal organiser, foretold that 'if a sectional Government were now returned, instead of the representative

National Government they had, it would appear the people, deep down in their hearts, approved of the Irregular policy.'[68]

Cumann na nGaedheal also appealed for unity directly to constituencies thought to be targeted by the smaller parties. Margaret Collins O'Driscoll said in a letter to the editor that the working classes would be best served by the return of a Cumann na nGaedheal government. She said that no one should vote for Labour, 'the party of Neutrals'.[69] Seamus Burke said that a sectional government could never fully address the needs of the population and the State: 'a Farmers' Government would probably find it very difficult to deal with the problems that confronted the country. They would only represent a section of the people.'[70] Cardinal Logue criticised independents as 'not always honest candidates. Many of them have their minds already thoroughly made up and raise the banner of independence to mislead the electors and get returned on false pretences.'[71]

Women were also urged against voting republican, even though Sinn Féin put forward more female candidates than Cumann na nGaedheal. Collins-O'Driscoll noted, 'the women of the country had been grossly maligned by the action of the women in the Dáil who had betrayed them and it was up to the women of Ireland to give the lie to the statement that all the women of Ireland were with de Valera.'[72] A Cumann na nGaedheal advertisement told the women of Ireland that a vote for Sinn Féin was a vote for 'burning of homes and of children, the rule of the bomb and the petrol can', whereas a vote for Cumann na nGaedheal would enable women to 'do their share to promote peace, order and prosperity in Ireland'.[73] Lady Arnott presided over a meeting of female electors at which she told women to use the power of the vote to promote their interests, but concluded that 'the destiny of this country depended on the character and ability of the men chosen'.[74]

The legacy of colonialism loomed over many of these calls for unity. Kevin O'Higgins observed that such unity would overturn colonial stereotypes of the Irish as divided, fissiparous, and ungovernable: 'we have to prove to the world that it was not true what our enemies said in the past, that the Irish people are incapable of governing themselves, and that the Irish people are a wanton, criminal, irresponsible people without sufficient cohesion for self-government.'[75] The nationalist parties understandably wanted to keep politics in a nationalist and postcolonial frame. They wanted to preserve, as much as possible, the unified nationalist front that had, after decades of intermittent resistance, finally won a form of freedom for the Free State. The smaller parties and independents, in contrast, wanted to move past this, creating a political culture whose leaders need not be nationalist heroes and whose rhetoric was less focused on lofty anti-English sentiment and more on bread-and-butter issues that affected ordinary people. They wanted, in short, a form of class politics that was common across the continent at the time. They offered not just specific policy platforms, but a reorientation of Irish politics that would be served by their election and their greater presence in the Dáil. Their political involvement pointed towards a particular definition of what all parties claimed to desire – a move away from the type of politics practiced by the former coloniser, and the creation of a new Irish system less bound to parties and backroom deals. This is why the small parties were important, despite their ultimate lack of electoral success and inability to ever form a government. They were arguing not just against particular Sinn Féin policies, but against the whole style of nationalist politics that developed in the nineteenth century and had been strengthened by the revolution. They wanted a politics less focused on the relationship with England or the Empire, and more directed to socioeconomic issues and ways that Ireland could modernise outside of the shadow of the Anglo-Irish relationship.

Voters, unfortunately for Labour and the Farmers, tended to think otherwise. While the Farmers' Party and Independents gained in the election, Labour lost seats.[76] Labour's postmortems concluded that 'the people voted politically'. A *Voice of Labour* editorial noted mournfully,

> the big issue in the elections was whether or not the Nation endorsed the Treaty. ... We have not yet emerged from the civil war atmosphere and it is not, therefore, surprising that many workers allowed themselves to be swept off their feet and blinded to the true interests of their class by the politicians of both Nationalist camps.[77]

The *Cork Examiner* attributed the Farmers' lesser showing to the fact that they ran too many candidates and that electors wanted a stable majority that did not rely on the smaller parties.[78]

Despite the seeming triumph of civil war politics, we should not let the teleology obscure the importance of the smaller parties in the election of 1923. There remained a tremendous amount of optimism in some circles that the Free State could both modernise along non-English lines and create a style of politics that was particularly Irish, without replicating either single-party nationalist hegemony or the British two-party system with all its perceived faults. A post-election letter from a Labour supporter still claimed, 'Ireland stands to-day on the threshold of a new era. New parties are springing up from the ruins of the old.' He believed that the masses would soon see the hollowness of Sinn Féin promises and start voting for Labour, concluding, 'now is the time to preach the doctrine of service and comradeship.'[79] This, to many, was a key aspect of the Irish revolution, the creation of a postcolonial Irish politics that differed from that of England. Smaller parties offered up a variety of visions for how this could come about, either through evolving a class-based system of politics or having a Dáil consisting of loose groupings of uncommitted independents.

The two Sinn Féin parties pushed back hard against this and ultimately prevented Labour or the Farmers from ever forming governments. But the election of 1923 shows how much belief remained that a true multi-party democracy could be created as Sinn Féin dominance waned. A Labour editorial noted, with a mixture of optimism and scorn,

> there is no doubt judging by the apathy and dullness shown on Election Day that the mass of the Irish workers are sick and tired of the present political leaders, and that the time has come for a new policy with new leaders ... [and] a clear-cut programme based on the hard facts of national, economic, and working-class needs.[80]

We know in hindsight that Fianna Fáil best articulated such a programme for voters over the next several decades, but the ultimate eclipse of the small parties should not blind us to the importance of the Labour and Farmers' Parties, as well as Independents, in creating democratic institutions and articulating alternative democratic visions in the New State's formative years.

CHAPTER 5

POLITICAL PROPAGANDA IN THE 1923 GENERAL ELECTION: METHODS AND THEMES

Elaine Callinan

The prevailing contradictory views and ideologies of the main political parties – Cumann na nGaedheal, Sinn Féin, the Farmers' Party and Labour Party – before and during this momentous 1923 General Election will be analysed in this chapter to provide insight into voter choices and party aspirations for the new Free State. Election day was Monday, 27 August 1923, and it was declared a public holiday to encourage voter turnout. In this first general election of the Irish Free State, established the previous December, campaigning began in earnest roughly four weeks prior to polling day.

Comparing the propaganda and electioneering tactics of the major parties across the constituencies in 1923 demonstrates that persuasion was used to alter attitudes and reinforce entrenched beliefs. An examination of the political campaigns reveals the similarities and differences in ideologies because they were embedded in the dialogue and conflicts that were presented in word, text, image and theme. Therefore, the methods of propaganda such as speeches, posters and newspaper advertisements (and others discussed later) will be investigated.

Methods of Propaganda

Political messages can be received and interpreted by different people in different ways, and the method of propaganda often determines the audience that is reached.[1] The main methods of communication to the electorate were political speeches, posters and handbills, canvassing, newspaper advertisements and political symbols. Political speeches were the most important in this era and every party candidate organised meetings in public spaces in their local constituencies to deliver their message. Unlike modern political methods such as radio, television and social media, this was one of the only means of face-to-face contact with the voting public in this era and where there was (often) a large audience. For instance, during W. T. Cosgrave's tour of his constituency in August where 'meetings by moonlight and torchlight' were organised, and where he carried out a 60-mile tour, addressing six meetings and finishing up 'again' at midnight, voters had the opportunity to listen to the candidate deliver policies and ambitions in person.[2] Sinn Féin's election campaign, according to the *Irish Independent*, proceeded 'with unprecedented intensity. An enormous number of meetings [were] being held in all the constituencies'.[3] As in past elections of this era – and as Daithí Ó Corráin points out in in his chapter (Chapter 7, pp 77–86) – the Catholic hierarchy and clergy were remarkably active during the election campaign, standing 'shoulder to shoulder with Cumann na nGaedheal'. Evidence of clerical attendance on platforms at public meetings demonstrated that nationalist parties believed that the clergy were a powerful force in swaying voter opinion.

The only way to gauge audience reaction (in an era of limited film or newsreel recordings) is through the commentary in local or national newspapers where crowd reaction was reported on, such as in the *Cork Examiner* for Labour's Michael Keyes in Limerick where his point was that Labour could give the country peace, security and prosperity to which there was 'applause'.[4] A sense of crowd numbers was also provided; for instance, the Farmers' Party candidate, Conor Hogan, at Ennistymon delivered a speech 'at a large meeting'; and in Limerick the Labour Party's meeting held at the O'Connell Monument was 'well attended' – and this shows that voters were interested in attending these meetings so public engagement with voters was crucial for parties and candidates.[5]

Speech delivery and audience interpretation of same took place in the arena of social interaction, and the processes involved occurred in the social context and this shaped the way in which individuals interacted and interpreted content.[6] This was important in election meetings because the conditions were an impending election and awareness of the speaker's intent was evident. The audience knew they were present at a meeting (whether private or public) to be persuaded or have their decisions reaffirmed. An Irish audience often had to wade through a myriad of sensory material before a speech began as platforms or indoor gatherings flaunted symbols and iconography of party identity such as flags and banners, and were preceded or concluded with music and processions.[7] For instance, in Tullow, County Carlow, Cosgrave's public meeting was headed by the local brass band and the location was at the 1798 monument, and in Rathvilly (a village near the Wicklow border) a large crowd was augmented by a pipers' band'.[8] In complete contrast the Farmers' Party campaign, according to the *Freeman's Journal*, was 'not marked by big displays, bands and flowery oratory' but with beliefs 'in economy and quiet efficiency'.[9] Using these two parties as examples demonstrates the contrast between the larger parties' desire for pomp and ceremony with the smaller parties advocating for direct messaging without diversions. The reason lies perhaps in the lack of funds of smaller parties to provide these added entertainments, but another reason can be found in the propaganda of, for example, the Farmers' Party who were regularly critical of 'a free-spending' and 'wasteful spending' Cumann na nGaedheal in relation to agriculture, so they were probably equally opposed to improvident spending on distractions to their key messages at public gatherings.[10]

A political candidate's public persona and image affected electoral propaganda outcomes, and this led the two main political parties – Cumann na nGaedheal and Sinn Féin – to promote the party leader who became the symbol of their cause and ambitions. In 1923 Cosgrave and Éamon de Valera became the spokespersons or message controllers of their respective parties, while the Farmers' Party and Labour were less reliant on a key leader. All political speeches contained narrative, and this was usually where a speaker set the scene to ultimately move the audience to a point of action, i.e., to vote in their favour. Cosgrave, on a tour of Carlow, alluded to the difficulties of sorting out the national finances in a volatile country because of past conflicts, and encouraged the electorate to move towards 'stable government' where 'no section of the community ought to put its interest before the interests of the nation'.[11] De Valera often focused on an historical theme at the outset by stating, for example, that 'the Sinn Féin candidates stand, as they have stood in every election since 1917, for the unity and untrammelled independence of Ireland'.[12] De Valera's powers of persuasion and emotional nationalism had in the recent past converted the more militant into political adherents to establish an interlude of peace until 1920. However, the civil war conflict over the Anglo-Irish Treaty had ruptured the Sinn Féin Party. De Valera's role was to convince the electorate to oppose the treaty, whereas Cosgrave needed to encourage support. Both leaders toured their own constituencies, bolstered party candidates in other constituencies, and were the leaders that personified the party line who could be referred to by other candidates, so they proved crucial in a politically divided Free State. Unlike in 1922 where Michael Gallagher points out that 'leading pro-treatyites did not tour the country appealing for support ... as did the anti-treaty leaders', tours with public speaking to large and small audiences was a central component of this electoral campaign.[13] Those in attendance at a large public meeting were able to experience the ambiance, but with large crowds it was often difficult to hear the speaker (this was a time before microphones). Messages were passed back by attendees, but many had to wait for the printed version in the local or national newspapers. Therefore, obtaining subsequent editorial in a newspaper was crucial for political parties and candidates to ensure the dissemination of accurate speech content.

As Basil Chubb pointed out, in the late nineteenth century there were whole communities of literate people who could afford to buy printed material and who had a vote, and this led to mass circulation papers, and 'as a result the whole context of politics and their conduct were greatly changed'.[14] Rising affluence among the middle classes provided customers for printed material, and these customers were voters. Provincial newspapers carried constituency election messages continuously and were largely used by local candidates, but it is impossible to assess with any certainty the real political influence of the provincial press as they were notoriously biased, but there were advantages and disadvantages. The political constituency message reached the defined target audience speedily; however a strongly biased newspaper's readership was the already converted as non-adherents had been alienated. Modern research suggests that newspapers with a known political prejudice were probably only partially successful as they did more to reinforce readers' existing opinions and failed to convert non-believers.[15] Richard Mulcahy pointed out that pamphlets and books had a similar difficulty in that they betrayed their origin, and so were read only by the already convinced. Newspapers, however, inspired 'talk', he said, and when details were good 'unbelievers' could be swayed.[16]

National newspapers were used to propagate the main party messages in general elections, but they also carried opinion pieces by staff correspondents. There were three main national dailies in Ireland that also produced weekly editions – the *Irish Times*, *Irish Independent* and *Freeman's Journal*. L. M. Cullen stated that the daily *Irish Independent* had reached a 100,000 circulation figure by 1917, and the total sales of morning dailies probably exceeded a half million copies by the 1920s.[17] Developments in the printing press facilitated sales increases and a few years previously the proprietor William Martin Murphy had reduced the price of this newspaper to a halfpenny to boost circulation,[18] and introduced better quality printing to improve advertising revenue by using five different type-faces (fonts) to enhance presentation.[19]

All newspapers regularly printed the speeches of political leaders and candidates, lending affirmative opinion and adverse commentary according to their bias. They were useful for disseminating ideas, critiquing political opponents, and giving voice to the ordinary voter in the 'Letters to the Editor' section. For instance, support for the Farmers' Party can be seen in a letter to the *Irish Independent* from a County Dublin writer (and no doubt a farmer) who complained bitterly against a 'Louth Farmer' who claimed that 'agriculture was in a precarious position' to advocate for 'a strong, virile farmers' party in An Dáil'.[20] Another later that month from an 'observer' offered 'Ulster Protestant's advice' by stating that unionists rejoiced 'in Republican successes only because they believed that the Republicans are more likely than anyone else to bring Ireland to destruction'.[21] These letters and political news demonstrated and influenced how ordinary people thought and consumed political ideas, and it encouraged the political elite to appeal to people through this medium. The importance of newspapers was emphasised by the pro-treaty Mulcahy who instructed that the 'object of propaganda is to induce everyone to think and talk about all the questions from your point of view' where 'first blood is all important'. In other words, it was crucial to be the first to propagandise opinion to convince. To do this, he believed that because 'propaganda enters the brain through the eyes and ears, viz., reading, pictures and talking', and even though newspapers should be the 'principal conveyance for propaganda', it was necessary to use books and pamphlets too. This was a propaganda philosophy that was applied by the two major nationalist parties in 1923. Mulcahy also emphasised that, 'the facts presented must be the 'Truth, the whole Truth and nothing but the Truth' and that the 'other side will … throw doubt on your real truths'.[22] Deciphering the actual 'truth' was the preserve of the public, and newspaper advertisements and editorial along with other methods of propaganda were the tools from which the truth had to be unravelled.

Newspapers were also the main forum for paid-for advertising, enabling candidates and parties to release short, targeted messages. According to Paul Neystrom, writing in 1914, advertising aims to 'attract attention' in the hope of developing a genuine 'interest' which would change to desire, and culminate with a 'decision to purchase' (or vote in the case of an election).[23] A 1910 article titled 'The Advertising Problem', published in *Leabhar na hÉireann* by the National Council of Sinn Féin, promoted the idea to separatist nationalists that 'good advertising pays and bad advertising oftentimes does not' – a 'good advertisement'…attracts attention, pleases the reader, and induces a desire to know more of the goods so advertised.' Good advertising, according to the article, 'included all recognised forms such as press advertising, catalogues, booklets, circulars, handbills, electric signs, billboard window displays, show cards, novelties, etc.'[24] Edward L. Bernays in discussing propaganda in 1928 generally maintained that the emotional responses that arise from propaganda 'limit an audience's choices by creating a binary mentality, which can result in quicker, more enthused responses'.[25] Therefore, politicians understood the importance of advertising and propaganda in this era, and even though newspaper advertisements were expensive, and short word count was essential and rarely was image used, they were a direct medium for candidates to reach their target audience. The scale of charges for small prepaid advertisements in the *Irish Times* in 1920 was £1 for twelve words or under with every succeeding word being 3½d.[26] The cost of an advertisement in the *Nationalist and Leinster Times* in 1923 was: Election addresses: 10s per single column inch per insertion; and, Notice of Meetings, etc.: 10s per single column inch per insertion.[27]

The political advertisement usually mirrored editorial style and often began with the headline 'to the electors' or 'ladies and gentlemen'. Good examples are those in the Cork Borough constituency where the Farmers' candidate, Timothy Corcoran, succinctly put forward the main party ideals of 'unity, peace and prosperity of our country', asserting the party's support of the 'treaty and constitution';[28] and, Cumann na nGaedheal used their concise advertisement to fire criticism at their opponents stating, 'the sectional and freak candidates [of Sinn Féin] are not prepared to shoulder the responsibility of Government. They merely wish to chip bits off the Government', and the advertisement concluded with the appeal to 'vote for the candidate who can deliver the goods'.[29] To defray costs oftentimes candidates from the same party shared advertising messages such as that in Cork East where three Farmers' candidates set out their main argument that 'agriculture is the only wealth producing industry in the country', closing with a strong call to action, 'vote for us and unity, vote for us and a prosperous peace'.[30]

There were limitations to newspaper advertisements and editorials and the main one, as Kissane points out, was the rigorous censorship of the media by the pro-treatyites.[31] Censorship had been strongly implemented during the Irish Civil War, but remnants carried forward into 1923. Sinn Féin charged the 'Free State Party' [Cumann na nGaedheal] of using its 'control of the armed forces to silence the press and propaganda their opponents improvised'.[32] Irish mainstream national and regional newspapers were largely pro-treaty, and this created difficulties for the anti-treaty Sinn Féin. Therefore, they needed to supplement party speeches with posters, circulars and handbills, and Cumann na nGaedheal had to adopt these propaganda tools also to counteract Sinn Féin messages. The most used was the poster, with dead walls across many Irish counties being decorated abundantly. As can be seen demonstrated on the cover of *Vying for Victory*, a powerful photograph of women and a child perusing the many messages on one such wall in Ennis, County Clare, shows posters that call for monster public demonstrations inviting the electors to 'come in your thousands', and others containing criticisms by Cumann na nGaedheal of Sinn Féin in harking back to more troubled times by asking 'who looted your ships, robbed your banks … murdered your sons'.[33]

Posters during the Great War were more colourful and printed on better quality paper as opposed to the later cheaper but flimsy political sheets that were mainly in black and white. Franklyn Haiman noted that posters communicate 'a sense of immediacy and of being surrounded by an event' that voters (in this instance) 'are not likely to get elsewhere'.[34] The content and themes of posters (which will be discussed later) between the two main rival parties demonstrated their animosity and rivalry, and the highly charged atmosphere of the election. As Ciara Meehan pointed out, posters had the appearance of enlarged newspaper advertisements and because they had both text and a visual message, they were a strong vehicle for spreading a message to a wide audience because they appeared in all manner of public spaces.[35]

The introduction of proportional representation in 1920 (1919 in Sligo) altered election posters because candidates now needed to capture first preference votes. Artistic and creative imagery did not disappear, but a new feature was the inclusion of candidates' names allied with their party and this was often presented in capital letters. The electorate now voted in numerical preference, numbered from one to the total number of candidates going forward in a constituency, so there was less space to promote policies or include creative imagery. Catchy headlines and memorable slogans became essential to capture voter attention. An example of this creativity was a Sinn Féin poster with a large image where the final line reads 'Voting for the Free State means keeping Ireland down. Don't prolong the agony!'[36] Of course, the call was to 'vote republican'.

Posters could not work in isolation as they held minimal details. Supplementing posters were handbills, booklets and pamphlets, and the door-to-door canvass. The *Freeman's Journal* reported that 'canvassers have begun vigorous operation in all districts ... The distribution of leaflets and the circulation of posters on a wholesale scale form an important part of the electioneering campaign, the electors being everywhere confronted with a bewildering array of appeals'.[37] Sinn Féin, however, accused the election of being a 'farce' because almost all their leaders, speakers, writers, organisers and election experts' were in jail, while Cumann na nGaedheal had its staff of 'officers and experts complete'.[38] They also complained that posters intended for distribution in the [Kilkenny] constituency were 'delayed in the post'.[39] Yet, according to the *Kilkenny People* 'there was a profusion of dead wall election literature', and some by the Sinn Féin Party were used in this constituency not only to promote policy, but to castigate Cumann na nGaedheal opponents. This newspaper reported that on Sunday morning 'the dead walls, bridges, hoardings and telegraph poles which contained lying and contemplable suggestions about Senator de Loughry and Sean Gibbons' had been erected. They maintained that although the name of the printer was not attached to the poster (although this was required by law) there was little doubt that the poster was issued 'on the order of the Sinn Féin Election Committee, and that 'some members of that committee were found in the act of posting up the placard'.[40] The *Irish Independent* and *Cork Examiner* noted that:

> Everyone is, of course, aware that in the recent election no party was so active, or made such full use of the peaceful condition of the country, as the Anti-Treatyites [Sinn Féin] who held meetings in every town and village. Everyone also will recall the other side of the picture – the determined, but fruitless, attempts to prevent Ministers and other treaty speakers obtaining a hearing at public meetings where noisy interrupters endeavoured to create disturbance.[41]

These mixed reports by national and provincial newspapers on electioneering activity really inform that constituencies had different practices and voters had diverse experiences of propaganda. For instance, the *Nationalist and Leinster Times* remarked that, 'in the matter of actual election organisation very little was done by any party. Such factors as personal canvass, literature, elaborate [*sic*] addresses, and any systematic demonstrations were largely missing from the elections of 1923. Band playing and flag waving were almost negative quantities.'[42] In contrast to this report, band playing was certainly evident in many constituencies, including Carlow-Kilkenny (an area where this newspaper was widely circulated), but the door-to-door canvass is harder to measure. Mel Farrell points out in his chapter (Chapter 2, pp 11–26) that there was an 'energetic canvass' in the Dublin constituencies, but it seems that in the counties of Carlow and Kilkenny public speeches rather than the canvass were to the fore. The canvass was (and still is) an essential component for checking the register of electors, for face-to-face contact by a candidate or a candidate's representative, and to ensure that a voter could be relied upon to attend the poll. In the General Elections of 1918 and 1922 (despite the split and subsequent 'pact' in the latter) Sinn Féin and the pro- and anti-treaty parties had a wealth of young men and women from the Irish Volunteers/Irish Republican Army and Cumann na mBan to conduct the canvass. The political split now forced the two parties to go head-to-head as polar opposites for the same voters, and loyalty from their supporting organisations was split also, ergo a reduced number of canvassers on both sides. Therefore, in 1923, the all-pervasive canvass of past years may not have occurred, and this may have cost both parties seats.

Candidates also used the postal system to deliver notices and propaganda handbills, but there were rules and restrictions around this. Under the Acts appertaining to elections, candidates were subject to the regulations of the Postmaster General, but were entitled to send, free of any charge for postage, to each registered elector for his/her constituency, one postal communication containing matter relating to the election only. The words 'Litir um Thogha' (election communication) had to be printed, stamped or legibly written at the top of the address side, and one day's notice had to be provided to the head postmaster of their town.[43]

An interesting and novel electoral approach was carried out by Cosgrave in 1923 when, as the *Cork Examiner* reported, 'a new chapter in electioneering' was opened by the use of the aeroplane. This allowed the Cumann na nGaedheal leader greater ability to attend a number of meetings with alacrity, being able to 'address meetings at Ennis, Clare and Carlow on the same day'. However, this also got him into hot water as he had used State property for a party-political event.[44]

In 1923, given the similarities in propaganda tactics and approaches, particularly by the rival nationalist parties, the electorate were not influenced so much by the methods used to entice support but rather were more persuaded by party policy, propaganda content and themes examined below.

Themes of Propaganda

The political scientist Harold Lasswell regarded propaganda 'content' as a set of 'messages' aimed at 'recipients' rather than as 'texts' to be interpreted by 'readers'. The underlying theory was that media generally produced powerful, direct, and uniform effects on people. This remained the prevailing perception and propaganda approach throughout the early twentieth century.[45] Propaganda content or themes can provide a broad indication of how the electorate interpreted political messages to cast a vote in favour of a political party or candidate. During the 1923 electoral campaign, dominant political actors introduced diametrically opposed opinions on common themes to uphold, condemn or highlight discordant stances. Fundamental lofty ideals were espoused by Cumann na nGaedheal and Sinn Féin to reinforce political ideologies. Smaller parties sought to push their future vision of Ireland based not on past national grievances, but on their core principles such as agriculture for farmers and workers issues for the Labour Party.

Farmers' and Labour Party

The political unity of the country, prosperity and a reduction in the cost of living, education and the provision of 'the greatest good for the greatest number of people' were some of the aims of the Farmers' Party. Agriculture was their priority, and this was pointed out in statements like, 'agriculture is the only wealth producing industry in the country'; and comparisons were drawn such as 'all other interests import. We export'. Therefore, to achieve economic success it was vital that the country had 'good rail and road facilities, a cheap and efficient postal service, and economy in public departments' to ultimately lead to a reduction in rates and taxes. During their public speeches the party wielded their green, white and yellow flag with a vividly red reaping hook as they maintained that they 'had enough of fighting' and 'represented the agricultural industry of the country'. The key argument was that it was an industry 'on which their prosperity must be built', and this included the subsidiary industries of 'tanneries, dead meat trade, beat and tobacco growing' to create wealth within ten years. Support of the treaty and constitution, economic administration, and agricultural interests were the primary propaganda issues, supported by other matters such as the right of political prisoners to vote (about which a resolution was passed at a meeting of the National Executive in July 1923); and, they were vehement in the claim that they would not enter into 'any pact with other political parties' and would 'stand alone in the elections'.[46] The end result shows that they increased the number of seats won and attained 9.8 per cent of the overall vote (although bear in mind the total number of overall seats had increased also). However, the impact of their propaganda on voters is difficult to evaluate, as there were other variables at play such as party loyalty on the one hand and voter apathy on the other. Given the number of candidates they put forward, against those put forward by Cumann na nGaedheal and Sinn Féin, the notion of a 'no pact' arrangement was somewhat bizarre, even in a pre-election environment.[47] While they did want to distance themselves from past nationalist hostilities, even if all their candidates had been elected they would not have had enough to form a majority government of 77 – they were going to have to align and form some kind of pact or compromise with another party and Cumann na nGaedheal was really their only choice because of the similar view on the treaty and constitution.

Labour candidates were caught between propagandising their own issues and taking a stance on the treaty. Speaking at a Labour meeting in Castlerea, County Roscommon, Liam Kelleher stated that the party was 'going into the Dáil'. The issue that confronted them was the oath of fidelity to the Free State and allegiance to the King, and this candidate claimed that 'we must go in and take the oath', but he qualified this by adding 'we would take a thousand oaths to help the workers'. In Strokestown, County Roscommon, Count Plunkett maintained that there would be no peace until the Free State Government was defeated and he maintained that Labour would be perfectly safe in the hands of 'our republican government being elected'. In Listowel, County Kerry, Cormac Breathnach (a Labour candidate not put forward) stated that Labour wanted Irish unity and their ideal was 'a Labour republic'. This posed a difficulty for voters because while it was not definitively stated that Labour and Sinn Féin would ally, it was implicit in the content of candidates' speeches. Or, at the very least, with insufficient candidates to form a complete Labour government, it could be understood that a coalition would be necessary, and the only choice was Sinn Féin. This proved advantageous in certain constituencies – County Roscommon being one – and disadvantageous in others where voters were not prepared to consider a Sinn Féin-led government. However, other Labour candidates were not as vocal on the issue of republicanism. Speaking at Glin in County Limerick Matthew Murphy strongly advocated for the fishing industry and Michael Keyes in the same constituency claimed the party could provide the necessary 'peace, security and prosperity' that the country needed.[48] Even though the number of Labour candidates doubled in 1923, the party attained less than half the vote achieved in 1922, winning only 14 seats. As Richard Sinnott pointed out, in 1922 Labour was the only alternative to the Sinn Féin panels; whereas there was greater electoral choice in 1923 and this was the difference between the two elections.[49] Furthermore, Labour was also hindered by internal divisions primarily due to Jim Larkin's hostility towards the Irish Transport and General Workers' Union, and as Niamh Puirséil states, 'Larkin detached so many of the workers who might otherwise have formed the backbone of Labour organisation in Dublin at precisely the time it was needed to establish its roots.'[50]

Cumann na nGaedheal and Sinn Féin

For Cumann na nGaedheal and Sinn Féin the overarching theme was acceptance or rejection of the Anglo-Irish Treaty. This had been the crucial issue in June 1922 where, in the contested constituencies, four-fifths of the electors voted in favour of the treaty, or 71 treaty candidates were elected as against 19 anti-treatyites. Despite the public vote, the country degenerated into civil war over this issue, and still by 1923 Sinn Féin maintained their determination of opposition. In a discussion with the Associated Press of America in July 1923, reported on in the *Irish Independent*, de Valera's contempt of the treaty was evident in his statement that the 'so called' treaty was 'no more binding on the honour or on the conscience of our nation than Pitt's Act of Union was. Each was ultra vires for the body of Irishmen that accepted it, and each was founded on fraud and force …'.[51] One of the key grievances (among a few others) was the oath, and de Valera vehemently proclaimed that 'elected Republican members will all refuse to take any oath of allegiance to the King of England'.[52] The Sinn Féin election manifesto was written by de Valera in a forceful tone of intense indignation against 'the propagandists who have been telling the world the base lie that the Irish people have, of their own free will, chosen to become a partitioned British province'. Speaking in Listowel, County Kerry, the wife of Tom Clarke and founder of Cumann na mBan, Kathleen Clarke, stated that 'the people of Ireland wanted absolute freedom … and not a treaty with England'. To promote unanimity both speakers made the association with an admired political predecessor, and this theme had been used by Sinn Féin politicians since 1918 to create continuity with the past. De Valera mentioned Padraig Pearse to drive forward the point that 'they know but one freedom … absolute freedom … of every sod of Ireland' in order to dispute partition. Kathleen Clarke, as the *Cork Examiner* reported, 'appealed to her hearers in the name of the martyred dead, from Wolfe Tone down …'[53] By linking the current Sinn Féin and their past anti-treaty and separatist aspirations a political strategy could be upheld. As Michael Laffan points out, Sinn Féin 'concerned themselves with abstractions rather than with material questions', and in regard to their 1923 manifesto this was certainly the case. Romanticisation and religious beliefs that linked in with Ireland' Christian population also featured in de Valera's speeches. For example, he claimed that:

> The love which puts the honour and glory of our motherland above all else on earth, the faith and the enthusiasm which inspires unwearied effort and unfailing resource, is with us. Sinn

Féin dominant once more will put Ireland again in the forefront of the nations – an apostle of enlightened Christianity in a heathen world, and a start of hope for all subject peoples.[54]

However, in other propaganda, such as political posters, they did address some of the everyday bread-and-butter issues that were pertinent to voters, which will be discussed later.[55] Labour candidates often spoke in similar fashion to Sinn Féin on the treaty issue. For instance, Edward Mansfield, a Labour Senator in Seanad Éireann, stated in Gort, County Galway that 'he didn't know what the treaty meant, as two clauses were inoperative, but partition, the English jumping off ground, would never allow freedom, and would always be a menace to Irish liberty and aspirations'. Murphy in Glin (mentioned earlier) went on to state that Labour 'expected to make a better fist of it than the other side [Cumann na nGaedheal] had done'.[56] Clearly this demonstrates Labour's averseness to an alignment with any party other than Sinn Féin. Even had all their 49 candidates been elected, they could not have secured a majority, and with only 14 in the end, it was an impossibility.

Cumann na nGaedheal counteracted Sinn Féin's negative treaty propaganda by highlighting that 'Ireland wanted to settle down and wanted more work' aiming to appeal to the war fatigue of the electorate. The way to make the most of the new-born state, they argued, was to cast a vote for their party that had policies 'on which the whole future prosperity of Ireland depended'.[57] One of the chief points made by Cumann na nGaedheal was that they were the party with members who had negotiated with the British Government, who were conversant with the facts, and were best qualified to complete the business. Propaganda aimed at addressing the future finances of the new state were strategically used to assure potential voters of sound administration under the treaty agreements. To manage the running of the state Cosgrave remarked on the 'big problems ahead' and explained that 'a good deal of money must be borrowed'. Political competence and stability, he argued, had to be portrayed to the 'people controlling great finance issues here and in other countries'. However, Cumann na nGaedheal was criticised for their past management of the financial conditions of the country by those outside Sinn Féin too. For example, William Archer Redmond who ran as an independent in the Waterford constituency, took them to task for paying £1,600,000 as pensions to 'capable and efficient civil servants'.[58] Cosgrave acknowledged that they were paying this amount in pensions, but that almost 1.5 million of it was paid to the ex-Royal Irish Constabulary and to pensioners, and that they were carrying it out as one of the conditions of the treaty.[59] The Farmers' Party were also concerned about public expenditure and advocated for 'strict economy'. Some of their candidates, such as Michael Doyle from Wexford, lauded the current government, referring to them as 'great men' that had 'carried their lives in their hands for the past twelve months', but when it came to farming and agriculture there was 'not one man in the front benches' that knew anything about it.[60] An advertisement in the *Cork Examiner* claimed 'economy means a reduced cost of living, a better return in capital, less unemployment, a happier country'.[61]

Promoting economic management and the bread-and-butter issues of life was designed to reassure party devotees and appeal to those who were unsure or not affiliated to any political party. While the distinguishing precepts of the treaty and the oath of faithfulness/ allegiance fuelled the initial thrust of political propaganda in 1923, the everyday matters pertinent to ordinary voters played a key role also. This was particularly evident in the posters of the two main parties. While the Sinn Féin manifesto focused on their lofty ideals, one poster added another section to the manifesto to explain why Sinn Féin should receive a vote. Interspersed with other messages about the Irish language and a promise to wipe out all internal dissension and bitterness arising from the past, Sinn Féin guaranteed to: administer the public services for the nation; reform the burdensome and expensive legal system; end unemployment by undertaking remunerative works of reconstruction, such as arterial draining, the utilisation of the water power and peat resources of the country, the improvement of docks and harbours, and the building of a Mercantile Marine. Other promises included: the development of the agricultural and fishing industries; the provision of houses for the workers; to foster and protect Irish industries; and reform the education system. A very visual poster titled 'Keeping Ireland Down' (briefly mentioned earlier) depicted a heap of hessian bags, wooden storage crates and trunks with titles printed on them such as 'Extravagance', 'Government Waste', 'Tim Healy £100 per day', '5% interest on F.S. share of English national debt £20,000,000 per annum', 'pension corruption', 'jobbery', 'Free State Loan Debt £10,000,000', to name a few. The English crown was depicted at the very top of all the crates and the female figure of Erin (Eiré) was attempting to crawl out from underneath the several heavy packages.[62] The message was 'voting for the Free State means keeping Ireland down'. The Sinn Féin remedy was to 'devote ourselves to social reform and to education', and to develop the economic and material strength of the nation.[63]

Keeping Ireland Down Poster, NLI, EPH C200, Image courtesy of the National Library of Ireland

Cumann na nGaedheal largely contradicted these Sinn Féin claims in public speeches, and in advertisement and posters they also focused on drawing comparisons that played on the public's fear over continued disruption and anarchy. As Mel Farrell points out in his chapter (Chapter 2, pp 11–26), their motto for the election was 'Safety first' and to 'strengthen those who have brought peace to the nation'.[64] One such advertisement (also used as a poster) set out to draw a clear distinction between the parties on the issue of unity and safety and opened with the headline 'The Challenge'. An immediate subtitle drew a comparison between 'The Government and Order' on one side versus 'The Irregulars and Anarchy' on the other. This was followed by a list underneath each one. On the government side it had: The ballot and majority rule, law with good order, security for life and property, right to live, right to work, with work to do. On the 'Irregular' side the list read: The gun, petrol can, the torch, and minority dictation, chaos and disorder, murder, arson, armed robbery and loot, burned houses, ruined roads and railways, broken bridges and ruined trade, unemployment and starvation. The solution offered was that the current administration 'has beaten anarchy' and 'the Cosgrave Government is alone strong enough to kill it'.[65] Ernest Blythe in Tralee, County Kerry, claimed that if they had yielded to past violence that 'there would now be "fellows swaggering around with guns, threatening the electors" but, we have taken care they will not start again'.[66] These propaganda messages did work in their aim to associate Sinn Féin with the violent evils of the past, particularly the Civil War. Public anxiety about a return to disorder, whether real or imagined, was fuelled by opinion pieces in the national dailies and regional press too. For instance, a *Dundalk Democrat* correspondent wrote, 'we must say whether we desire to be governed by our fellow-countrymen, under the constitution of the Free State, or whether we prefer to renew the disastrous conflicts of the past three years, to throw away the prospect of peace and order won for Ireland by the treaty.'[67]

Violence had been a difficulty in past electoral contests, but surprisingly in 1923 despite the discord between Cumann na nGaedheal and Sinn Féin the overall conduct was peaceful.[68] This may have been due to the penalties for disorderly acts under the Electoral Abuses Act which was publicised by the Government Publicity Department. This act stated that 'any person who at a lawful public meeting in a constituency … acts in a disorderly manner … is liable, on summary conviction, to a fine of £100'.[69] Regardless, a few did not heed the law and there were threats and violent exploits in some areas such as Ramsgrange in County Wexford where in the week prior to the election date, the Farmers' Party entered the village and were met at the crossroads 'by a hostile crowd of young men and boys'. The Director of Elections, N. J. Murphy, decided to call off the meeting, but before his car could be started, he was 'set upon and assaulted with clenched fists'. He stated that 'rotten eggs, and sound ones too, rained upon me, and I was covered with the contents of the eggs from the top of my hat to my boots'.[70] There were also a few heated outbursts at public political meetings. For example, the Cumann na nGaedheal candidate in Goresbridge, County Kilkenny, was 'heckled by a young man', and as the party was leaving there were 'some shouts for de Valera heard'. In Rower village, in the same constituency, 'some angry words between members of the crowd led to blows.' Interrupters were either 'chased away by a section of the crowd' or 'antagonists were separated', and the meetings became peaceful.[71] On the other side, Sinn Féin accused their opponents of tampering with their election campaign, and some included 'raids on the Sinn Féin headquarters, the houses of Mrs

Childers, Dr Lynn, O'Hanrahan, R. H. O'Connor, Miss Barton, and Madam Markievicz'. A public meeting in Grange, County Louth, was attacked by the Civic Guard and a meeting in Omeath in the same county was surrounded by soldiers who 'took all the literature'. It was alleged that soldiers stoned a meeting at Kenmare, County Kerry, attacked a meeting in Strandhill, County Sligo, and attacked a group of republicans in Tramore, County Waterford. In Carndonagh, County Donegal the *Irish Independent* reported that 'sticks and stones were brought into play while anti-treatyites were speaking'.[72] The fear of violence or actual violence had an impact both on propaganda and electoral turnout. Daunted and perhaps frustrated by the threat of violence and intimidation some voters decided to abstain on polling day. Voters may also have absented themselves from public meetings leaving all the parties with reduced numbers and a loss of propaganda opportunity.[73] However, even though rivalry between candidates was keen in contested constituencies, there were only very few instances of actual violence and only a few minor skirmishes.

In conclusion, the astute propaganda campaigns of the 1923 General Election reinforced not only entrenched political ideals but created earnest combat between the two clearly opposing paradigms of nationalism. It is difficult to evaluate the impact of propaganda because there were other variables at play such as everyday economic issues, the 1921 Treaty, and simply a desire to return to normality after a decade of conflicts: and all these played into voter decision making. The purpose of propaganda is to manipulate behaviour, and the war of words in this elections campaign was as influential as those pointed out by other scholars in assessing major conflicts such as the Great War or the Anglo-Irish War 1919–21.[74] Propaganda, as a form of communication, was (and is) influenced by the technological devices for sending messages that are available in a given time, and elections in the 1920s by comparison to modern elections were limited in their methods of communication.[75] Sinn Féin and Cumann na nGaedheal had used similar methods of propaganda, but the former had focused their content largely on the ills of the treaty and condemnation of 'any foreign authority in Ireland', whereas the latter looked more to the future.[76]

In speeches and in print Sinn Féin and Cumann na nGaedheal had excelled by utilising propaganda that had consistency of messages and slogans and by using a variety of themes, and they were vocal and visually present in their constituencies. In contrast both the Farmers' and Labour Parties banked on public speeches which required an audience to turn out. The strident propaganda of the 1923 campaign aided in altering public opinion, and perhaps more so amongst wavering voters or those not aligned to a political party. Ultimately Cumann na nGaedheal with their appeals for unity, peace and a sound economy, won the day. As Basil Chubb points out, 'there is no denying the importance of the mass media for politics' because 'it is essential to an understanding of how political attitudes are formed and behaviour is shaped'.[77] Other propaganda methods also impacted on this election to sway attitudes, such as person-to-person communication. The civil war atmosphere still prevailed so the big issue in these elections was still whether voters did or did not support the Anglo-Irish Treaty. What 1923 proved, even with the variety of propaganda methods and themes and sometimes adversarial messages, was that electors wanted a stable majority government that did not rely on the smaller parties in order to take the Free State into the future.

CHAPTER 6

'THE ONLY HOPE WAS TO WORK THE TREATY': LOCAL NEWSPAPER COVERAGE OF THE 1923 GENERAL ELECTION IN KERRY

Owen O'Shea

It has been correctly noted that the 'principal conduits of information and framers of public opinion in the second decade of the twentieth century were newspapers and word of mouth.'[1] Newspapers were 'the unrivalled medium of communication' in Ireland at the beginning of the twentieth century, and, during the revolutionary period, 'played a key role in framing the public discourse'.[2] Because of negligible competition from other media, the role of newspapers in building awareness and influencing opinion, including political opinion, 'cannot be understated.'[3] Moreover, the space devoted to politics in the press at this time was 'unrivalled by any other news item.'[4] Regional and local newspapers had a particular influence: while many in the business class 'leafed through the national dailies', the majority of people turned to their local newspaper for information.[5] These publications were 'central to the dissemination of ideas and opinions, and to shaping the public mindset.'[6] Yet, the role of newspapers – regional newspapers in particular – in influencing political discourse and, in particular, their effect on electoral outcomes, has been the subject of relatively few studies, at least until recent years.[7] Alan McCarthy has examined the influence of newspapers in County Cork between 1910 and 1923 while the role of the press in the regions in revolutionary Ireland – until 1921 – is provided in monographs by Christopher Doughan and Elaine Callinan.[8] A wider survey of the Irish regional press between the late nineteenth and early twenty-first century is contained in a collection of essays edited by Ian Kenneally and James T. O'Donnell.[9] How local newspapers approached the reporting of the election campaign of 1923 as well as what they actually reported had a critical impact on the outcome of the 27 August poll, the first general election after the civil war. In Kerry, where the civil war was more brutal, violent and protracted than any other county, newspapers were uniquely placed to guide and influence political opinion, act as a force for calm and stability, engender the importance of electoral participation, and direct voters towards or away from a particular political party or philosophy.[10] These endeavours presented challenges for journalists, columnists and editors in a county which was weary and punch-drunk from the violence and bloodshed of 1919–23. This chapter will examine how the Kerry newspapers which re-emerged after the civil war approached the election campaign of 1923, what advice they offered to voters, and how, crucially, they emphasised the importance of the democratic process and the primacy of the ballot over the bullet in the aftermath of the bitterly divisive fratricide of the previous year. It is concerned less with what was said by candidates and dutifully regurgitated in lengthy columns but more with how electioneering was reported and presented in the context of the party-political allegiances and opinions of newspaper editors and owners. Finally, it will assess what impact these matters had on the result of the election itself.

The newspaper landscape in Kerry in the summer of 1923 was a much depleted one in a county which had a very large number of publications in circulation at the beginning of the century. In 1902, for example, there were nine local newspapers published in Kerry.[11] Four of these had ceased publication by 1920. None of those which remained would endure, without a breach, the turbulence and turmoil of 1919–23. *The Kerryman* and its tri-weekly sister Tralee publication, *The Liberator*, fell victim to a rampage by the Black and Tans: its printing presses were blown up and destroyed following the killing of a senior Auxiliary officer, Major Mackinnon in April 1921.[12] Two of the others, which were published by the Quinnell family, the *Kerry Weekly Reporter* and the *Kerry News*, were also forced to cease publication. The only journal to survive the war of independence was the *Kerry People*, which was edited by Maurice P. Ryle. During the civil war, the *Kerry People* provided 'accurate and balanced coverage of the conflict', but 'its independent editorial line did not endear it to republicans.'[13] It was suppressed by anti-treaty forces in August 1922 when it published a message, on its front page, from the National Army chief of staff, Richard Mulcahy to the Kerry Command of the army. Within days, the printing press of the newspaper at Barrack Place in Tralee was dismantled and the 'vital parts of the machine were taken away' rendering publication of the newspaper impossible.[14]

The anti-treaty constituency in Kerry had been afforded a temporary platform through a short-lived newspaper, the *Kerry Leader*, which was published in Tralee for several months during 1922. One of the very few explicitly anti-treaty newspapers anywhere in Ireland at the time, it was co-founded and edited by Seán Moynihan, later a personal secretary to Éamon de Valera, assistant editor with the *Irish Press*, and a senior civil servant.[15] The newspaper was suppressed by Free State forces following their arrival in large numbers in Kerry and after its refusal to publish a Free State 'proclamation'. Moynihan and the newspaper's manager, Eamon O'Connor were interned, amid accusations of 'silencing possible criticism of the policy and actions of the Free State authorities and their agents.'[16] The suppression of the *Kerry Leader* deprived those on the anti-treaty side of a newspaper which both facilitated and advocated their position and such a platform would not be restored until the end of the decade when the Fianna Fáil-supporting *Kerry Champion* was founded in 1928 by the former anti-treaty TD, Paddy Cahill.[17]

There were no newspapers published in Kerry in the period between August 1922 and June 1923, which deprives readers (and historians) of locally published newspaper accounts of most of the civil war period. The first publication to re-emerge a few weeks after the end of the war was the *Kerry People*, though extant editions for the months which followed are extremely rare. Despite hopes in 1921 that the demise of *The Kerryman* and *The Liberator* would last just six months, neither resumed publication until August 1923, just weeks before the general election of 27 August, something which was 'universally welcomed.'[18] Information regarding newspaper sales in this period is sparse. *The Kerryman*, however, did publish what they claimed to be 'certified' sales figures and, given its subsequent dominance in the market – it is the only newspaper from this period which continues to be published to this day – the details are informative. When it resumed publication, *The Kerryman* was selling 1,500 copies per week. This figure rose quickly to 3,933 in January 1923 and 8,286 in December 1924.[19] Actual readership, as opposed to sales, can be reasonably assumed to be multiples of the latter.

The editorial approach of the Kerry press in the months after the civil war and in the weeks before the 1923 General Election incorporated a number of attitudes and ambitions. There was a combination of expressing a desire for securing and maintaining peace; the hope that the horrors of the civil war would be confined to history; strong support for the treaty of 1921; condemnation of those who opposed the treaty and anti-treaty combatants during the civil war; and political support for the Cumann na nGaedheal party and the government of W. T. Cosgrave. The return to some semblance of normality in daily life was hoped for and demanded by newspaper editorials and commentators as soon as the conflict ended and as the election approached. This was combined with calls to move on from, or even forget, the bloodshed and the bitterness which it inspired. This deliberate suppression of invoking what had occurred, and talking about what had occurred, was a phenomenon which would pervade attitudes to the civil war among the people of the county for generations and was often encouraged by the press.[20] In June, the aspiration of the editorial in the *Kerry People* was for peace and progress and the writer set the tone for much of what followed in the Kerry press during subsequent months:

> The nine months have been very tragic ones for Ireland. It would be well if their memory could be blotted out altogether. The people should try at any rate to forget what has happened and to look forward to the future with confidence and with hope. The comparative calm that obtains at the present moment in Ireland looks like an assurance that we are nearing, if we have not already reached, the normal. God grant that this may be so. Business is proceeding 'as usual' and the fact that the railways, with all their ramifications, are able to get through their daily routine is a sure indication of normality.[21]

The sentiments were echoed in *The Kerryman* stable. The first editorial of *The Kerryman* following its re-emergence in August declared a confidence that 'the worst is over and that our beloved country is destined for a glorious future.'[22] It was not just the editors who appealed for calm and progress and expressed the hope that the violence of the previous years was at an end. The local 'Notes' columnists from various parts of the county who supplied copy to *The Kerryman* and *The Liberator* injected political discourse with the same messages. The author of the 'Castlemaine' column, for example, struck a note of optimism, suggesting that there was a growing sense of security: the 'sound of the rifle and bomb grows more and more to be but a bitter memory … it is surely not full time to try to forget and forgive' while the 'Annascaul' column noted 'the return of normal social conditions.'[23]

From the moment it resumed publication, *The Kerryman* adopted a clear pro-treaty position. This was nothing unusual in the press across the country at the time with almost all of the mainstream Irish press in the 26 counties supporting the accord to varying degrees.[24] *The Kerryman* stance on the prevailing constitutional question was embedded by its owners as much as it was a feature of editorialising. It was owned by cousins Thomas and Daniel Nolan from Tralee and Maurice Griffin, its managing editor, a native of Dingle. Griffin, who most influenced the newspaper's political ethos, was active in Sinn Féin and was a member of Tralee Urban District Council. He was jailed for a period after the Easter Rising.[25] The newspaper was largely sympathetic to Sinn Féin before the rebellion.[26]

While it was appalled at the loss of life during the Rising, the newspaper praised the rebels and their objectives.[27] Its Tralee publication, *The Liberator* was 'one of the earliest of the regional papers to come out in explicit support of the [1916] rebels.'[28] In the years before Independence, *The Kerryman* 'firmly directed public opinion towards the aims of the Irish republican and the Fenian brotherhoods.'[29] It had also directed a 'lot of poisonous rhetoric' towards the Irish Parliamentary Party.[30] The localised circulation of *The Liberator,* which was published three times each week, in the largest town in the county offered a further platform for the political commentary and editorialising of *The Kerryman*, much of which was replicated verbatim. The pro-treaty stance adopted by Griffin and the Nolans was most apparent in its condemnation of the anti-treaty party and its advocacy of Cumann na nGaedheal. *The Kerryman* management and editors took the view, in the words of Dan Nolan, son of founder, Thomas, that the only option was to back the treaty:

> the publishers were strong-willed enough to take the Treaty side in a by then predominantly Republican Kerry. The country was on its knees in every respect following the Anglo-Irish struggle and the bitterly contested civil war. My father [Dan Nolan] and his colleagues felt that the only hope was to work the Treaty. [31]

Moreover, there were editorial efforts to exonerate the outgoing government, for example, for the partition of Ireland: 'it is not fair to blame either the present government or the Irish signatories of the Treaty for this state of things.'[32]

After the civil war, the *Kerry People* also positioned itself firmly in the pro-treaty camp. In seeking compensation for the suppression and destruction of his newspaper at the hands of the IRA in August 1922, editor Maurice Ryle explained the loss he and his employees had suffered, in a letter to Piaras Béaslaí, a pro-treaty TD for Kerry. Ryle wrote:

> Outside our ordinary trading losses we have missed about £1,000 worth of printing and advertising work, which would have come to us from the Army and Government had our Office been allowed to function…We went down in the service of the Free State and have been brought to the brink of financial disaster.[33]

When it was finally in a position to publish its opinion on the events of 1922–3, *The Kerryman* ensured that the blame for the origins and prolongation of the civil war was laid firmly at the door of the anti-treatyites. 'Love of country is not best expressed by attempts to compass that country's destruction,' noted *The Liberator* editorial of 9 August 1923. 'Surely,' it added, 'it is possible for men and women to be patriots without having to give vent to their love of country in a vehemently violent way'.[34] Every citizen, be they 'Republican, Free Stater, Laborite or Farmer – his manifest duty to his country is to build it up, not to pull it down.'[35] The same columnist condemned the civil war as an 'incomprehensible folly – amounting almost to morbid perversity' which left the new state in 'the most critical situation that could possibly confront a nation just emerged from subjection into freedom.'[36] The commentary about the devastation of the civil war, and specifically the destruction and disruption caused by anti-treaty forces in Kerry was not without some justification. Though it was not documented in the local press during the war, the toll of IRA looting, robbery, damage, disruption and destruction – which subsequently generated over 1,000 claims for compensation from individuals and businesses in Kerry –

was widespread.[37] There was a noticeable absence, however, of any similar condemnations of the many atrocities and extra-judicial murders presided over by the Kerry Command of the Free State army in 1922–3. The Kerry editors were particularly mute in this regard.

Support for Cumann na nGaedheal was immediately evident in the columns of *The Kerryman*, despite its insistence, many years later, that it held 'no brief for any of the political parties – which would prove hugely consequential for elections and their contestants'.[38] In an editorial a fortnight before polling, readers were urged to 'complete, not wreck the marvellous work of those countless great heroes of ours who died so willingly so that Ireland might live.'[39] There were those who wanted to 'go another round' over the concessions won in the treaty but others who were keen to 'develop the country intellectually, materially, and from a Gaelic viewpoint than to indulge in further conflict.'[40] The inference was that those who wanted to re-open the civil war were hellbent on chaos while those keen to build the Free State were the true Gaels and had the vision and ideals to progress the country. There were also apologias on behalf of the Cosgrave government which, it was argued, could hardly have achieved utopia as the country descended into civil strife. Voters needed to remember that:

> the present Government took up office in a most difficult situation and under circumstances which precluded anything in the nature of economical administration of the affairs of the country. An Executive endeavoring [sic] to function under conditions with which we have, unfortunately, become only too familiar for the past 12 months could not be expected to become too well acquainted with perfection.[41]

Even more explicitly, an editorial declared that the right-thinking voter would make the correct choice come polling day: those 'who are capable of forming mature and shrewd judgement express complete confidence in the return of the Cumann na nGaedheal candidates,' and specifically, 'with Mr Finian Lynch at the head of the poll.'[42] In the same vein, it was believed that right-thinking voters would 'acquit themselves' in the polling booths with the result being a greater 'profit to the nation' which was facing its greatest ever crisis. Few readers could have doubted where the editors and proprietors stood on the electoral choice before the people.

Despite expressing clear biases about the major constitutional and party-political choices before the voters, newspapers left readers in no doubt about their support for resolving differences with ballots rather than bullets. The general election of 1923 would be the first time that voters went to the polls in Kerry since 1910 – each of the elections in the interim had not been contested – and on a much wider franchise. It was the first election in which everyone over the age of 21 could vote with the Free State extending the vote to women between the ages of 21 and 30. Many citizens had never cast a ballot and the experience of participating in the democratic process was alien to them. The newspapers wholeheartedly encouraged participation in the poll and promoted the ballot as the best means for expressing political opinions. All editors called on readers to exercise their right to vote and emphasised the importance and significance of the poll. A week before polling, readers of *The Liberator* were reminded of the 'far-reaching consequences' of their decisions and that, on polling day:

> the people of Ireland will be engaged in making a choice pregnant with consequences of the

greatest moment in this ancient nation. This is the first occasion on which the people of Ireland are offered the opportunity of deciding for themselves as to the character of the composition of their National Assembly.[43]

This language of persuasion about the duty of citizens to vote and thereby using parliamentary democracy to address and resolve political differences was hugely important following the divisions of the civil war.

Coverage of the election campaign consisted of a large number of reports on the meetings and activities of the candidates, commentary on the parties and their policies, details of the arrangements for polling, and the publication of a limited number of party advertisements as well as the statutory notices regarding the election. The Kerry constituency was contested by 15 candidates including four Cumann na nGaedheal, four Republicans, three independents (including Thomas O'Donnell, a former Irish Parliamentary Party MP), and two each for the Farmers' Party and Labour.[44] Reports on the electioneering of Cumann na nGaedheal were by far the most extensive and frequent. Meetings and canvassing conducted by the party usually received a column or more of newsprint. Most of a page of *The Kerryman* edition of 18 August was devoted to a Cumann na nGaedheal meeting in Cahersiveen.[45] The following week, and in the only such case of its kind, significant space was devoted to a list of all those who had signed the nomination papers of each of the Cumann na nGaedheal candidates.[46] The party's activities were also more positively portrayed than those of the others. Fionán Lynch, for example, had 'a very successful collection' for his election fund in Cahersiveen and the collectors were 'remarkable spirit of enthusiasm' who contributed, which 'speaks well for the reception and support which Mr Lynch will have when he visits his constituents in South Kerry.'[47] Cumann na nGaedheal meetings and campaigning, such as the canvass by candidates John Marcus O'Sullivan and James Crowley, were invariably described as a success.[48] Whether this was party propaganda willingly regurgitated by the press or a series of descriptions applied by the editor, the effect was the same: Cumann na nGaedheal was portrayed as a dynamic and successful party whose message was gaining electoral traction.   While Cumann na nGaedheal events were widely published, anti-treaty meetings and electioneering were rarely mentioned. This lack of coverage must be considered in the context of the major difficulties faced by the anti-treatyites in mounting a meaningful campaign. The campaign was constrained by the absence of three of their four candidates, Tomás O'Donoghue, Paddy Cahill and Austin Stack were in jail, while another, Thomas McEllistrim, was on the run from the authorities. The inability of those contenders to hold meetings and appeal to voters through the pages of the press put Sinn Féin on the back foot immediately. But where Republican campaigning was reported, it was minimal and sometimes reported dismissively. A public meeting in Killarney which was addressed by Professor William Stockley (Sinn Féin TD for the National University of Ireland) and other prominent republicans was mentioned in a one-line report.[49]

Plenty of dismissive language was used to talk about the Republican campaign. It was 'rumoured' that the Republicans had held a convention to select candidates, implying something underground or underhand on the part of the anti-treatyites.[50] Reporting on an anti-treaty meeting during Fair Day in Kenmare, *The Liberator* correspondent commended the Civic Guard for carrying out their duties 'in a most creditable manner' when fighting erupted during the rally. The Sinn Féiners, it was noted, in a front-page report, 'got a bad reception, which shows that their policy is not favoured much in the district.'[51] This sort of reference to the anti-treatyites was a running theme and the inability of many of the Republican candidates to respond directly because of their forced absence did little to counteract it. Generally, where they were mentioned, the speeches at anti-treaty meetings were usually reported without any descriptive comment save for a reference to Charlotte Despard being prevented from 'getting a hearing' during a melee at a Republican meeting in Kenmare although it was reported that Mary MacSwiney's address in Tralee was 'very largely attended.'[52]

During the campaign, it also became practise for columnists to undermine, belittle or demean those from other parties if their message did not fit easily with the prevailing editorial ethos. It was perhaps because parties like Labour and the Farmers' Party were defined by issues other than the constitutional question and the civil war split, and tried to infuse the discussion with more tangible bread-and-butter issues, that they were not treated with the same adulation as those in Cumann na nGaedheal. There was a clear attempt, editorially, to confine the discourse to the treaty – other issues would be dealt with when a new Dáil and government was formed. This stance was echoed in many editorials: many of the 'side issues' advanced by Labour and the Farmers' Party would have to be determined at a later date rather than at a time of national constitutional turbulence.[53] Farmers' Party candidates were considered acceptable and worthy of support by the press: if elected, they would not be 'found wanting in ability.'[54] Both that party and Labour did receive space in the columns – the selection of their candidates and some of their meetings were reported though not to the same extent as Cumann na nGaedheal and anti-treaty Sinn Féin. However, in the main, the message was clear: the 1923 poll should be a straight vote on the major constitutional issue of the day and be decided between the proponents and opponents of the treaty. That over three quarters of Kerry voters gave a first preference to the two main parties in August 1923 suggests that this message resonated with the county's electors.

One of the features of the 1923 election was regular outbreaks of violence between supporters of the different parties. This offered reporters and readers alike reportage of greater entertainment value and political colour than much of the other more turgid reporting of speeches and party meetings and journalists did not resile from relaying the outbursts of fisticuffs to their readers with eloquence and dramatic verbiage. The *Kerry People* comment in mid-August that the outlook for a peaceful election seemed 'very dubious' was prescient.[55] Editors made commendable efforts to dissuade electors from disruptive behaviour. Ten days before polling, the 'Tralee Topics' writer in *The Liberator* evoked the divisions, not of the recent civil war, but of the Parnell era, to remind readers of the perils of violence:

> Surely it is possible for men and women to be patriots without having to give vent to their love of country in a vehemently violent way ... I remember fairly well the rather ferocious bitterness engendered by the Parnell split, when life-long friends fell out, and brother was ranged against brother and father against son, when things were said and done which were nothing but unpleasant memories afterwards.[56]

Some political representatives emphasised the same message: ahead of a speech by Mary

MacSwiney in Tralee, Cumann na nGaedheal published an appeal to its supporters to refrain from disorder, claiming it stood for liberty of speech and good order. The notice issued to the press was signed by Dr Brian McMahon Coffey, chairman of Tralee Cumann na nGaedheal and M. Ó Ríobhirdan, its secretary.[57]

Where violence did erupt, the drama was reported with plenty of detail and colour. Not only were heckling and interruptions at election events very common, there were also a small number of episodes of bloodshed. In Dingle, there was chaos at a pro-treaty meeting which was attended by the four Cumann na nGaedheal candidates:

> Boohs, political catch-cries such as 'Up Stack' and 'Up De Valera' came from different sections of the crowd. The interrupters came in for rough handling, and they stoutly defended themselves with sticks. At times terrible confusion and excitement prevailed. There were many free fights, and sometimes it looked as if there would be a general stampede.[58]

When a meeting at Kenmare was being addressed by republican campaigners Charlotte Despard and Kerry Sinn Féin county councillor, Albinia Brodrick, a ruckus involving fighting and egg-throwing required the Civic Guard to produce their batons.[59] Elsewhere, *The Liberator* correspondent shared a vivid description of a melee during a Cumann na nGaedheal meeting in Cahersiveen when women carrying black flags and bearing dummy coffins – representing the republican dead – marched through the town. The coffins were seized and smashed by police and Cumann na nGaedheal supporters. A local man, Eugene O'Neill, was shot in the leg and another man was arrested by the Civic Guards.[60] The extensive report under the headline 'A dose of their own medicine' continued:

> Peaceful persuasion to get the demonstrators to 'move on' proved unavailing and the volunteers resorted to sterner methods by pushing them off. The disturbers resisted and blows were freely exchanged between the male section of the interrupters and the volunteers. The women demonstrators joined in the free using of their flag staffs on the heads of the volunteers ... They struck out vigorously with their clenched fists and being met with similar 'arguments' by some of the sturdier section of the male belligerents while the women continued to parry and strike with their flag staffs ... A running fight continued on towards the market. Here a hail of stones was kept up for some minutes.[61]

The declaration by *The Liberator* a week after polling that a feature of the election campaign was the 'total absence of disturbance' did not reflect the reality.[62] It did, however, betray the prevailing attitude of the local press which insisted on a peaceful election and the primacy of the ballot box. That there was not greater disturbance on the hustings just a few months after the end of the civil war was quite remarkable.

A critical aspect of newspaper coverage of elections in this period was the publication of political advertisements. As Callinan attests, candidates and parties had no control over the 'free propaganda' they obtained in the newspapers: they realised that coverage of their election messages, speeches and meetings was not always guaranteed and that electoral success also necessitated the purchase of advertising space in the newspapers.[63] During the 1920s, regional newspapers increasingly recognised the commercial potential of advertising by the political parties, reminding election agents to 'place orders as early as possible.'[64] A small number of advertisements appeared during the 1923 campaign in Kerry, including those of Cumann na nGaedheal, Labour and one of the independent candidates. The extent of advertising reflected the capacity of those parties to pay for those notices. For example, a total of nine large advertisements for Cumann na nGaedheal were published in *The Liberator* as well as two advertisements advising the public how to vote and best use the PR-STV system to the advantage of the party. Cumann na nGaedheal adverts often occupied almost a quarter of a page in *The Liberator* and *The Kerryman* and two or three different adverts sometimes appeared in the same edition.[65] In its first edition on resuming publication, *The Kerryman* carried three large advertisements for Cumann na nGaedheal and four in the edition of the following week.[66] Full-blown partisan rhetoric was ventilated in the advertisements of Cumann na nGaedheal which was not slow to politicise the civil war for electoral benefit. One such notice evoked the atrocities committed locally against Free State soldiers during the civil war, the shooting dead of TDs Seán Hales and Michael Collins and the economic impact of the Republican campaign:

> ONE CIVILIAN MOTOR DRIVER MURDERED AT BALLYSEEDY
> ONE CIVILIAN MURDERED, ROCK STREET, TRALEE
> TWO RAILWAY MEN DASHED TO DEATH IN ARDFERT
> FIVE IRISH SOLDIERS BLOWN TO PIECES AT KNOCKNAGOSHEL
> NINE RED CROSS MEN MURDERED IN KERRY
> 200 CORPSES OF IRISH SOLDIERS IN GLASNEVIN
> COLLINS AND SEAN HALES ASSASSINATED
> LITTLE EMMET MCGARRY ROASTED TO DEATH
> RUINED LIVES, BROKEN HEARTS, DIVIDED HOMES
> FIFTY MILLIONS OF WEALTH DESTROYED
> IF YOU WISH TO GET RID OF THIS CALAMITOUS SPOILED CHILD
> VOTE FOR THE CUMANN NA NGAEDHEAL CANDIDATES[67]

However, this was a rare foray into the politicisation of specific incidents of the conflict for electoral purposes. For the most part, during the 1920s, and in subsequent decades, the tragedies of Kerry would not be an explicitly stated feature of party advertisements.[68]
Labour published a small number of advertisements to promote their candidates. Their message focussed on free speech and 'liberty, equality and fraternity' as well as more practical matters such as industrial stability, improved prices for farmers, and the need for free higher education.[69] But constitutional matters were also referenced with a demand for the release of all prisoners 'before Election Day' and calls for a united Ireland 'with the abolition of all obnoxious oaths and tests.'[70] The only other candidate to publish a paid-for advertisement during the 1923 campaign was Independent candidate and chairman of the Tralee Board of Guardians, Jeremiah McSweeney. He attempted to appeal to voters of all hues and, in a catch all advert, insisted that he was unfettered by allegiance to any political group. McSweeney claimed to be the son of a farmer and his people were 'living by the land', he was a supporter of the Town Tenants groups in the county, and the release of prisoners would be his 'first effort' if elected.[71]

Voting in Kerry took place at 260 polling stations with 90,156 electors eligible to vote, slightly less than the number of registered voters for the uncontested 1922 poll.[72] The so-called 'Pact Election' of 1922 had returned, without opposition, three pro-treaty and five anti-treaty candidates for the Kerry-Limerick West constituency. A new constituency encompassing County Kerry was created for the 1923 poll. As such, the 1923 contest represented the first opportunity which Kerry voters were afforded to express their support for or opposition to the treaty and to issue a verdict on the first government of the Free State. Concerns were expressed in the press about the condition of the electoral register: one writer in *The Liberator* suggested after the election that, in Kerry, 'some entitled to vote had no vote at all, whilst others of doubtful age, who could be taken as knowing no more about the issues concerned than the man in the moon, much less the sense to care, helped to swell the quota.'[73] Any deficiencies with the register were never tendered, however, as a reason to invalidate or undermine the process.

The final result saw all of the Republican candidates – Austin Stack, Thomas McEllistrim, Thomas O'Donoghue and Patrick Cahill – elected, and they filled four of the seven available seats. Stack, the most-high profile Sinn Féin candidate in the county, headed the poll on 10,333 first preferences, almost 19 per cent of the total. Nationwide, the anti-treatyites polled 27 per cent of first preferences but in Kerry, almost half of all voters backed Republican candidates, proving that there was 'a huge reservoir of political support for the anti-treaty wing of Sinn Féin in the county.'[74] At 45 per cent of first preferences and 3.6 quotas, the anti-treaty vote in Kerry was the second highest in the country, behind the party leader's Clare constituency on 47 per cent, and well ahead of the Munster average of just under 31 per cent.[75] The remaining three seats were filled by Cumann na nGaedheal TDs, Fionán Lynch and James Crowley and newcomer, UCD professor, John Marcus O'Sullivan. Cumann na nGaedheal secured 17,808 first preferences and 32.5 per cent of the valid poll but their tally of 2.6 quotas delivered three seats. Theirs was a lower percentage of the vote attained by the party nationally at 39 per cent.

Over 16 per cent of first preferences were secured by Labour (7.8 per cent) and the Farmers' Party (8.5 per cent) between them. Both were pro-treaty parties and therefore, as shown in Mel Farrell's chapter, much of this vote was effectively denied to the main pro-treaty party in Kerry. But it also suggests that a significant tranche of voters were not persuaded to support either of the treaty parties nor be influenced exclusively by the divisions it inspired – or the newspaper editorials which focussed on these delineations. Nevertheless, the two main treaty parties had received 78 per cent of the poll in Kerry, making the treaty, which had been the dominant issue in the newspaper coverage and commentary on the election, 'the paramount political issue for eight of ten voters in Kerry.'[76]

Despite all of the editorial encouragement to voters to engage with the democratic process, approximately 35,000 of eligible Kerry voters chose not to cast their ballot. With 54,845 valid votes cast, turnout in Kerry was 60.8 per cent, just slightly ahead of the national figure of 59 per cent.[77] The turnout in a county which had experienced many greater horrors and a more protracted conflict than other counties can be considered significant. Such was the degree of intimidation, criminality and disruption to civilian life during the war and in the months which followed, electoral participation in Kerry might well have been expected to be lower.[78] Jeffrey Prager suggests the low turnout generally had much to do with the apathy identified by other contributors to this volume, and a distrust of the new state's political institutions. Prager points to a pattern of lowest turnout in constituencies in which Sinn Féin support was strongest.[79] Based on the results which emerged in Kerry, this suggests that Republicans – despite the absence of many of their candidates from the campaign trail and a lack of financial resources were better at, in modern parlance, getting their vote out. That they achieved this in the face of a hostile press adds an even greater significance to that achievement.

In the days immediately following polling and as the votes were tallied, the Kerry press maintained a conciliatory and respectful tone. There were reports on the cordial remarks of the candidates, both elected and defeated. For example, the words of Fionán Lynch, who spoke on behalf of his Cumann na nGaedheal colleagues, in which he said that he 'trusted that the constitutional procedure which had brought the opponents of the Government to the use of the ballot box would be pursued, and that all parties would take their share in the administration of the affairs of the nation' were characterised by the local editorial writer as 'a felicitous note of friendship.'[80] The press columns accepted the results of the general election as an expression of popular will: the votes of the people must be characterised as 'the considered verdict of the people.'[81] However, while the votes were still being counted, *The Kerryman* identified two options for the country, insisting that one of those was deeply fraught with danger:

> If the voters decide for a Republic, well, their decision, as a national pronouncement of policy, is entitled to the respect of every Irishman and woman. Should the electorate declare in favor [sic] of the Free State form of Government in accordance with the Constitution, it need not be labored [sic] that such decision is entitled to the very same respect. But the work which the latter verdict would set before the Irish people would be nothing in comparison with the problem which would necessarily have to grapple with as a corollary of their pronouncement in favor of a Republic.[82]

Moreover, if de Valera's TDs declined to take their seats in parliament and abstentionism prevailed among republicans, this would be met with the strong opposition of the 'stern, unbending Cosgrave administration'. There could simply not be 'two Governments in the country at the one time'.[83] So, although voters in Kerry voted in far greater numbers for anti-treaty candidates than pro-treaty nominees – by a margin of almost 3:2 – and although Republicans held four of the county's seats to Cumann na nGaedheal's three, the county's newspapers insisted that only the latter could provide the stable government which the country needed. Though not explicitly stated, there was a belief that most electors, on this occasion in Kerry, at least, had made the wrong choice.

If the approach of the Kerry press towards the election campaign was broadly pro-treaty and supportive of the Cumann na nGaedheal party, there was an immediate and noticeable shift in the editorialising and reporting within days of the poll. What had been a largely supportive and rather benign approach to the governing party until polling day was replaced by calls to get on with the business of governing now that voting had been completed. Curiously, the type of bread-and-butter issues which concerned the people of Kerry in the autumn of 1923 were noticeable by their absence from the reportage and the editorials before the election. Apart from very rare references to problems such as housing – 'one of our many local problems' – the constitutional question about the direction of the new state was put front and centre.[84] This was framed around arguments against the inclusion of too many non-aligned candidates on the ballot in the interest of maintaining a focus on the treaty and its implementation: 'the present National question situation is too critical to permit of [sic] many side issues or sectional interests being considered.'[85] Writing about Galway in the decade after the civil war, Úna Newell suggests that the 1923 election was about politics, not economics, it was a binary choice between Free State and a Republic, sectional interests were waived and 'candidates were defined by the treaty split'.[86]

73

This was replicated in Kerry, where there was an apparent effort to set aside debate on the social and economic problems while the voters tussled with the politics of the treaty and the direction of the country, politically, in the aftermath of the civil war.

Immediately following the declaration of the result however, the very issues which had been absent from the political discourse in the news columns for several weeks were prioritised in the commentary. There was a demand for political leaders to shift their focus from constitutional matters – which were deemed to have been settled following the formation of the new Cumann na nGaedheal government – and to concentrate on the social and economic challenges facing the country. *The Liberator's* front page insisted, for example, that it was necessary to 'make an honest effort to settle down and try to transact some serious business'.[87] There was now a need to deal with the 'less sentimental and more material aspect of questions vitally affecting our country.'[88] Among the issues locally requiring remediation were acute distress in the congested districts, problems in the fishing industry, inadequate prices for agricultural produce, and industrial disputes.[89] Nationally, the immediate aftermath of the election was dominated by cuts to teachers' pay and a reduction in the old age pension – these 'rotten' and 'projected experiments' should be abandoned.[90]

The same demands were made of the new parliament. 'An Auspicious Start' is how *The Liberator* greeted the first meeting of the Fourth Dáil. There was 'much constructive work to be done, and the labor [sic] involved in making good the calamitous destruction of last year and a half will be prodigious.'[91] The newly elected deputies needed to concentrate on areas such as the waste of public monies, poverty and unemployment, and the depressed economic situation in Kerry and beyond. In an editorial in September 1923, which was typical of its kind, the *Kerry People* writer opined that, 'In the whole course of her chequered history Ireland has never had to face, from the economic and financial point of view, so momentous and even menacing a situation as to-day'. Demanding political discussion on a range of issues, the newspaper insisted that 'Dublin Castle with its 40 Boards' was too costly, insisting that the 'pruning knife' be taken to the multiplicity of departments. It concluded that local authority elections were needed as early as possible to ensure those bodies were 'manned by the best business ability in the country, [and] may endeavour to bring relief to a sadly burthened people.'[92]

Achieving cost savings was a constant theme for editors and correspondents in the aftermath of polling. When the army was being reduced by 10,000 members, there were no pro-rata cuts at senior officer level; why was the vice-chairman of the Senate on a salary when the Deputy Speaker of the House of Commons was not; why did the Governor General's office cost £37,000 per annum; and why were TDs salaries not being reduced.[93] These criticisms were fuelled by one of the most controversial decisions ever taken by an Irish government – the reduction, by a shilling, of the old age pension which *The Liberator* described as a 'rotten' decision and roundly condemned by countless local correspondents.[94] The press clearly saw itself as a voice and advocate for the wider public on such matters. 'It is well to see,' observed a Killorglin correspondent, 'that public opinion as expressed by the Press is against this as well as the OAP [Old Age Pension] reduction.'[95] Meanwhile, *The Kerryman* insisted that the difficulties in agriculture required urgent intervention, insisting that the government 'had better realise, sooner than later, that our chief, and virtually our only industry must get assistance of a very material character in this time of stress.'[96] And there were also more personal and practical concerns: a letter writer who described himself as a 'loyal Free State citizen' bemoaned profiteering, the lack of jobs, and the fact that 'the workman's beer and tobacco are still costing him war time prices, and are his only luxury.'[97] Thus, whereas the approach of the local press prior to the general election had been largely supportive of the Free State government and the continuity it offered at a time of crisis, there was a shift towards a more questioning and critical attitude towards government after the poll. This was coupled with demands for substantial progress on a wide range of issues as well as maintaining peace. So while Cumann na nGaedheal could apparently be assured of sympathetic coverage during election campaigns, they would be readily condemned and criticised if they did not achieve results when returned to power.

In conclusion, the Kerry press was not unusual in adopting a pro-treaty stance after the civil war, as Ó Drisceoil has documented in the *Atlas of the Irish Revolution*.[98] Politics aside, it could be reasonably argued that newspapers, as commercial enterprises and employers, supported the governing party and the political status quo for financial reasons. Much of their advertising revenue was derived from retailers and businesses, the majority of whom supported Cumann na nGaedheal at this time and much of their sales revenue will have derived from those with enough disposable income to purchase a newspaper (*The Kerryman* cost two pence at the time). Cumann na nGaedheal has been widely referred to as an organisation which drew its support from the middle and upper classes and whose members were usually influential figures, 'local notables' or 'big noises' in their communities.[99] Local networks of influence in Cumann na nGaedheal were dominated by lawyers, doctors, merchants and large farmers.[100] Those who filled the top officerships in the party's branches in Kerry fell into the same category. There was often an 'influential assembly' at meetings arranged in the county in the 1920s to organise new branches: this would include 'business men, farmers, national teachers etc.'[101] Newspaper owners and editors would have been part of the same influential class. In this sense, newspapers were reflecting the political biases of their advertising base even if this was not fully reflective of the views of the wider readership and citizenry.

The electoral consequences of how local newspapers covered elections at this time should not be overstated. Callinan has pointed to research which suggests that newspapers with a known or evident political allegiance and prejudice sometimes had limited success in persuading voters one way or the other.[102] Readers of the Kerry newspapers during the 1923 election cannot have been unaware of their editorial biases. But the re-emergence of three newspapers just four months after a brutal civil war and so proximate to the election of August 1923 – the first contested election in Kerry in 13 years – which had a vastly increased electorate, in a county which has been deprived of locally-published newspapers for much of the fratricidal conflict, had a short but very sharp impact. Calls for calm, stability and progress in a county ravaged by the events of 1922–3 coupled with strong messages on the importance and necessity of democracy and the electoral process provided a crucial antidote to the preceding turbulence and ensured that voters were aware of the magnitude of the decision they faced.

The editorialising and reporting of August 1923 can be said to have significantly buttressed the Cumann na nGaedheal vote in the constituency and ensured that the party secured one third of all votes casts and three of the seven available seats. During the campaign, the party was afforded unquestioning and laudatory coverage from the press which reinforced the new party's core vote and persuaded undecided voters of the merits of what Cosgrave and his peers were offering the country. The same editorial biases deprived Republicans, already constrained and at a disadvantage in their electioneering capacity, of the opportunity to gain any traction in the mainstream press. The derision directed towards the anti-treatyites, combined with the minimal coverage of their campaign was one of the many obstacles in the party's path, which was already stymied by a lack of resources and the imprisonment of many of its candidates. At no point were the anti-treaty candidates afforded a platform to outline their policy positions in the same way as were their main opponents.

There would not be counterbalance or an alternative to this editorial line in the press in the county until 1928 when the strongly pro-Fianna Fáil *Kerry Champion* was founded, and which contributed, in no small part, to the party's significant dominance of Kerry politics in the early 1930s.[103] By 1932, Fianna Fáil held five of the seven seats in the constituency and the party would go on to dominate politics in the county for decades. Had there not been such a strong pro-treaty editorial line in *The Kerryman*, *The Liberator* and the *Kerry People* in 1923, the republican vote in Kerry might well have been even higher in the August election and it may well have set anti-treaty Sinn Féin – and later Fianna Fáil – on a sharper and speedier trajectory towards that electoral supremacy in Kerry.

CHAPTER 7

'RETURN THEM TO POWER WITH SUFFICIENT STRENGTH TO COMPLETE THEIR WORK'[1]: THE ROMAN CATHOLIC CHURCH AND THE 1923 GENERAL ELECTION

Daithí Ó Corráin

In his classic political science work on Irish elections, Cornelius O'Leary contends that the general election for the fourth Dáil in August 1923 was the first since 1910 'to be held in what approximated to normal political conditions'.[2] While such an observation was possible with the benefit of hindsight, few contemporaries in 1923 would have agreed. Given that the election took place just three months after the end of the Irish civil war with the Irish Free State still on a war footing, the campaign was inevitably dominated by the Anglo-Irish treaty of 1921, fratricidal conflict, and the future political and social stability of the state. As Michael Laffan has observed, the government campaigned 'on a "safety first" programme, associating itself with Ireland's independence and democracy'.[3] Bill Kissane goes further by suggesting the government's chief ploy was 'to frighten the voters' into thinking that their interests and the safety of the state were at stake.[4] The outgoing government was powerfully endorsed by the Roman Catholic hierarchy and the vast majority of Catholic clergy. At its most fundamental, at issue for churchmen was the need to uphold the authority of the state, to safeguard the stability of the political system, to place the arduous task of national reconstruction in capable hands, and to ensure that justice and peace would prevail after the sufferings of the civil war. Bishop Michael Fogarty of Killaloe claimed that 'the issue really at stake in this election is national safety or national death'.[5] The Catholic hierarchy and clergy were remarkably active during the election campaign. They championed the record of W. T. Cosgrave's ministry and encouraged the electorate to pass a positive verdict on it.

That the Catholic hierarchy stood shoulder to shoulder with Cumann na nGaedheal was not surprising. Between the signing of the treaty in December 1921 and the 1923 General Election, the stance of the Catholic bishops was characterised by obeisance to the legally constituted government, advocacy of majority rule, support for order and social stability, condemnation of the partition of Ireland, and abjuration of republican political violence. Both individually and collectively, the Catholic hierarchy were committed, in Patrick Murray's compelling phrase, to 'sustaining' and reinforcing the authority of a nascent Irish state and were committed to the survival of the treaty settlement.[6] In April and October 1922, powerful statements were issued by the hierarchy that condemned the actions of the anti-treaty IRA. The October pastoral sought to strip the republican campaign of any legitimacy, to appeal for obedience to the legitimate government, to threaten the removal of the sacraments from those engaged in unlawful rebellion, and to appeal to republicans to pursue their grievances through constitutional means.[7] During the civil war, there was no public episcopal condemnation of the government's execution policy (although several bishops appealed in private for clemency) or the conduct of the National army. Michael McCabe suggests that had the bishops overtly disagreed with aspects of the government's policy, it may have occasioned questions about its legitimacy or lent credence to the anti-treaty cause.[8] The hierarchy faced significant criticism from republicans for its position, including an appeal to the pope.[9]

During the early months of 1923, several episcopal pronouncements emphasised the necessities of stable government, constitutional political action and unimpeded elections. For instance, in his Lenten pastoral in February 1923, Archbishop Thomas Gilmartin of Tuam urged, 'for the gun, the revolver, the bomb and the mine, substitute argument. For terrorism substitute an appeal to the dignity and intelligence of the voter'.[10] The pastoral of Cardinal Michael Logue of Armagh was even more forthright. Describing the government as all that stood 'between us and absolute anarchy', he looked forward to the return of peace when the people would have the opportunity of making their electoral views known on a wide franchise. To be effective, such an election must be

> free from violence, from coercion, from unfair devices, from absurd 'pacts' which would make it a selection, not an election. All parties should be free to advocate their principles in press, on platform, in committees by peaceful canvass, and by any other means legitimate in a lawful election.[11]

As the end of the civil war came into view in May 1923, similar sentiments were expressed by Archbishop John Harty of Cashel. He prayed for a peace that will 'recognise the legitimate authority of the Government that is elected by the people', 'a peace that will ensure that the law of God shall be observed' and one where political controversies 'can be carried on without any personal ill-feeling and all public questions can be settled in the ordinary constitutional way, by a free vote of the people'.[12] In the event, Harty's prayers were answered as the election campaign was a remarkably peaceful one despite its proximity to the civil war.[13]

Cumann na nGaedheal's election manifesto emphasised the need 'to secure and to safeguard the status of national sovereignty to which you have attained ... by supporting with your united strength the party whose programme stands for the realisation of the immense possibilities the ratification of the Treaty and of the Constitution open up for our country'.[14] That message reverberated in the electoral pronouncements of churchmen. The most common medium of episcopal comment during the election campaign was through letters addressed to election meetings. Four broad themes can be discerned in these statements: a concern for law and order, urging the continuation in government of the Cosgrave ministry, a fear of political fragmentation, and to a lesser extent engagement with the policy provisions in the Cumann na nGaedheal manifesto.

Several bishops stressed the debt owed to the outgoing government for upholding the authority of the state. In a letter to a pro-government meeting in Tralee in late July, Bishop Charles O'Sullivan of Kerry praised the 'exceptional tenacity, firmness, moral and physical courage' which Cosgrave's government 'brought to the self-sacrificing and unflinching performance of their duty', even at 'risk of grave unpopularity' as they 'unflinchingly held the Bearna Baoghail [the breach] for Ireland'.[15] Bishop Fogarty of Killaloe, with whom Cosgrave stayed when campaigning in Ennis, claimed that the government had 'rescued our island from anarchy, and triumphantly vindicated public order and justice regardless of their own lives or popularity ... It now rests with the people to build a strong Ireland upon these foundations'.[16] Bishop Patrick Finegan of Kilmore enjoined electors in Cavan to show gratitude to the government for vindicating 'the right of the majority to rule', thereby upholding 'the first principle of democracy'.[17] One of the most ringing endorsements came from Bishop Patrick Morrisroe of Achonry in a letter to a meeting in Ballaghadereen, County Roscommon on 19 August:

> Every man and woman who has the vote should feel a conscientious obligation of recording it for the candidates who are most likely to promote the general good of the entire community. The late government have restored peace at imminent risk to their lives, they have brought order out of confusion. Their administration of public affairs has been marked by statesmanship of the highest order.[18]

These statements referred implicitly to the personal losses suffered by members of the government. Cosgrave's uncle was killed in September 1922 in what he believed was a personal attack and the Cosgrave family home was burned in January 1923.[19] The following month Dr Thomas F. O'Higgins, father of Kevin O'Higgins the minister for home affairs and vice-president of the executive council, was killed during a raid on his home in Stradbally, County Laois.[20]

When Frank Aiken, IRA chief of staff, issued a final order for republicans to dump arms on 24 May 1923 there was no formal truce or surrender of weapons. Some prelates were concerned that as long as a considerable quantity of arms lay outside government control then in the words of Bishop Finegan, 'a recrudescence of the terror is possible'.[21] Archbishop Gilmartin also drew attention to the issue of arms in a letter to a Cumann na nGaedheal meeting in Castlebar on 5 August. This was a particular concern for him as low intensity anti-treaty IRA operations continued in parts of Connacht, particularly in Mayo, for the remainder of 1923. Gilmartin hoped that the forthcoming election would produce 'a Government strong and able enough to complete the task of rescuing the country from anarchy, terrorism and commercial ruin'.[22] He criticised those who had opposed the treaty for not forming 'a constitutional opposition instead of organising an armed revolt', which in the circumstances was a crime. For Gilmartin it was the duty of the electorate 'to make the repetition of such a crime impossible'.[23] To that end, an essential precondition for peace was that all arms be brought under the control of the government. Notably, the 1923 Public Safety Act, passed at the end of September 1923 in one of the new government's first actions following the opening of the fourth Dáil, contained detailed provisions on the control and licensing of firearms.[24] These were strengthened further under the Firearms Act in 1925.

Almost all of the bishops insisted on the need for the Cosgrave ministry to continue in government. This was not tantamount to an uncritical endorsement of the government's record but rather a plea that the future of the Free State be placed in trustworthy hands. In this way, political and social stability could be consolidated and secured. At a meeting in Grand Parade in Cork city on 8 July 1923, attended by Cosgrave, Eoin MacNeill and Ernest Blythe, a large crowd heard a letter from Bishop Daniel Cohalan of Cork. Although the prelate 'made it a rule not to interfere in politics', nevertheless he stated his belief that Cosgrave's ministry should be allowed to carry on.[25] The bishop counselled, presciently as it transpired, that time was required for all departments of state and the army, in particular, to be trained to submit to the civil authority:

> In five years' time, the great public departments and services won't care who are the ministers of Government, but during the period which immediately follows a revolution the personnel of a Ministry counts for much in securing and fostering the loyal submission of all services and of all citizens to the civil authority.[26]

Similarly, electors in Tipperary heard Archbishop Harty's conviction that a 'change of Government at the present moment would lead to instability and want of confidence in the stability of the young nation'. The archbishop hoped, therefore, that the poll would 'result in a majority for the Government which has successfully steered the ship of state into a safe harbour'.[27] Cardinal Logue warned of the dangers of mismanagement. He maintained that the safest course was to support the outgoing government which 'may have made some mistakes but have done wonders during the past year to reorganise the country, establish order, secure peace, and lay a solid foundation to build up the future prosperity of the country'.[28] In a letter to a Cumann na nGaedheal meeting in Mullingar, Bishop Laurence Gaughran of Meath warned that 'the work of the nation is yet only half finished'. Given that the most important portion of that work remained, he asked if it would therefore be 'folly as well as ingratitude to take out of the hands of men so capable the destinies of the country that they have so safely guarded?'[29]

The 1923 General Election was the first election fought on a universal adult suffrage. It was also the first in which every constituency was contested with 375 candidates standing for 153 seats; some 19 groups competed for votes.[30] In some episcopal minds such a broad field might produce a fragmented and unstable political system. Cardinal Logue warned voters at a meeting in Dundalk to be 'on their guard' against 'so-called Independent candidates' who may be 'returned on false pretences'. His advice was not to 'follow too many particular interests' or 'run after Independents, however fair their promises may be'.[31] The cardinal's letter drew a spirited criticism from Ralph Brereton Barry, a lawyer from a unionist family background and a future Fine Gael election candidate.[32] He took issue with Logue's inference that independents were in reality in alliance with one political party or another. He maintained that independents stood in the belief that TDs were 'wanted in the Dáil who will offer a sane and reasoned criticism of the decisions and actions of the executive, who will not represent exclusively class interests nor act as voting machines in accordance with Mr O'Higgins' nod'.[33] Brereton Barry suggested that some of those who sat on the fence, in the cardinal's phrase, did so to avoid indulging in futile recriminations about the civil war. He closed his letter with the remark that 'His eminence will doubtless recall recent periods in Irish history when the fence was by no means so untenanted.'[34] Bishop O'Sullivan warned of the danger of particular economic classes safeguarding their own interests when it was paramount that a strong national government be established that would be 'sufficiently strong and independent to be able to refuse to subordinate national to purely section interests'.[35] Likewise, Bishop Fogarty took issue with independents and smaller parties that were capable of detaching votes from Cumann na nGaedheal. He attempted to focus minds by suggesting that a robust ministry backed up by a strong parliament would not be achieved from 'a Dáil of shreds and patches of broken interests'.[36] In an uncertain political climate, such episcopal concerns were not without foundation. As John Regan has argued, the 'possibility of a large, even a majority, anti-treaty party entering the Dáil, coupled to the uncertainty surrounding the allegiance of many of the Labour party, Farmers' party and even some of the treatyite deputies to the treaty settlement' demanded a large and cohesive pro-treaty party in the Dáil.[37] From December 1922 de Valera and Austin Stack had busied themselves with the creation of an anti-treaty political organisation and 'the cessation of the republican military campaign ensured that the considerable efforts of its proponents could now be focused on political agitation'.[38]

A handful of bishops engaged specifically with the legislative record of Cumann na nGaedheal and the policy commitments outlined in the party's election manifesto. Bishop Finegan of Kilmore was a case in point. In a letter to a Cumann na nGaedheal election meeting in Cavan on 5 August, attended by Cosgrave, Finegan gave prominence to the settling of 'the long standing and vexed land question on terms just to the parties primarily concerned'.[39] This was a reference to the 1923 land act which aimed to complete the transfer of holdings begun under the British government in the nineteenth century. A bill was introduced in May and became law on 9 August, less than three weeks before polling day. Notably, those who had engaged in violence against the state were excluded from the provisions of the act.[40] Finegan also mentioned the boundary question and financial relations with Britain – vital issues that the incumbent government was best equipped to address and which should be the first consideration of the Cavan electorate. Bishop O'Sullivan of Kerry also made explicit reference to the boundary with Northern Ireland and fiscal relations with Britain. He suggested that the settlement of those policy areas involved not merely 'national honour' but 'the whole economic development of our country'.[41] This further buttressed his argument against the danger of electing a parliament representative of sectional interests. Bishop Gaughran also claimed that the government 'deserves well of the country' given the 'amount of useful legislation enacted'.[42]

With the exception of Bishop Fogarty, bishops generally refrained from *ad hominem* criticism of republicans. In a move that ultimately proved counterproductive in electoral terms, de Valera was arrested in Ennis on 15 August and subsequently lodged in Arbour Hill prison.[43] Four days later, Fogarty strongly condemned him in a letter to an election meeting in Ennis. He described de Valera as 'the man of all others … responsible for the shame, ruin and bloodshed of the past 12 months, and who has the hardihood now to say he never stood for destruction'.[44] The bishop had been a staunch ally when de Valera, then a political novice, was first returned for East Clare in July 1917 and celebrated the funeral mass for republican hunger-striker Thomas Ashe in September 1917.[45] During the War of Independence, Fogarty was the bishop closest to Sinn Féin. However, relations with de Valera broke down over the treaty and civil war to the extent that Fogarty developed an almost pathological dislike of the future Fianna Fáil leader that mellowed little during his lengthy episcopacy. In what appears to have been a coordinated move, when Cosgrave addressed the Ennis meeting he was accompanied by Daniel F. Cohalan, the Irish-American nationalist leader and judge of the supreme court of New York who had clashed with de Valera during the latter's sojourn in the United States in 1919–20. In the event, de Valera was returned with 17,762 votes (more than two quotas) compared to

8,196 first preferences for Eoin MacNeill, the minister for education and the only Cumann na nGaedheal candidate elected in Clare. De Valera's massive surplus helped secure a second republican seat for Brian O'Higgins, even though he initially polled only 114 first preference votes and was in last place.[46] The remaining two seats in Clare went to Labour and the Farmer's Party.

A small number of bishops extended their involvement in the election beyond open letters to the public or subscriptions to electoral funds by recommending or nominating candidates. For example, Patrick Foley, bishop of Kildare and Leighlin, commended the candidacy of W. T. Cosgrave and Tom Bolger in the Carlow-Kilkenny constituency. The prelate and Bolger had been contemporaries at school. Foley confidently pronounced that the performance of the outgoing ministry provided 'a guarantee of future success which no other group of politicians who are seeking the suffrages of the electors can furnish'.[47] Bishop James Naughton of Killala went a step further by proposing Joseph McGrath, minister for industry and commerce, as a candidate in North Mayo.[48] This was a rare example of nomination papers being endorsed by a member of the hierarchy.

The clergy followed the lead of their bishops and were active in a variety of ways during the election campaign in support of Cumann na nGaedheal and the Free State. After the official launch of the party at a convention in the Mansion House in Dublin on 27 April 1923, attended by some clergy, priests were active as party officers and organisers.[49] For example, Fr P. J. Doyle, a curate in Naas, was one of 24 members of the general council of Cumann na nGaedheal.[50] When a branch of the party was set up in Bray in early May, Fr Joseph Hickey, the local curate, was elected president.[51] In County Cavan there was a push to establish branches in July ahead of the constituency convention on 7 August. Fr Martin Comey was elected president of the Killygarry branch and Fr John McDermott was elected chairman of the Belturbet branch.[52] The party's constituency committee in Clare was chaired by Fr Charles Culligan, curate in Kilkee, with Fr P. J. O'Sullivan of St Flannan's College, Ennis, as honorary secretary. Canon William O'Kennedy, president of St Flannan's who had been imprisoned on Bere Island in 1921, was appointed director of elections.[53]

Several election candidates were nominated, seconded or assented to by priests. While this was not restricted to those running for Cumann na nGaedheal, the party's candidates attracted greater clerical backing than other parties. In the County Dublin constituency Kevin O'Higgins was proposed by Fr Peter Dunne, parish priest of Howth, for Cumann na nGaedheal and in the same constituency Canon Christopher Grimes, parish priest of Rush, proposed John Rooney for the Farmer's Party.[54] A similar pattern obtained in the constituencies of Leix-Offaly, Monaghan, and Wexford. In Leix-Offaly, Seán Kelly of Cumann na nGaedheal was proposed by Monsignor J. Murphy, parish priest and vicar-general of Maryborough, and seconded by Fr Patrick Doyle, a curate in Maryborough, whereas Fr John Gorman, parish priest of Philipstown (now Daingean), proposed Patrick J. Birmingham for the Farmer's Party.[55] Neither candidate was elected. In the Monaghan constituency, Ernest Blythe was proposed for Cumann na nGaedheal by Thomas Toal and seconded by Canon Andrew Maguire, parish priest of Carrickmacross. His running mate Patrick Duffy was proposed by Senator Bernard O'Rourke and seconded by Fr Philip Mulligan, parish priest of Tydavnet. The Farmer's Party candidate, Hugh Maguire, was also nominated by a priest as was James Johnston who stood as an independent.[56]

In the Wexford constituency, clergy nominated Osmond Grattan Esmonde and Thomas McCarthy for Cumann na nGaedheal. The two Farmer's Party candidates – Michael Doyle and Michael Jordan – were proposed by Fr J. Quigley, parish priest of Tagoat, and Fr A. Forrestal, parish priest of Newtownbarry, respectively.[57] Remarkably, in Limerick four of the five Cumann na nGaedheal candidates – James Ledden, John A. Smyth, John Nolan and Patrick Walsh – were proposed by priests; Dr Richard Hayes, who topped the poll for Cumann na nGaedheal, was the exception.[58]

There are also examples of clerical support for republican candidates. Among those who nominated James Colbert, brother of the 1916 martyr Con, in the Limerick constituency were Fr Thomas Wall, a curate in Foynes, and Fr Cornelius O'Sullivan, a curate in Monagea.[59] Colbert won the fourth seat. In the Galway constituency, Barney Mellows was proposed by Canon Patrick Moran, parish priest of Claregalway, and seconded by Fr James Kelly of Spiddal; they also put forward papers for Louis O'Dea and Frank Fahy.[60] All three republican candidates were elected. In addition, the republican Colm Ó Gaora was proposed by Fr Thomas Burke, a curate in St Joseph's, Rahoon in Galway city.[61] At the Cumann na nGaedheal selection convention in Clare on 30 July, Canon O'Kennedy's resolution that Eoin MacNeill be invited to stand for Clare was passed unanimously. When MacNeill agreed he was proposed by Fr John McInerney, parish priest of Kilrush and vicar-general.[62] Not to be outdone, de Valera was proposed by Patrick Keran, parish priest of Ballyvaughan, who also nominated Michael Comyn and Brian O'Higgins as anti-treaty candidates.[63]

Clergy, and especially parish priests, were prominent at election meetings where they chaired proceedings, introduced speakers and openly endorsed the Cosgrave ministry. A meeting in Claremorris on 1 July addressed by W. T. Cosgrave, Kevin O'Higgins, and Patrick Hogan, minister for agriculture, was chaired by Dean Thomas F. Macken, the local parish priest and vicar-general.[64] When Cosgrave attended a meeting in support of the government in Tralee on 22 July the clergy came out in force. Among the platform party were David O'Leary, parish priest of Tralee and dean of Kerry, who chaired the meeting; Fr T. J. Lyne, administrator of Annascaul; Fr Timothy Trant, parish priest of Ballymacelligott; and Fr P. J. Brennan, parish priest of Castlemaine.[65] When Cosgrave visited Cavan on 5 August, Fr Martin Comey chaired the meeting and eulogised Arthur Griffith as the father of Irish freedom. He was joined on the platform by Fr Peter Lynch, parish priest of Crossdoney, Fr Bernard Brady, parish priest of Belturbet, and Fr John O'Reilly, a curate in Cavan town.[66] At a local level, hundreds of election meetings were chaired by priests.

A notable feature of the 1923 General Election not replicated to the same extent in subsequent contests, for various reasons as explained below, was the clerical inclination to pronounce their pro-government partisanship. Examples abounded. At an election meeting in Clonmel in early July, Fr Daniel F. Walsh, the local parish priest, wrote to state that the fate of Ireland was in the balance and that 'it was the duty of the people to stand by the Government which had done so much in such a short time against such dreadful odds'. Similar sentiments were expressed by Innocent Ryan, parish priest and dean of Cashel, who urged 'all lovers of a free and independent Ireland to rally to the support of the people's government'.[67] Canon T. Cummins, parish priest of Roscommon, presided at a meeting in Market Square, Roscommon in August where Cumann na nGaedheal candidates opened their campaign. He told those assembled that his advice was the same as that of Cardinal Logue 'to vote for the Government every time' because:

> This election was not a choice between candidates: It was a choice between the questions whether Ireland was to live or die. The Republicans had done their worst already by rifles and bombs and the petrol can, and they asked people to add to that destruction by their votes ... Mr de Valera wanted them to destroy the liberty they had won because of the shadow of a name. This modern Samson, blinded by folly, having pulled down the pillars of the State and involved himself in the wreck of fifty million pounds, wanted their votes to resurrect him.[68]

When Fr P. Gaynor, a curate in Birr, presided at an election meeting addressed by Cumann na nGaedheal candidates Francis Bulfin, Patrick Egan and Seán Kelly, he stated that one of the reasons that led him to support the treaty was that it held out more hope of achieving a north-south unity than did a republic.[69] His colleague Fr Joseph Houlihan, chaired a subsequent meeting in nearby Kinnitty where he served as curate. He pronounced that his bishop Dr Fogarty, his parish priest and himself would each vote for the government.[70]

Some priests published letters in the press in support of particular candidates. For example, on 27 August, polling day, the *Freeman's Journal* published a letter from Fr Patrick Daly, parish priest of Castlepollard, which endorsed Patrick W. Shaw, a Cumann na nGaedheal candidate in the Longford-Westmeath constituency. The priest trusted that the voters would have the patriotic spirit to recognise what the government candidate represented:

> You stand for ordered government versus anarchy. You stand for the protection of life and property; you stand for the building up of the ruins that strew the country; you stand for the resurrection of Ireland, for its restored moral and financial status; you stand, in fine, for the Government that has, in face of obstacles almost insurmountable, given us in these days a taste of the liberty and prosperity for which our father sighed.[71]

Despite such emphatic clerical support, the poll was topped by republican Conor Byrne who secured 5,299 first preferences to 5,147 for Shaw in second place.

The result of the poll in Longford–Westmeath raises the broader question of how significant the support of the Catholic Church proved to Cumann na nGaedheal. While it is impossible to provide a definitive answer, some observations can be advanced. The election result was somewhat disappointing for Cumann na nGaedheal, notwithstanding its rather offhand approach to electioneering and underdeveloped branch structure. It secured 39 per cent of the vote and 63 of the 153 seats. Despite the manifest difficulties that they faced, not least the fact that as many as 10,000 were interned at the end of the civil war, republicans secured 27.5 per cent of the vote and 44 seats.[72] In fact, the republican share of the vote had increased since the 1922 election by 6 per cent, despite the warnings of hierarchy and clergy, whereas that for Cumann na nGaedheal rose by just 0.5 per cent.[73] Labour won 14 seats and the Farmer's Party secured 15. The church's warnings against returning independents to the fourth Dáil did not prevent 63 candidates from seeking votes under that banner. Independents secured 15 seats and 9.4 per cent of the total vote. The number of seats retained by them remained relatively steady until the snap election of 1933.[74] The election result suggests that the political influence of the church was not particularly decisive, although the ruthless excesses of the government's prosecution of the civil war and the fact that all constituencies were contested on a wider franchise than 1922 must also be taken into account when considering the magnitude of the republican vote.

In many respects the outcome of the election and manner of the contest eased the anxieties of the hierarchy. The result endorsed the treaty, the constitution and the Irish Free State which the bishops had vehemently defended during and after the civil war. The principle of majority rule invoked in 1918 and defended in 1922 was secured in 1923. Second, the abstentionist policy of republicans ensured that Cumann na nGaedheal possessed a commanding majority in the Dáil, thereby delivering the hierarchy's cherished aim of political stability. In September 1923, Archbishop Edward Byrne of Dublin sent invitations to Cosgrave and to members of the Oireachtas to attend a solemn votive Mass to the Holy Spirit to ask Divine guidance on their deliberations. This took place in the Pro Cathedral in Dublin on 3 October.[75] It signalled a return to a normality of sorts.

Third, republican candidates and voters embraced constitutional politics in a largely peaceful campaign. In this sense, as Bill Kissane argues, the election proved to be a 'mechanism of deradicalisation' because it marginalised political violence and revealed a consensus on the primacy of democratic politics.[76] During the largescale republican hunger strike in October 1923 episcopal appeals to the government instanced republican adherence to constitutional methods. Writing privately to Cosgrave, Archbishop Edward Byrne of Dublin stated that any deaths from hunger strike would be 'a downright calamity for the country' and would cause 'such revulsion as to shake the very foundation of the state'.[77] Cardinal Logue was even more forthright when he intervened publicly the following month. Doubting the morality of the republican protest, he appealed to them to abandon it in favour of a 'more reasonable, natural and lawful means of … advocating their political views'. But the cardinal also urged the government, which did not yield, 'not to do things by halves and by driblets, thus prolonging the agony' and to release the untried and unconvicted because the 'leaders of the so-called Republican party have declared that they are prepared to abstain from violence and seek to secure their political aims by constitutional means'.[78] The embrace by republicans of constitutional politics satisfied the episcopal desire to draw patriotism away from the gun. By the end of 1923 the vast majority of republican internees had been released and all had been freed by the autumn of the following year. Furthermore, an amnesty was declared for crimes committed during the civil war. For these reasons Kevin O'Higgins told the Oxford Union in October 1924 that the country was now more 'normal' than at any time since 1912 or 1913.[79]

Widespread clerical involvement in politics and the comingling of democracy and popular Catholicism stretched back to the era of Daniel O'Connell, its original architect. Although the decrees of the plenary synod of Maynooth in 1900 forbade priests from entering political disputes at public meetings and in the press, it was largely ignored during the tumultuous years of the Irish Revolution. Between 2 and 15 August 1927, a plenary synod was held at Maynooth to bring Irish ecclesiastical decrees from earlier synods into conformity with the new code of canon law promulgated in 1917.[80] The new decrees received the sanction of the pope in June 1928 and were promulgated by the Irish Catholic hierarchy on 17 November 1929.[81] In communicating the decrees to the laity, the hierarchy highlighted a medley of dangers that imperilled the faith and morals of Catholic Ireland: 'the dance hall, the bad book, the indecent paper, the motion picture, the immodest fashion in female dress'.[82] Their lordships also made reference to politics. While welcoming 'party zeal and frank criticism' in public affairs, the hierarchy appealed to the people 'to cast out for ever the spirit of rancour and animosity, wherever it has found a lodgement ... and put in its place a 'spirit of forbearance and conciliation'.[83] The Maynooth synod also made it clear that 'political addresses, election harangues and all such discourses in church' – set down in canon 139 of the code of canon law – were forbidden on pain of suspension.[84] Increasingly from the mid-1930s, secular and political matters not touching on faith and morals were left to the laity. By 1937, 'the Church had disengaged itself from active participation in the electoral process in the South'.[85]

In a letter read in churches in Cork on the morning of the 1923 General Election, Bishop Cohalan suggested that the electors should vote for those who would cooperate in establishing statehood and stable government in the country, for those who would give security to life and home and property, and who would restore social life in the land in conformity with God's commandments.[86] The Catholic hierarchy and the vast majority of clergy naturally invested in the political party that promoted the vista of a Catholic democratic state. Tom Garvin suggests that at a time when the legitimacy of the state remained in dispute the government was reassured by 'the superabundant reserves of political legitimacy enjoyed by the Catholic Church'.[87] W. T. Cosgrave appears to have agreed. In a letter to his friend Bishop Fogarty in December 1923, he ascribed Cumann na nGaedheal's success to the support of people in 'high and important positions throughout the country'.[88] He could afford to indulge episcopal *amour propre* because the result of 1923 General Election vindicated the triumphant alliance of the church and his government.

CHAPTER 8

'WITHOUT DISTINCTION OF SEX': THE ROLES OF WOMEN IN THE 1923 GENERAL ELECTION

Claire McGing

The 1923 General Election was hugely significant for Irish women in the context of their rights as citizens in the new state. In 1923, all adults over the age of 21 had the right to vote for the first time – a pledge fulfilled by the Provisional Government, led by W. T. Cosgrave, in 1922. The achievement of 'votes for women', and the contrast in the status of women in Ireland compared to Britain and other European democracies, contributed to the excitement of the 1923 election campaign. The press reported that women across the country turned out to vote in high numbers. However, in terms of access to national office, women accounted for only five of the 153 elected members of Dáil Éireann. The four republican women TDs continued to abstain from the chamber. This left Margaret Collins O'Driscoll in Cumann na nGaedheal as the only female figure in the Fourth Dáil (1923–7).

Therefore, the 1923 General Election was highly gendered in its process and its outcome and legacy for women in Ireland.[1] This chapter draws on a range of sources, including press reports, the parliamentary record and archival sources, to provide a rounded picture of women's participation and representation in the 1923 General Election; as voters, activists, candidates and TDs. After outlining the history of women and politics in Ireland from 1918 to 1922 – with a particular focus on the impact of the divisive debates on the Anglo-Irish treaty and how this bled into discussions on the enfranchisement of younger women – the chapter details the implementation of universal adult suffrage, without any resistance, as part of the drafting of the Free State constitution in 1922. The following sections examine the myriad roles played by women in the 1923 General Election, the gender dynamics of the campaign, and the impact of women voters on the results. As the only woman TD to take her seat in 1923, Margaret Collins O'Driscoll's parliamentary career, and the challenges she faced in her role, will be discussed. The conclusion considers the longer-term impact of the 1923 election on gender politics in Ireland, reflecting the need to incorporate gender as a central theme in the commemorative process of this period. What did the parliamentary vote mean for women citizens? Did enfranchisement substantively improve their lives, as suffrage campaigners had hoped it would?[2] How did the 1923 election influence opportunities for women to participate in elected office? The chapter represents one of the first gendered analyses of this critical, but often overlooked, election in the history of Irish elections.

Women's participation in Irish general elections, 1918–22

After several decades of campaigning, the passage of the Representation of the People Act 1918 marked an important victory for suffrage activists in Britain and Ireland.[3] The legislation extended the franchise in parliamentary elections to men over the age of 21, whether or not they owned property, and to women over the age of 30 who met minimum property (essentially a class barrier) or education qualifications. In Ireland, restrictions on suffrage remained in place until 1922, when all women were granted the right to vote under the terms of the Constitution of the Irish Free State. Regarding political representation, the Parliament (Qualification of Women) Act 1918 granted women in Britain and Ireland over the age of 21 the right to stand as candidates for national office. The House of Commons had to hurriedly pass the legislation in November 1918 due to legal uncertainty about whether women were permitted to contest the upcoming general election in December.[4] Takayanagi advises that the radical nature of this legislation and its broader significance for gender equality have been overlooked in favour of a celebration of partial voting rights.[5] This was reflected at commemoration events to mark the 'votes for women' centenary in Britain and Ireland in 2018.[6]

Fifteen women unsuccessfully contested the 1918 General Election in Britain. Across the Irish Sea, nationalist women lobbied Sinn Féin to run women candidates – a campaign that had commenced in 1917 when prominent female activists demanded equality of status for women in the organisation.[7] Women's rights activists were disappointed to learn that Sinn Féin placed only two women on the ballot: Constance Markievicz in the Dublin Saint Patrick's constituency and Winifred Carney in Belfast Victoria (a majority Unionist constituency). The 1918 General Election was a landslide for Sinn Féin, who won 73 out of 105 seats. The only woman elected, Constance Markievicz, became the first-ever female MP (and TD) – a symbolic victory for gender politics after the recent passing of the two Acts – but she refused to take her seat in line with Sinn Féin's policy of abstention from Westminster. In January 1919, Sinn Féin members founded a separate parliament in Dublin called Dáil Éireann – the assembly of the 'Irish Republic'. The Dáil was established in defiance of the British government and declared illegal in September 1919; it met secretly after this. Significantly, Markievicz was appointed to cabinet as minister for labour (which included responsibility for social welfare).[8] This made her only the second woman in the world to hold a government appointment. However, as a woman, she did not receive this ground-breaking role without a struggle, reporting that she had to 'bully' the men and threatened to defect to the Labour Party if not given a cabinet post.[9]

The 1921 General Election was held under the terms of the Government of Ireland Act 1920. The Act established separate Home Rule Parliaments in Northern Ireland and Southern Ireland.[10] All 128 candidates in the South were unopposed: 124 in Sinn Féin and four Independent Unionists. The 124 Sinn Féin TDs constituted themselves as the Second Dáil. Women party members and lobby groups called on Sinn Féin leaders to recruit more women to contest the election.[11] 'Votes for women' had not translated into opportunities for Irish women (bar one) to enter parliament in 1918. Former suffrage campaigners now turned their attention to candidate nominations; as the Irish Women's Franchise League (IWFL) argued, 'Republican and Labour forces have now a fresh opportunity of giving practical expression to their pledge of equal rights'.[12] In the end, Sinn Féin selected six female candidates and thus TDs with no actual polling taking place. The 1921 election represented a significant increase in the number of women TDs in just three years (from one to six). It would take until the 1977 General Election before this figure for women's seat-holding was reached again. Constance Markievicz was returned to office in 1922, representing the Dublin South constituency. No longer the lone women's representative, she was joined by Kathleen Clarke in Dublin Mid, Mary MacSwiney in Cork City, Dr Ada English in the National University of Ireland (NUI) constituency, Kathleen O'Callaghan in Limerick City and Limerick East and Margaret Pearse in Dublin County.[13] Despite no age restrictions, no women under 30 were nominated to run. Notably, four of the six women TDs in the Second Dáil were relatives of prominent male republicans who lost their lives in the nationalist struggle between 1916 and 1921. Scholars have traditionally characterised these women as 'virtual surrogates for the dead' – in other words, as symbols of tradition and guardians of memory.[14] Newer feminist analyses attempt to counterbalance this older narrative, emphasising how this first generation of women TDs were independent thinkers and activists in their own right, schooled in the republican tradition – even an influence on their male relatives.[15] Yet, it is equally valid that their lineage afforded them opportunities not available to other nationalist women to participate in parliamentary politics – Kathleen O'Callaghan and Margaret Pearse stated they had been elected because of their dead men.[16] Constance Markievicz and Dr Ada English were the only female deputies not to lose a male relative in the conflict. Still, despite their objections to this gendered rhetoric[17], they were often generalised as 'bereaved women' like the others.[18] The fact that all six women were said to have worn black during the debates contributed to this narrative.[19]

The women deputies played a prominent role during parliamentary deliberations on the Anglo-Irish treaty in December 1921 and January 1922. It was the first issue of national importance on which women's voices were heard in parliament. All of the women spoke against the terms of the treaty, claiming to 'know the women of Ireland' in doing so.[20] Pro-treaty deputies also regarded themselves as representative of female electors. They accused women TDs of 'rattling the bones of the dead' to justify their stance[21], and questions were even raised about their mental abilities.[22] The women TDs understood the symbolism attached to their family histories and, despite their low numbers, it afforded considerable influence over the discourse. However, they also sought to assert their own political agency in opposing the treaty. Kathleen O'Callaghan stated, 'the women of An Dáil are women of character, and they will vote for principle, not for expediency'.[23] In a lengthy speech of opposition, Dr Ada English argued that she 'had no dead men to throw in my teeth as a reason for holding the opinions I hold' and strongly disputed the argument that elected women only held their opinions because of grief or anger.[24]

The six female TDs ran in the so-called 'pact' general election when it was held in June 1922. An election was required to be held under the terms of the Anglo-Irish treaty. The Labour Party, running for the first time, did not select any female nominees. The only women elected were Mary MacSwiney in Cork City and Kathleen O'Callaghan in Limerick City (she was unopposed), both running for Clann na Poblachta (anti-treaty Sinn Féin). Kathleen Clarke reflected on the result, 'we all paid in our temerity in voting as we did. We were all women who had worked and suffered for the freedom of our country'.[25] Pro-treaty candidates received over 75 per cent of the vote in total. Anti-treaty deputies refused to take their seats and civil war broke out shortly afterward. The anti-treaty boycott gave uncontested control of parliament to the pro-treaty members of Sinn Féin, enabling W. T. Cosgrave to establish the Second Provisional Government. The results of the 1922 General Election, which was effectively a de facto referendum on the treaty, showed that despite their arguments to the contrary, the women of the Second Dáil did not represent the views of ordinary Irish women (at least those aged over 30 with the qualifications to vote).

The position taken by all of the female TDs on the Anglo-Irish treaty had significant, negative consequences for women's political representation in the early years of the Irish Free State and beyond. As they abstained from the Dáil, women TDs had self-excluded themselves from serving in politics at a time when the norms of parliamentary democracy were being established in Ireland. They were also deprived of first-hand political experience in legislative matters. Deeper than this, their fervent opposition to the document had nurtured a view within pro-treaty circles that republican women were too inflexible and bitter for public life – they were described as 'abnormal individuals'[26] – and some commentators even blamed women for the outbreak of civil war.[27] This view was copper-fastened when Cumann na mBan became the first nationalist organisation to vote to oppose the treaty, by a large margin, and its members had widely campaigned against the terms in the 1922 election.[28] More broadly, Knirck concludes that 'this characterisation spread to republicanism as a whole, as the movement was feminised in Free State propaganda'.[29] In other words, the political arguments of anti-treaty women became a critical factor in the marginalisation of all those attached to republicanism, regardless of gender.

If the anti-treaty side created a space, if limited, for elected women in its ranks, pro-treaty politics was highly male dominated at the upper echelons; no pro-treaty women appeared on the ballot paper in 1922. In the aftermath of the Cumann na mBan vote on the treaty, a group of women resigned from the organisation. In April 1922, these women established a new organisation, Cumann na Saoirse, to advocate for the pro-treaty side.[30] Ward writes that almost all of the members were related to members of the Provisional Government.[31] The group's 'immediate policy' was to assist in the return of pro-treaty candidates at the 1922 General Election.[32] Members repudiated the narrative put forward by female TDs that the women of Ireland, as a whole, opposed the treaty.[33] During the civil war, while anti-treaty women resumed their activities in support of the men in the IRA, members of Cumann na Saoirse organised fundraisers for the pro-treaty side and did propaganda work. When the civil war ended in May 1923, the executive saw no reason for the organisation to continue, having fulfilled its objective of supporting the treaty. Many of its members went on to join the new Cumann na nGaedheal party.[34] Three of the organisation's senior members, Jennie Wyse Power, Alice Stopford Green and Eileen Costello, were appointed to the Free State Seanad in 1922 – they would oppose much of the gender discriminatory legislation introduced by the Free State government in the years that followed.[35]

The implementation of universal adult suffrage in 1922

In the aftermath of the split in Sinn Féin over the treaty, in March 1922, Kathleen O'Callaghan proposed a motion to grant full electoral equality to women voters at the 1922 General Election. It was estimated that women aged 21 to 30, if enfranchised, would account for about one-seventh of the electorate.[36] A former member of a suffrage society, O'Callaghan remarked in her opening speech:

> I cannot believe that there is in this Parliament of the Irish Republic a single Deputy but holds with me that we ought now to remedy this injustice to a section of Irishwomen. During these last years of war and terror, these women in their twenties took their share in the dangers. They have purchased their right to the franchise and they have purchased their right to a say in this all-important question before the county. Without their votes or their voice, nobody can say that the will of the people of Ireland will have been ascertained.[37]

The debate on the motion repeated much of the gendered discourse that arose during the earlier deliberations on the treaty. Despite the claims from each faction to represent Irish women's views, no one knew what political direction female voters would take; some believed that younger women were more strongly opposed to the treaty than their older counterparts.[38] In the course of the debate, pro-treaty deputies who had long favoured granting voting rights to women, including Arthur Griffith, were arguing against the motion, while anti-treaty TDs with no record of supporting gender equality issues, such as Éamon de Valera, found themselves advocating for full suffrage. Anti-treaty members were accused of trying to 'torpedo' the treaty, motivated by republican ideology rather than a genuine concern for women's rights – a charge also placed on the suffrage societies who had lobbied Griffith on this issue.[39] On the other side, deputies responded that if the pro-treaty TDs truly believed themselves to be representative of women, they had no reason to fear the enfranchisement of younger women – would a large women's vote in favour of the treaty not strengthen its ratification, rather than weaken it, they argued?[40]

The pro-treaty side deferred to practical challenges to defend their position on O'Callaghan's motion; the Dáil had no power to alter the law on the franchise; the validity of the poll would not be accepted by the British government and put the treaty in jeopardy; and it would take at least eight months to update the register.[41] When the vote was taken, it was defeated on predictable lines, with 38 votes in favour and 47 against. Arthur Griffith pledged that his government would fully enfranchise all women voters after the 1922 General Election.[42]

The constitution of the Irish Free State, which came into effect in December 1922, granted suffrage to all women on equal terms with men in Article 14. Historians have commented on the significance of this reform, placing the Free State several years ahead of other European nations.[43] Press reports widely hailed the new constitution's democratic principles and ethos. An editorial in the *Cork Examiner* provides an example:

> The Irish Constitution as already formulated is admittedly democratic in its conception and principles, and Dáil Éireann has already given a lead by bringing adult suffrage into being which the Mother of Parliaments [British Parliament] may someday be forced to follow. The new franchise based on adult suffrage, the abolition of plural voting, and the adoption of Proportional Representation in every contested election of more than two members in either House of the Oireachtas, provide a splendid example of Ireland's first steps following the achievement of her national freedom.[44]

During its deliberations, the Constitution Committee (which had no women members) completed a review of women's voting rights in other constitutions worldwide.[45] In practice,

Article 14 reflected a promise that had already been made by the Provisional Government and, in the years before, a commitment to universal suffrage in the 1916 Proclamation. The 'pact' signed by Michael Collins and Éamon de Valera in advance of the 1922 General Election agreed that, if the post-election government were to collapse, the consequent election would 'be held as soon as possible on Adult Suffrage'.[46] Thus, Article 14 and, subsequently, the 1923 Electoral Act, which established the Irish Free State electoral law, were widely anticipated by the press and enacted without any real opposition in parliament.[47] In September 1922, before the ratification of a new constitutional framework but in anticipation of an election soon after its enactment, Ernest Blythe, minister for local government, moved a Dáil resolution to immediately prepare a new electoral register as it would take six and a half months to compile and admit 400,000 new electors. Again, the general consensus on universal suffrage was evident, with the minister remarking that 'giving the same franchise to women is a matter so generally accepted here that there is not likely to be any discussion with regard to it'.[48] Announcing the new constitution, W. T. Cosgrave declared, 'the pledge of Arthur Griffith has been fulfilled'.[49]

While unarguably hugely significant for women's rights, Article 14 has tended to overshadow the more contentious issue of Article 3 in the gender history of the period. A draft equality provision in Article 3 was watered down on several occasions before the final wording was agreed. According to Mohr, 'there can be little doubt that the 1922 Constitution, and Article 3 in particular, proved weak and ineffectual in protecting the vision of equal rights reflected in the drafts produced by the Constitution Committee'.[50] Despite a reference in Article 3 to the privileges and obligation of citizenship 'without distinction of sex', campaigners were concerned that the constitution sought to limit women's rights to 'mere "political" equality' and women of their public identities in the economic and social spheres of the newly independent state.[51] Their fears would, ultimately, be founded after 1922. With the two anti-treaty women TDs in abstention, no female voice was heard during the Dáil debates on the 1922 constitution.

1923 General Election

The 1923 General Election has been described as the first 'normal' election contest in Ireland.[52] The civil war was over, although many republicans remained interned, and the bones of the new Cumann na nGaedheal party, established by pro-treaty members, were in place. Polling day was designated a public holiday to encourage voters to go to the polls. Farrell remarks, 'given its proximity to the civil war, the campaign was remarkably quiet. While republicans were free to organise and campaign, as was typical of the period, all meetings were subject to heckling and interruptions'.[53]

Recruitment of women candidates

As in previous general elections, gender equality campaigners advocated for the recruitment of female candidates in 1923. Interestingly, women's activists also considered running a panel of independent women in Dublin to advance women's issues in the Fourth Dáil (which they felt had been neglected by the outgoing members).[54] In the end, the platform did not materialise. Seven women were selected to run across the state, a decrease of one since 1922 despite a larger number of seats in the chamber. Sinn Féin nominated five women: Constance Markievicz (Dublin South), Mary MacSwiney (Cork Borough), Dr Kathleen Lynn (Dublin County), Caitlín Brugha (Waterford) and Kathleen O'Callaghan (Limerick). On the pro-treaty side, Cumann na nGaedheal selected Margaret Collins O'Driscoll, a national teacher and sister of the late Michael Collins, to run in her local constituency of Dublin North. Notably, the *Belfast Newsletter* reported that Mary Collins Powell, another sister of Michael Collins, had planned to run in Cork Borough. She withdrew her name as she 'wasn't strong enough to fight the election' and was replaced on the ticket by Professor Alfred O'Rahilly.[55] The fact that Cumann na nGaedheal's two female aspirants for office, with only one ultimately on the ballot paper, were sisters of Michael Collins shows his potent symbolism in the party after his death. Again, it speaks to the powerful representation of 'mourning women' in the politics of this period – but this time on the pro-treaty side.

Partisan appeals to women voters

Campaign literature on the pro-treaty and anti-treaty sides generally sought to appeal to voters as a homogenous group; constitutional issues, the impact of the civil war and the economy were the main issues of the day. In a small number of cases, Cumann na nGaedheal made direct appeals to women voters, tactically using its position as the party that granted full suffrage. A national advertisement in the *Freemans Journal* asked voters to 'show you are worthy of the franchise' by voting for Cumann na nGaedheal candidates and subscribing to the party's election fund.[56] At the constituency level, the Cumann na nGaedheal ticket in Cork Borough encouraged female electors to return the party to government. The two candidates, James Walsh and Alfred O'Rahilly, appealed to the traditional domestic concerns of women – employment opportunities 'for your men in Cork', reducing inflation and housing provision. Women going to the polls were reminded that, 'When things go well or ill in the Homes, you have to pay the piper. Women voters of Cork! You can now call the tune'.[57] However, this approach to campaigning was not commonplace in Cumann na nGaedheal as the party, like Sinn Féin, sought to mobilise the electorate on the basis of the national interest, not narrow sectional concerns.[58]

Women exercising their right to vote

On the eve of the election, the *Irish Times* published figures from the Department of Local Government which estimated a total electorate of 1,789,293.[59] Gender-disaggregated statistics, where available, showed that women accounted for between 43 per cent and 49 per cent of voters in the constituencies.[60] Therefore, women electors were seen to 'have much to say to the ultimate results' – and there was excitement in the press about an election being run for the first time on the basis of universal suffrage.[61] A number of special public meetings were organised for female voters to hear pitches from local candidates and encourage turnout.[62]

Without official turnout data by gender, press anecdotes provide a key qualitative indicator of historical election turnout. National newspapers suggested that turnout rates among women were very high in the Dublin constituencies, with their political engagement and interest in these areas positively noted. As the *Irish Times* observed in Dublin North:

> The number of women entering the booths was remarked, and from the duration of their time inside it was concluded that most of them had made themselves familiar with the process of voting and exercised their franchise in a businesslike way. Another noticeable feature was the large number of women personation agents acting on behalf of republican candidates.[63]

Similarly, an *Irish Independent* report on Dublin South observed a high percentage of females turning out at the polls – perhaps motivated by the presence of Constance Markievicz on the ballot paper: 'Women voters equalled – if they did not actually outnumber – the men'.[64]

Women citizens outside of Dublin also exercised their voting rights, often in numbers comparable to men, as reports on constituencies as diverse as Donegal, Monaghan and Limerick suggest.[65] Fewer news items were filed about gendered participation rates in rural areas. More generally, there were reports from some rural polling stations of voter apathy and the 'dullness' surrounding election day in August 1923 compared to previous general elections – a situation contributed to, in part, by bad weather in parts of the country.[66]

Election results

Cumann na nGaedheal won 39 percent of the vote and 63 seats in the 1923 contest. While this figure represented a gain of five seats since the June 1922 election, in a context where the number of seats in the Dáil had increased from 128 to 135, it was a disappointing result for the new party. It did, however, record a number of stand-out electoral performances at the constituency level. Significantly, in the Dublin North constituency, Margaret Collins O'Driscoll was elected for the party (along with three of her male running mates; all were beneficiaries of General Richard Mulcahy's large vote surplus). She would be the only female deputy to take her seat in the Fourth Dáil. With Sinn Féin boycotting the Dáil chamber, Cumann na nGaedheal had a comfortable working majority to form a government.

Sinn Féin increased the proportion of the anti-treaty vote. In terms of women's representation in the party, Constance Markievicz (Dublin South) and Mary MacSwiney (Cork Borough) were both re-elected and joined by Dr Kathleen Lynn (Dublin County) and Caitlín Brugha (Waterford). The latter represented the first of a generation of women TDs to succeed their late husband in the Dáil – a phenomenon referred to as the 'widow's mandate' by political scientists.[67] Following her husband's death at Free State troops' hands in 1922, Caitlín Brugha 'was to play a very public role as the widow of an unrepentant Republican martyr [Cathal Brugha], standing in his Waterford constituency in 1923 for Sinn Féin'.[68] Meanwhile, Kathleen O'Callaghan failed to retain the seat she had held in County Limerick since 1921, and she would never run for public office again after 1923.

The 1923 General Election was interpreted as a second endorsement of the treaty, albeit with a drop in support, by a larger electorate.[69] It is difficult to discern the impact of women voters, especially those under the age of 30, and if they contributed to the rise in support for anti-treaty candidates. At a national scale, though, the pro-treaty parties' collective strength suggests that a majority of female electors voted on similar lines to men, as they had in 1922. Once again, the republican women TDs, who abstained from parliament, were unlikely to have been representative of the average female voter.

'Anything I was asked to do I did it': Women as activists in the 1923 election campaign

Beyond voters and candidates, what else do the sources tell us about women's participation in the 1923 campaign? The Irish Military Service Pensions Collection (MSPC) is the most detailed archive available on the activities of women in the Irish revolutionary period from 1916 to 1923.[70] Importantly, for the purposes of this research, many pension applications refer to election activities between 1918 and 1923. In relation to the 1923 General Election, almost all of the relevant applications were submitted by republican women. In their own words, they shared the extent of their work during the campaign. Women assisted candidates,[71] canvassed,[72] raised funds,[73] distributed literature,[74] put up posters,[75] made speeches,[76] prepared and served food for canvassing teams,[77] provided nursing and first aid,[78] granted facilities for meetings in their homes or businesses,[79] acted as personation agents[80] and resisted attempts by Free State supporters to break up republican meetings.[81] A small number of files allege the harassment of women at the hands of Free State supporters during the election campaign.[82]

It is evident that republican women viewed electioneering as an extension of their other duties at this time, including campaigning and fundraising for interned prisoners and their dependents following the cessation of the civil war. As Margaret Gallery stated, 'anything I was asked to do I did it'.[83] For Nora McMahon, electioneering was simply another way to work against the treaty.[84] Many republican candidates were still interned in August 1923, and those on the run faced the risk of arrest whenever they appeared in public.[85] For this reason, women activists were central to the republican campaign at the constituency level – as pointed out by many applicants. For Delia McArdle, 'Cumann na mBan did all the work during this election as the men were in prison'.[86]

Other women went to participate in the election campaign following their own release from prison. Lily O'Brennan, who was a founder member of Cumann na mBan, was arrested in October 1922 and jailed until July 1923, after which she went back to Cork to work for the election.[87] May Casey claimed she travelled from Dublin to Longford for convalescence following a 14-day hunger strike in prison and campaigned for republican candidates.[88] Mary Agnes Byrne travelled to Clare in August 1923 after her release from prison by the North Dublin Union on medical grounds; she 'resumed service in Clare on release immediately'.[89] Byrne assisted in preparations for Éamon de Valera's visit to Ennis. In her application, Byrne detailed how she was on the speaking stand at the meeting when National Army forces arrested de Valera, and she provided first aid to those injured. She claimed to experience physical abuse herself during the encounter:

> [I] defended him on platform when enemy turned guns on platform. [I] remained beside him, till enemy knocked and pushed me off the platform with rifles. Assaulted.[90]

In another case, Maire Comerford was released from Kilmainham Gaol, where she participated in hunger strikes, in the summer of 1923. Making herself available, Comerford was sent by IRA officers to Cork to support the election campaign – and subsequently re-arrested while collecting deposits for candidates:

> Sent to Cork to do election organising – nearly all our men were in jail at the time. I had the whole county. Took orders from IRA officers in each area. Arrested Fermoy; released Cork.[91]

'I was not elected on the question of sex': The parliamentary role of Margaret Collins O'Driscoll TD

As discussed, Margaret Collins O'Driscoll was elected to represent the constituency of Dublin North in 1923, in the process becoming the first Cumann na nGaedheal woman TD. A first-time candidate (and the only female on the party ticket), she was politicised after her brother's death in August 1922.[92] Details of how she became a candidate are vague; the party's archives from this period are sparse, while the press did not report any substantive information bar her name. Still, there is no doubt that her lineage was a critical factor for selectors – as was the case for several women on the republican side. When first elected, she took her seat in mourning dress, calling attention to the loss of her brother.[93]

With republican deputies in abstention, Collins O'Driscoll served as the only female TD in the Fourth Dáil (1923–7). She was re-elected in 1927 (June and September elections) and 1932, losing her seat in 1933, after which she retired from party politics. Again, she was the sole woman TD in the Sixth Dáil between September 1927 and 1932. In 1932, she was joined on the government benches by Mary Reynolds who successfully contested the election for Cumann na nGaedheal in the Leitrim-Sligo constituency following the murder of her husband.[94] Alongside her parliamentary role, Collins O'Driscoll was elected as vice-president of Cumann na nGaedheal in 1926 (replacing Jennie Wyse Power) and held this position until 1927.[95] She was appointed to a party committee on Registration and Electoral Reform in 1925.[96]

Collins O'Driscoll spoke on the Dáil record at least ninety times between 1923 and 1932.[97] When the Free State government implemented a series of discriminatory legislative reforms to restrict women's rights, Collins O'Driscoll, a government party member, strictly adhered to the party line. McNamara and Mooney state that she held the record among private members for attendance at divisions during her tenure in politics.[98] A primary school teacher (alongside her parliamentary career, she had a teaching job until 1928 when she retired on health grounds) and a former principal of a girls' national school in Clonakilty, County Cork, she was regarded by political colleagues as an authority on education issues.[99] She frequently referenced her professional experience when speaking on matters related to her occupation as an educator. A diligent constituency worker, Collins O'Driscoll increased her share of the vote at each successive election (bar 1933), and it is said that she addressed 'hundreds of public meetings' as a TD.[100]

In terms of gender politics, Collins O'Driscoll was significant as the only female voice in the lower house for several years. There were, however, women representatives appointed to the Free State Senate.[101] She sat on the government bench in the 1920s and early 1930s as her party introduced legislative reforms to restrict women's participation in the new state's public, economic and social affairs. A group of female senators strongly opposed this regressive legislation. One of them was Jennie Wyse Power who, in 1925, resigned her membership of Cumann na nGaedheal over restrictions to women sitting on juries.[102] By contrast, Collins O'Driscoll was a supporter of government policy throughout her tenure – though she was frequently lobbied by women's organisations to oppose gendered legislation.[103]

Coleman concludes that her parliamentary career was 'characterised by adherence to the Cumann na nGaedheal party line and a conservative attitude to social issues'.[104] Her biography suggests that she was personally committed to equal opportunities for women – in 1921, the family moved from Cork to Dublin so her daughters could receive their third-level education there – but her position on social policy reflected the views of Irish society at large.[105] When Collins O'Driscoll raised women's causes on the floor, her focus usually centred on improving women's lives in traditional settings – for example, employment opportunities for girls to train as dressmakers to reduce emigration[106] or tax cuts on household goods that would materially benefit housewives.[107] She occasionally sought to bring what she regarded as a uniquely female perspective to the chamber; in 1928, she spoke 'as a family woman' in a speech in favour of vaccinations and referred to her experiences with her own children.[108]

As for reforms that diminished women's rights, Collins O'Driscoll voted in favour of the 1924 and 1927 Juries Bills, which restricted jury service for women, but she did not contribute to debates on legislation fervently opposed by women's rights activists – was she not comfortable doing so? In the area of morality, she firmly expressed her approval of the 1928 Censorship of Publications Bill, which banned indecent literature and publications on birth control. She stated, 'no vote I have ever given here, or will ever give, will be given with more satisfaction than the vote I will register in favour of this bill'.[109] In one of her most notable contributions, Collins O'Driscoll explained her support for the Civil Service Regulation (Amendment) Bill in 1925. The legislation confined state examinations for civil service posts to men:

> There is no one in this Dáil more interested in this Bill than I am… During the past few days I have been canvassed by very influential members of my sex to vote against this Bill… I cannot see that it infringes our rights under the Constitution in any respect. I am not enamoured of this Bill. I am by no means in love with it, and I must admit it limits to a certain extent the appointments for which women are eligible. It might be asked why I am voting for the Bill… When I was elected to this Dáil I was not elected on the question of sex… The more I study this Bill the more I see that I would be injuring my sex by voting against it. The number of appointments women would be excluded from would be very small and the Minister has given us a good explanation… All I can say to those people who canvassed me to vote against this Bill is that women, when the next election will come on, will have an opportunity to return women on the Government ticket to this Dáil who will have the power to amend this Bill if it is passed… I ask the Minister and the Government to limit the number of appointments as far as possible for which women would be ineligible under this Bill.[110]

Collins O'Driscoll's support for the Bill reads as cautious, and she sought to disentangle her vote from her gender identity. As a bearer of the much-respected 'Collins' name and its intimate associations with the Free State, in addition to the need to observe party discipline, this legislation may have put her in a challenging position. Did she feel conflicted about her vote? Interestingly, in 1924, in the less visible setting of ministerial questions, she had argued against restrictions on the appointment of 'lady doctors' at the Grangegorman

Mental Hospital, which was located in her constituency. She asked the minister if he was aware 'that this is in direct violation of Article 3 of the Constitution of Saorstát Éireann' in relation to women's citizenship rights.[111] Did the lower stakes of ministerial questions empower her to advocate for equal opportunities for professional women? Had a concerned citizen or lobby group approached her to raise this issue? We can only speculate about her intentions, but her views were at odds with the position she took months later on senior civil service appointments.

After the vote: Gender politics in the Irish Free State

In the years before enfranchisement, suffrage campaigners in Britain and Ireland had been optimistic that the parliamentary vote would bring about significant changes in women's lives. While a momentous gain for women, this chapter has demonstrated that universal adult suffrage, implemented for the first time in the 1923 General Election, did not lead to increased opportunities for women to run for office, nor to many significant policy advancements in gender equality. In the 1920s and 1930s, the fragility of the advances won by Irish women in earlier years became apparent, as Cumann na nGaedheal and Fianna Fáil governments legislated to undermine women's rights as equal citizens – as gender equality campaigners had feared would happen when the Irish Free Constitution was agreed upon in 1922. While gender roles in the revolutionary period were relatively fluid, in the post-revolutionary era they were rigid.[112] As for political representation, no general election between the 1930s and 1970s returned more than five women TDs at a time. Most of the women TDs had to rely on political dynasties to overcome gender-based barriers; they were selected to mobilise a 'sympathy vote' in the constituency.[113] Like Caitlín Brugha in 1923, though she never actually sat in the Dáil as a republican, the majority of female TDs were widows of men who died while in office. For the most part, they were 'obedient party women' who did not oppose gender discriminatory legislation when it was placed in front of them.[114]

As the centenary of the 1923 General Election is commemorated in Ireland, it is essential to take a wide definition of women's activities as citizens in the election and after the event. The centenary of all women being granted the vote, regardless of age or class, is cause for a huge celebration, particularly when so many turned out to exercise their rights in 1923. Universal suffrage in place for the first time in 1923 was a major milestone, especially in comparison to other European democracies. Importantly, this chapter has also shown that women, mostly on the republican side in the available sources, played a critical role as election activists and campaigners at the constituency level. However, the commemoration of political events of this period should also reflect on the formal and informal barriers that were put in the way of women participating in politics and society in the new state. Analysis should move beyond 'votes for women' to include 'seats for women' and 'policies for women' in our gendered assessment of historic general elections.

CHAPTER 9

THE AARIR AND THE 1923 GENERAL ELECTION IN THE UNITED STATES

Regina Donlon

The Easter Rising of 1916 happened just a few short weeks before the 50th anniversary of the first Fenian invasion of Canada in 1866.[1] The timing is merely coincidental, yet its significance is prodigious as it embodies a half-century of reciprocal transnational republicanism between Ireland and its diaspora. The Fenian Brotherhood, as distinct from its Irish counterpart, the Irish Republican Brotherhood (IRB), represents the first significant foray of Irish-America into the republican discourses of the motherland. Over the course of the next 50 years, successor organisations, including, among others, Clan na Gael, the Friends of Irish Freedom (FOIF) and latterly the American Association for the Recognition of the Irish Republic (AARIR) each made important impacts on that republican discourse with varying degrees of success. Accordingly, this chapter examines the interactions between the AARIR and Irish republicans during 1923, and in particular, in the period before the 1923 Irish Free State General Election. In so doing, this chapter synchronously uncovers an organisation in flux as it sought to maintain its role and dominance in the United States, while simultaneously striving to assert its legitimacy and relevance on Irish affairs. Ultimately, by 1923 the death knell had already tolled for the AARIR and the 1923 General Election simply represented one final opportunity for the diaspora to interpose on a society it no longer fully understood.

In assessing this half-century of transatlantic republican discourse both Irish-America and Irish Americans' interpretation of what an Irish Republic should be evolved with each new wave of Irish immigrants that settled in the United States during that period. As republican rhetoric became more hard-line in Ireland, so too did its American counterpart. This relationship largely revolved around the raising of funds in return for influence in Ireland and, more specifically, over Irish republican ambitions. There is no doubt that the bond between Ireland and its American diaspora was symbiotic during this period, but it is equally important to note that Irish Americans also used Irish nationalist rhetoric to promote a sense of ethnic exclusivity in their host communities as well. To that end, each of the main Irish American republican organisations founded between 1865 and 1920 had a bifurcated agenda – the creation of an Irish republic on one hand and on the other, the consolidation of its own position in American affairs, both at local and national levels. By the time the AARIR was founded in 1920, Irish-American politicians had perfected the art of unifying the diaspora behind the banner of Irish republicanism as it worked stealthily within local communities to strengthen its own position locally. The advantages of this approach were also two-fold. It gave the diaspora an opportunity to stay connected to the homeland, while membership also provided a sense of ethnic solidarity and projected strength and unity within the host community itself.[2] By 1920, organisations like the AARIR consisted of some of the most powerful and influential businessmen and professionals from Irish-America, Edward L. Doheny and John F. Finerty being just two examples. Doheny, an oil tycoon, was the first national president of the AARIR and nephew of Young Irelander Michael Donhey, while Finerty, was a lawyer and ultimately Doheny's successor as AARIR president. These men and their contemporaries, coupled with the power of the AARIR and its predecessors, highlighted how far Irish-American republicanism had come from the days of the attempted Canadian invasions of the 1860s and 1870s.[3]

By the mid-1870s Clan na Gael had become the natural successor of the Fenian Brotherhood and by 1916 it too had been largely replaced by the FOIF, founded at the third Irish Race Convention in New York. Each of these organisations fulfilled roles quite specific to the communities they served as well as to the evolving nationalist narrative in Ireland. Ultimately, it fell to the FOIF to promote the cause of Irish Republicanism during the revolutionary period itself. Kenny suggests that at its peak in 1919 the FOIF had a membership of 275,000 and managed to raise an estimated ten million dollars for the nationalist cause.[4] However, given the complexity of the organisation's dual purpose, to promote Irish-American interests stateside as well as to provide leadership for republicans back in Ireland, the organisation was distracted in its objectives.[5]

De Valera spent a number of months touring the United States during 1919 and 1920 and gradually became frustrated with John Devoy and Daniel Cohalan's pre-occupation with gaining the right to self-determination for Ireland as part of the Versailles Treaty negotiations. This campaign resulted in Irish Americans petitioning their state representatives and senators seeking their help in gaining recognition for Ireland, thereby creating visibility for and enhancing the political position of Irish-America. It was at this juncture that the complexity of the transnational relationship between Irish and Irish-American republicans became unsteady. Cohalan, and to a lesser extent Devoy, believed that formal international recognition for an Irish government was essential to its international legitimacy, whereas de Valera viewed it as a distraction from the true purpose of the FOIF organisation, which he determined was the raising of funds to help Ireland in its war of independence against Britain.[6] Thus, in an attempt to re-focus Irish-American minds, de Valera, with the help of another prominent Irish-American republican, Joseph McGarrity, founded the American Association for the Recognition of the Irish Republic in November 1920. The organisation was designed to replace the Friends of Irish Freedom and ultimately give Ireland, specifically de Valera, more control over diasporic involvement in the independence movement. The new organisation was largely welcomed in the United States with local newspapers such as the *Cordova Daily Times* reporting from Washington that, 'Irish leaders from all parts of the country had been summoned' to form an organisation 'designed to supplant' the FOIF and 'give De Valera a vehicle for working out plans for the recognition of the Irish republic.'[7] Within the space of three weeks, the new organisation had gained a strong following in New York with the *New York Tribune* reporting that:

> members of eighty branches of the Friends of Irish Freedom bolted that organisation at a meeting last night ... and joined the ranks of the newly organised American Association for the

Recognition of the Irish Republic ... A resolution was adopted denouncing the past control of the Friends of Irish Freedom. This organisation was attacked by various speakers for its alleged failure to give support and cooperation to Éamon de Valera.[8]

However, given the relationship between Ireland and Britain it was met with suspicion by the British press which recorded that 'a new Irish organisation ... was established at a conference summoned by Mr de Valera in a session which was almost continuously secret for 15 hours. It adopted a policy, a name and a constitution.'[9] Interestingly, the news of the AARIR's formation went largely unreported in the Irish press until it eventually appeared on page four of that Friday's *Freeman's Journal* when the same circular published by the *Sheffield Evening Telegraph* the previous day was reprinted.[10]

The formation of the AARIR was a key moment in Irish-American nationalism as it was the first time that Irish republicans had sought greater control over how Irish-America engaged with the independence movement. In some ways it marked the coming of age of the Irish movement itself as de Valera was adamant that the organisation should focus on the needs of Ireland instead of simultaneously fostering its own Irish-American agenda. The new organisation was headquartered in Washington DC, with a secondary propaganda office in Chicago.[11] Brundage claims that at its peak, the AARIR had a membership of over 700,000, while Kenny suggests it was closer to 800,000.[12] Either way, this made it the largest Irish nationalist organisation in American history and within the diaspora as a whole. The association issued membership cards similar to many of its predecessors in a tried and tested strategy of creating ethnic unity. Its stated objective was to gain US recognition for the Irish provisional government, but ultimately, this was never achieved. Despite this, it was a very powerful force in Irish nationalist discourse in America and as Brundage noted 'nothing on this scale had happened before – nor for that matter, would it ever happen again. Irish-American nationalism had hit high tide'.[13] While it might well have been high-tide for Irish-American nationalism, it was also a time of international crisis and tumult as the realities of the Versailles Treaty became apparent. This, coupled with a lull in the migration flow from Ireland to the US during the war years, meant that many of the members of the AARIR had emigrated before the First World War and had consequently left Ireland before the war of independence had begun. Their image of an independent Ireland, coupled with the importance of republican ideologies in an American context more generally, meant that members of the AARIR arguably had a different interpretation of what an Irish republic might look like in 1920. This image often contrasted with that of those who stayed at home and were attempting to make a republic a reality.

The AARIR enjoyed initial success and coordinated the sale of Irish Republican Bond certificates raising more than five million dollars in the process although only a fraction of this would actually make its way to Ireland. For the rest of 1920 and much of 1921 the AARIR were on the crest of a wave. Membership was high, funds were easily raised, and bonds were selling quickly. However, with the signing of the treaty, support for the organisation began to dwindle. Many AARIR members supported the treaty and viewed it as the 'stepping stone' that Collins suggested it was. Yet, by the time the civil war began, anti-treatyites had managed to take over the organisation, as those who supported the treaty saw no further need for their continued membership, and the fate of the AARIR seemed sealed. Membership began to fall slowly as those who supported the treaty felt they could no longer align themselves with the association's aims. Simultaneously, the organisation was beset with in-fighting and jostling for local autonomy as some local branches wanted their own independence to deal with local issues or in some cases to lend their support to Collins. The once impressive membership of 700,000 fell staggeringly to just 13,870 by 1925 despite repeated calls by the association leadership for support.[14]

Thus, as 1923 began the organisation was in an increasing state of disarray. By this time, John F. Finerty, a second generation Irish-American lawyer who represented de Valera during the Irish Republican Bond litigation proceedings was the association's president. Thomas W. Lyons was the national secretary and spent much of his time during this period attempting to recruit membership into the organisation and J. J. Hearn had been appointed as the national Treasurer. Assessing the correspondence of the organisation for the year 1923, it becomes apparent that despite de Valera's best efforts, this organisation had also succumbed to the bifurcated model of its predecessors as infighting, internal funding difficulties and membership woes befell the association by early 1923. Despite this, the AARIR did play a relatively important role in shaping republican rhetoric in the months before the 1923 General Election, but at times its perception of its own self-importance to the republican cause gave the organisation a false sense of security and the association's longevity was compromised as a result.

The year 1923 began on a positive note for the association as it requested 'states and councils to organise a vigorous campaign of boycott [of English goods and insurance] in their respective states and districts.'[15] This strategy formed part of a policy of recognition for the Irish republic and was designed to hurt English business interests in the United States. The boycott was seen as a patriotic service to America as Irish Americans would favour domestically produced goods and services over foreign, specifically English, ones and in so doing continue to further cement the ethnic community's position as faithful Americans while simultaneously supporting the cause of Irish freedom. Members were informed that 'the boycott is a most effective weapon' and they should 'use it with a vengeance'.[16] The importance of the boycott was difficult to underestimate as it had long been part of the weaponry of Irish rebels. However, its success in this particular instance was negligible as the majority of Irish Americans overlooked the call and continued to seek the best value possible for their goods and services.[17] Despite this, the association persisted, and a special meeting was called for late February 1923. Adelia Christy, a prominent AARIR member from Cleveland and one of the organisation's vice presidents, implored Finerty to hold an event in the Midwest as she felt that 'there are some of us in the West and the Middle West who do not think that New York and Philadelphia are the only places on the map and fear that the AARIR may meet with the same fate as the Friends of Irish Freedom.'[18] This was an astute observation as committed republicans in the Midwest and West were often frustrated at the eastern focus of the association and felt that a significant event such as a national executive meeting would help to gain recognition both for the association in the United States and also for the cause of Irish republicanism itself. Christy's request was granted, after some internal political manoeuvring, and so on 25 February 1923 the national executive met at the Morrison Hotel in Chicago. The meeting was especially important in terms of recognition for the association and its cause because de Valera's appointed envoy, Laurence Ginnell, had been secured as one of the guest speakers. This further enhanced the legitimacy of the association and helped to position it further within republican rhetoric. The meeting was a significant success for the organisation as it took its first tentative steps towards reorganisation. Over 400 delegates from 45 states attended the meeting which discussed potential new directions for the association, a new membership drive, a financing strategy for the national office, the success of the boycott of English products and introduced an intensive drive for the Irish Republican Defence fund which would close on 24 April. Monies collected under the AARIR was to be transmitted to Ireland via Laurence Ginnell as the association was wary of repeating the mistakes of the Irish Republican Bond sales a few years previously.

Although the national executive meeting in late February suggested that the organisation was in the process of reforming and re-establishing itself as a powerful force in transatlantic Irish republicanism, the association's national committee was almost continuously battling sinister internal disputes between local councils and indeed between local councils and the national executive itself. This clearly did little to help the association to restructure itself and consolidate its position as the primary voice of Irish republicanism in the United States. It was also a clear indication of Finerty's fragile position as president of the association and the suspicion with which he was held by the grass roots members. Until such time as these internal disputes were dealt with and the national executive regained its authority, the success of the organisation in achieving any of its public-facing goals was going to be minimal. In early January, Frank Horgan, a member of the national executive from Boston wrote to Finerty detailing infighting within a local council in the city and suggested that there could be a proposed coup within the council by more radical members. Horgan noted that 'their vicious activities have disgusted John Harrigan to such an extent that he is determined to resign at this state convention.'[19] Finerty intervened and Harrigan remained as chairperson of the council, but these local disputes had a distracting impact on the business of the association.

Although Finerty managed to deal with the situation at a local level, a more serious incident arose in March 1923 when Jeremiah O'Leary, an AARIR member from New York wrote to Finerty outlining that one of the officers at a local branch in New York proposed, and had passed, a resolution calling for Finerty's immediate removal by de Valera.[20] The matter escalated and resulted in an emergency meeting of the national executive being called on 7 April 1923 to formally deal with the issue. Finerty's response was to bring the New York local council officer, Michael A. Kelly, before the national executive and have a formal hearing on Kelly's actions. Finerty accused Kelly of violating the associations constitution and he was required to appear before the national executive on nine separate charges ranging from misconduct and insubordination to misappropriation of funds and 'efforts to use the society for political purposes of a personal nature.'[21] Of particular offence to the AARIR executive was Kelly's involvement in the organisation of the St Patrick's Day parade in the city which 'espoused and defended the alleged Free State government of Ireland which [was] presently engaged in carrying out a war of extermination against the Irish Republicans and against the Irish Republic.'[22]

At the meeting on 7 April, 16 states were represented although Kelly failed to appear. New York was represented by John Mangan who acted as an intermediary between Kelly and the national executive. Just before the meeting began, a settlement was reached in which the outstanding dues from the local New York council for 1921 and 1922 were written off and the dues for 1923 were to follow within ten days. In return for overlooking the misappropriation of AARIR funds, Kelly agreed to retract his resolution calling on de Valera to remove Finerty from the position of president of the association.[23] Other members of the national executive were outraged that the situation had been allowed to develop to such an extreme. John Larkin Hughes, a representative from New Jersey stated that the hearing would 'create a scandal without any benefit' and ultimately have a negative impact on the public perception of the organisation.[24] This debacle consumed the business of the national executive for over a month when its priorities lay elsewhere and ultimately negatively impinged on more pressing objectives, such as fundraising for Ireland and gaining recognition and legitimacy for the cause. However, it did also present a salient example of how the organisation was beginning to unravel at a local level and perhaps suggests that the influence of the AARIR had already started to disappear as early as April 1923.

While Finerty was busy trying to convince grass roots members of his own legitimacy as the association's president, the national secretary, Thomas W. Lyons was equally busy trying to enhance the organisation's membership. As early as 9 January, Lyons sent a circular to all states calling for the re-enrolment of old members and announced a drive for new ones.[25] The success of this enterprise is difficult to decipher, but by April the association had received subscriptions and membership dues from 18 states. The largest contribution came from Massachusetts where the state representatives were making regular lodgements of $200, while the smallest contributions came from Kansas where dues of only $1 were received.[26] Presumably, the national executive was disappointed with these returns and there was a renewed effort to recruit and re-enrol members in May 1923. A circular issued to all AARIR officers challenged members by asking: 'are you doing your utmost to enrol every available member in your district? You are pledged to help the republic, and this is the crucial moment.'[27] The next national meeting of the association had been scheduled for late July 1923 and Lyons was adamant that a large attendance was necessary to ensure further recognition and legitimacy for the association. Again, four days later, on 25 May, Lyons attempted to rally the troops by issuing another notice to AARIR membership. In this example, the republican rhetoric was passionate, but importantly exposed one critical flaw in the AARIR's strategy, namely an over-indulgence in its own self-importance and its own perceived crucial role in the ultimate success of the Irish republican project. Lyons wrote that:

> it is now quite obvious that if public sentiment, especially in America, is manifested strongly enough that happy conclusion [the right of the Irish people to decide their government], is possible of achievement ... [We] are now convinced that if those in America who are interested in Ireland will come forward at this time and make known to the world that they agree with President De Valera's terms to abide by the result of a free election by the people of Ireland, and that such an election is the only fair and just method of deciding the issue. The Free State will be forced to agree to the plebiscite as proposed ... We have it on the most reliable authority that every move of the present so-called Free State Government is gauged by American opinion.[28]

Meanwhile, Finerty had travelled to Ireland to take depositions from witnesses in the Irish Republican Bond litigation which was pending in the US courts. While there, he used this as an opportunity to report back to Irish Americans on the lived experience of republicans in Ireland during this period. In late June 1923, again with a view to recruiting members for the July convention, he issued a statement claiming that he 'found the Republicans more determined than ever to maintain the Republic and to use whatever means, political or military, or a combination of both as may from time to time seem the most effective for this purpose.'[29]

Despite the public confidence portrayed by Thomas Lyons and John Finerty, J. J. Hearn's financial reports offered a harshly realistic interpretation of the association which was devoid of republican rhetoric and the 'glorious end' to which Lyons and Finerty often referred. Much of the correspondence from the organisation focused on the need to raise funds, both for the republican cause in Ireland and more acutely for the efficient running of the national office. In early January, as part of a circular communication to all members, local branches and state organisations were called on 'to secure voluntary contributions to the national office.'[30] These, it seems, were not particularly forthcoming as the financial statements of the national organisation up to June 1923 highlight. It also appears that the general membership of the organisation was suspicious of the national executive as a number of letters to and from AARIR members in January 1923 disclose. Finerty is especially concerned with reassuring the membership that 1923 represents a new era for the association informing Mrs Margaret Walsh of Cuyahoga Falls, Ohio that 'our financial embarrassment doesn't by any means indicate that the organisation generally throughout the country is defunct … the condition is due chiefly to the failure of some states to turn over the national assessment for 1921 and 1922.'[31] A similar explanation was given to Joseph Burtchall of Philadelphia a few days earlier when he raised concerns about the misappropriation of funds in the past and was told by Finerty that 'the majority of the national executive is now perfectly sound and I assure you that while I am national president, I intend to see the constitution lived up to in 1923.'[32] Clearly, grass roots members felt that the association had ample funds and were suspicious of further misappropriation under Finerty's leadership. However, Hearn's reports highlight that the national executive struggled to exist from one month to the next. In the financial report given to AARIR officers at the national executive meeting on 7 April, the national office had only $22.41 cash on hand and a balance on hand of only $154.16 to keep the national office operational.[33] Throughout the summer of 1923 the situation worsened and at the national executive meeting in Washington DC in mid-June 1923, Hearn reported that the cash on hand was only $5.54 and the balance on hand was a mere $48.88.[34] Aside from the fact that these figures are troubling, they also highlight a number of important observations about the association. Firstly, the AARIR is quite obviously not fit for purpose by June 1923. Secondly, there is quite clearly a disconnect between the public perception of the organisation and the realities which the national executive experienced and thirdly, the AARIR has evidently not managed to consolidate its position as the voice of Irish-American republicanism and therefore it is questionable how useful the association really was to the republican cause in Ireland by late summer 1923.

These internal struggles stood in stark contrast to the perceived wealth of the organisation externally. Irish-America had long been the reliable financial donor to the motherland's embattled fight for freedom and the stereotype compounding that image was difficult to challenge. A case in point was a letter sent to Finerty by John Castellini in early January in which Castellini chastised the national executive for seeking more money from Irish-Americans for the republican cause noting: 'Last July she [Ireland] needed $100,000 to finance the candidates running for election … in less than six months you, as head of the Irish missions in this country ask for ten times that amount … it seems to me that you should lose that notion that some people have, that gold grows on the streets here in America.'[35] Thus, given all of the internal struggles and infighting, the financial difficulties, the distrust of grass roots members and the constant battle to achieve recognition and legitimacy it is surprising that the organisation continued to be the voice for Irish republicanism in the United States. It does, however, also highlight how out of touch de Valera was with the Irish-American diaspora and how irrelevant they had become to Irish republican rhetoric.

Irrespective of the internal implosion of the AARIR stateside, there were a number of significant interactions between the AARIR and Irish republican leaders in the months leading up to the 1923 General Election. In early January, there was criticism from republican forces in Ireland, specifically from Sean Moylan, Commandant General of the Southern Division of the IRA, who according to Frank Horgan claimed that leadership of the organisation was 'inefficient' and according to Horgan, Moylan seemed to 'labor under the impression that we have contributed no money to Ireland since the date of the truce'.[36] However, some of the other correspondence highlighted the function of the organisation in its most valuable sense. On two occasions, Finerty was petitioned by members of the AARIR to make representations to the US president, Warren Harding, about the unjust capture of American citizens by British forces in Northern Ireland and the army of the Irish Free State.[37] In June 1923, the Kevin Barry Council of the AARIR based in Washington DC again requested Finerty to petition president Harding to 'protest to the British government against the atrocities now being perpetrated against republicans and the catholic minority in north east Ulster.'[38] However, very little seems to have emerged from these petitions. The AARIR also published an official response to W. T. Cosgrave's interview on 11 February 1923 with the British publication, the *Daily Mail,* in which Cosgrave 'declared himself ready to agree to a proposal that De Valera should advise his followers to surrender their arms on condition that the question of the Republic or Free State should be left to the electors'.[39] Finerty claimed that Cosgrave had made a spurious offer of an election and gave a 'misleading press interview' while encouraging republicans not 'to lay down their arms while the republic is threatened,' no doubt buoying republican morale in Ireland in the process.[40]

The influence of Laurence Ginnell as Special Envoy of the Irish republic to the AARIR was an important development, especially in terms of giving the AARIR renewed validity and authority in the months after its re-organisation. However, Ginnell's death in April 1923 again fractured the relationship between the AARIR and its Irish counterparts. Before his death, Ginnell did make one final important contribution to the association when he attended the special national executive meeting in Chicago on 25 February. At this meeting the Irish Republican Defence Fund drive was launched, and all monies raised were to be funnelled through Ginnell to the republican cause in Ireland. However, Ginnell's death on 17 April led to some confusion within the AARIR in terms of where the funds raised should be distributed to. Ultimately, it was decided that any funds raised for the Irish Republican Defence Fund should be sent to J. J. Hearn who would then forward them to republican sources in Ireland. The results of the drive were illuminating although it is not clear if Hearn only handled funds from Ginnell's death until the drive formally closed on 19 May 1923 or if he handled all monies raised as part of the drive. On 16 June, at the national executive meeting in Washington, Hearn provided the national executive with a report on the Defence Fund drive noting that he had received funds from 11 states including: Minnesota, West Virginia, Massachusetts, Pennsylvania, Tennessee, Texas, New Jersey, Washington, Washington DC, California and Ohio.[41] The largest donation was for $600 from Pittsburgh, Pennsylvania and the smallest was $11.06 from Seattle, Washington.[42] The total raised was $1706.08, a disappointing return considering the fundraising proficiency of the organisation just a few short months before.[43]

Undoubtedly the proposed election was the main political interest of the AARIR in 1923. In this instance, the association assumed an authoritative, almost paternal tone in its communications, both with its membership and with republicans in Ireland. In a statement issued after the special national executive meeting in Chicago in February, just a fortnight after Cosgrave's interview with the *Daily Mail*, Finerty warned Irish republicans not to 'tolerate another sham ... don't tolerate an election the sole purpose of which would be to mislead the outer world again.'[44] By June, Finerty's rhetoric had become even more virulent, when he openly criticised the prospect of a general election upon his return from Ireland in mid-June. He told republicans in his statement of 22 June that:

> it is the business of republicans at present ... to present a constant menace to England and her Free State and obtain for the people of Ireland a fair chance to choose between the Free State and the Republic ... the only choice presented ... to anyone ... is not between the Republic and the Free State, but between the Free State and extermination ... It is clear that at an election held under such conditions, no fair choice is given to them [republicans] and it is the growing recognition of this fact ... that makes the downfall of the Free State inevitable.[45]

The ferocity of this statement and these sentiments again highlights the increasing lack of understanding and unity between Irish republicans and their diasporic counterparts. Certainly, de Valera was going to insist on a policy of abstention, but Finerty and the AARIR seemed to overlook the importance of participating in the democratic process, which was ironic given the attitude of his own homeland to such matters.

As the prospect of a general election became more apparent, the AARIR appeared progressively more detached from Ireland. This was partly due to the fact that the new Special Envoy to the United States, Donal O'Callaghan, the Lord Mayor of Cork had only been in the position for a number of weeks before the August election and was only confirmed at the July meeting of the national executive in Boston. An election drive was initiated but with little apparent success. On 30 June, Finerty received a letter from Thomas D. O'Connor, secretary of Cumann na Poblachta (American Delegation) outlining the funding requirements of the republican party in any forthcoming election. 'The Irish Republican Party', he wrote 'intend to contest every constituency in the interest of the Republic. To do this, a considerable amount of money will be required – contesting 128 [*sic*] seats at a cost of at least $1500 per seat would mean close to $200,000 and then there are the usual and other expenses ... in all about $300,000 is needed.'[46]

The AARIR fell far short of this figure, and it seems the association was in a state of dysfunctional disarray when the election was eventually called. Any remnants of leadership from either John Finerty or Thomas Lyons had all but disappeared and events in Ireland leading up to the election simply added to the chaos in the United States. Upon hearing of de Valera's arrest at Ennis on 15 August, Finerty and Lyons sent Cosgrave a telegram in which the dignity and gravitas that had characterised both men's correspondence up to that point had been replaced with a tone of exasperation and frustration. They accused Cosgrave of 'tyranny' and stated that only 'stupidity … could hope longer to delude the world into believing you want peaceful solution in Ireland when you arrest de Valera while he is engaged in attempting to obtain a peaceful expression from the electorate even though … your threats … make a fair election impossible.'[47] Meanwhile, individual councils in the United States appeared to have undertaken fundraising activities for the election entirely independently from the association itself. On 21 August 1923, less than a week before the election, Tom Connaughton from the Benjamin Franklin Pledge Council in Cleveland wrote to Finerty stating: 'we cabled Cosgrave and the Chief, told Cosgrave that his action in arresting Dev was the best thing for the election fund that we have sent £500 to help his defeat.[48] To the chief we said, 'keep your heart, your friends in the US are backing you".[49] At this juncture any and all discipline within the association seemed to have well and truly disappeared.

Given the events of election week, it was difficult to see how the AARIR could proceed. Upon the appointment of O'Callaghan as special envoy in July the association agreed that a further reorganisation was needed 'to secure the advancement of the objects of the association … [and] to facilitate this reorganisation … the Envoy of the republic was unanimously given control of the scheme [or reorgansiation].' Finerty's position in the organisation was significantly diminished and he was appointed as a member of the advisory body. Lyons and Hearn maintained their positions as national secretary and national treasurer respectively. O'Callaghan faced a significant challenge in trying to reorganise the association as the divergence between the Irish-American interpretation of an Irish republic and the practicalities of being a republican in the Irish Free State were simply too conflicting to be reconciled.

Once all the votes had been counted, the republicans had won 44 seats, increasing their previous tally by eight seats. For their Irish-American counterparts this electoral success had little consequence. The AARIR had reached its peak and was on a rapid descent towards irrelevance. As Carroll argues, 'it had lost the support of the vast numbers of Irish Americans across the country, whether from disillusionment about the apparent dogmatism of the Republicans in Ireland or from the dictatorial methods of the forces running the organisation in the United States'.[50] Arguably, it was neither disillusionment nor dictatorial methods that were entirely to blame for the association's demise. The AARIR had fallen victim to the same afflictions that impacted many of its predecessors. Ultimately, it was a bi-functional organisation with two competing, albeit complementing agendas, namely the consolidation of Irish American presence within the host society and a leadership role in the Irish republican experiment. This meant that the leadership had to contend with infighting, challenges with internal funding and membership decline all in the context of trying to seek recognition and legitimacy for the association externally. Simultaneously, the organisation was expected to fundraise for republican activities in Ireland and provide a paternal-like guardianship as Irish republicanism evolved. This eventually led to the association having a misconstrued interpretation of its own relevance that resulted in it falling out of touch with both its members and those it was designed to aid. By the end of 1923 the AARIR had lost the confidence of its membership and although it was not fully disbanded until 1925, it was only the most ardent and committed Irish-American republicans that were affiliated with the organisation after the 1923 General Election. As Joseph Burtchall, the perceptive, straight-talking grass roots member from Philadelphia stated: 'I believe I am safe in predicting that the American Association for the Recognition of the Irish Republic HAS PASSED INTO OBLIVION and that Moses himself could not re-establish it on its once lofty plane.'[51]

CHAPTER 10

IRELAND AND THE 'END OF THE EUROPEAN CRISIS,' 1923–24

Gearóid Barry

It was the photograph of General Richard Mulcahy that was surprising: amongst the meagre handful of items yielded by an electronic search of Gallica, the BNF's (Bibiothèque Nationale de France) digital collection, for the search terms 'Irlande, 1923' is a photograph, distributed by the contemporary French news agency Rol, taken in Dublin in June 1923. The scene is of an unidentified army barracks yard where uniformed National Army soldiers stand to attention for the raising of the Irish tricolour, army chief and minister for defence Mulcahy ready to lead the salute to the flag.[1] As a photograph partly intended for an international readership – and thus distributed to foreign news agencies – this veritable *tableau vivant* projects the image of a stable secure state with a regular army, calmly entering the community of free nations. The holding of (largely) peaceful elections in August 1923 would be another good news story from Ireland, the Free State government hoped, as the country prepared to enter the League of Nations in Geneva that September.

This chapter situates the end of the Irish civil war and the Irish Free State's general election of August 1923 in a European context. Notwithstanding the fratricidal conflict of the Irish civil war of 1922–23, the speedy move in Ireland's case from civil war to electoral competition as the normative arena of politics is remarkable, if not completely unique, in European context. The argument of this present chapter is that to put Ireland's post-civil war election in European context, we must begin by acknowledging the legacy of the First World War, a war that in many senses failed to end in 1918 but whose aftershocks were felt across Europe up until at least 1923. Three major structural factors affected politics in both new and long-established states in Europe in the early 1920s: the shadow of the Russian Revolution of 1917, the complicated process of demobilisation after the First World War and the 'wars after the War' that scarred parts of Europe between 1918 and 1923. These are considered in turn in the first two sections of this chapter as a prerequisite for any survey of 'democratic' Europe in 1923. Cognisant of these structural factors, the 'roadtrip' around the European democratic landscape that follows is set against the specific backdrop of events in Europe mid-1923. At that juncture, Italian democracy was not yet quite dead even if, in retrospect, a consolidation of Benito Mussolini's fascist rule was underway. A major flashpoint of the year 1923 was the French-led occupation of the Ruhr district of Germany, which began in January 1923, and which touched off a wave of economic and political crises in Germany that might well have toppled the democratic Weimar Republic in August 1923. Germany's democracy proved more resilient than Italy's.

Thus, whilst the state of European democracies in 1923 was often ambiguous, the story was not completely bleak everywhere. All the same, the unresolved issues of the end of the War generally poisoned the well of political 'give-and-take' and served, even before 1923, to make some form of authoritarianism or military hegemony feasible, indeed likely, in former combatant nations such as Turkey and Hungary, and to undermine democracy's longer-term prospects in others.

Before embarking on such a grand tour encompassing Ireland and Europe, however, it is worth reflecting briefly on signposts provided by existing scholarship on the emergence of the Irish Free State. As far back as 2007, historian Alvin Jackson's superlative contribution on Ireland, north and south, in a volume dedicated to the 'twisted paths' of Europe's interwar history set out the complicated ways in which the two states in Ireland conformed with and departed from wider narratives of Europe's 'dark interlude'; in the process Jackson sagely disabuses readers of some negative myths about the Irish Free State as an exceptionally benighted polity.[2] More recently, historian Mel Farrell has provided us with an indispensable guide to the creation and evolution of the party system in the Irish Free State on foot of the civil war in his study *Party Politics in a new Democracy*.[3] Though the global dimensions and ramifications of the Irish Revolution itself have been recently confronted in the historiography, it is perhaps political scientists such as Bill Kissane – or, most recently, the productive pairing of historian Mícheál Ó Fathartaigh and political scientist Liam Weeks – who have done the most to put the foundation of the Irish state and the formation of its party system under the transnational microscope. These scholars have reminded us that, in comparative terms, Irish politics bore the imprint of unique circumstances, the Irish Free State being both a successor state of empire like Finland but also a British Dominion like Canada.[4] Some of these same European examples recur in this chapter below as they come to terms with the shift in understanding of sovereignty and legitimacy the War provoked.

'Democratic' Europe in 1923: the shadow of a (Soviet) gunman?

The 'wars after the [First World] War' experienced in Europe in the years 1917–1923 were often interlinked with the reverberations of the earth-shattering Russian Revolution of 1917 and of the Russian civil war that followed between 1918 and 1922. Lenin's Communist regime, with its explicit aim – through the Comintern established in Moscow in 1919 – of bringing about world revolution meant that the Russian Revolution acted like a magnetic field in European politics in the early 1920s, attracting imitators but equally repelling others in whom it inspired fear and loathing. Indeed, the Russian civil war of 1918–22 was the largest (and, on account of foreign intervention against the Bolsheviks, the most internationalised) of the so-called 'small wars' of these five post-war years which, added together, cost an estimated four million lives in Europe.[5]

The First World War itself is now increasingly studied as a global 'war of empires'; after all, it mobilised millions of the colonial subjects of European powers as never before and, by 1918, it had also brought down four major dynastic land-based multi-ethnic empires by sweeping away Romanov, Habsburg and Hohenzollern empires and seriously undermining the Ottoman one. The proliferation of violent conflicts in Europe and Asia Minor in the years 1919–23 was, as Robert Gerwarth and Erez Manela put it, all 'part of the same process of the realignment of global patterns of power and legitimacy' of the period 1911–23.[6] From 1918, therefore, it was the nation-state that would be the normative political unit for Europeans (if not for their subject colonial peoples overseas). Indeed, well before any top-hatted politicians gathered at Versailles in January 1919, new states had come into existence: Poland commemorates 11 November [1918] as its independence day. By the same token, in large parts of eastern and central Europe, the fall of empires often also left a power vacuum creating what historians now refer to as a 'shatterzone of empire'.[7] This post-1918 vacuum was often filled by violence.

The years 1919–22, therefore, were replete across Europe with violent transfers of power, accompanied by 'latent or open civil wars' often fought with creedal ferocity. In his study *The Vanquished*, Robert Gerwarth argues that War itself had raised more political problems than it solved and that the novel factors of Bolshevism and anti-Bolshevism combined with heightened ethnic antagonisms brought to the fore by imperial disintegration in the 'shatterzones' of empire to inject a radical edge to the violence of these new post-armistice conflicts. Indeed, W. B. Yeats' famous poem *Nineteen Hundred and Nineteen* captured something of this spiral of hatreds: the great poet 'viewed Ireland's predicament as part of a much wider European malaise, an ongoing conflict that originated in the world crisis of 1914–1918 while also being distinct from it.'[8] Gerwarth points to 'at least three distinct but mutually reinforcing, and overlapping, types of conflict' that occurred across Europe in the aftermath of the First World War. These included national and social revolutions such as those that occurred in Russia and to some degree in Hungary, civil wars such as the Finnish and Irish example and also interstate wars such as the Soviet-Polish War of 1920 and the Greco-Turkish War of 1919–22.[9]

Different types of armies and armed groups, from the conventional to the paramilitary – defined as 'military or quasi-military organisations and practices that either expanded or replaced the activities of conventional military formations' – fought these wars.[10] Though 'paramilitarism' had precedents in European history, in the years 1919–23 it perpetuated 'War in Peace', to quote a contemporary newspaper heading that Robert Gerwarth and John Horne borrowed for the title of their suggestive volume on the subject. In that same volume, Julia Eichenberg draws very interesting comparisons between the military strategies of pro-independence Polish and Irish nationalists in their respective countries in this same troubled period.[11] The most violent 'shatterzones of empire' tended to be on the frontiers of defeated former empires where territories, often with ethnically mixed populations, were now up for grabs. The territory of Silesia, disputed by Germans and Poles, was one such flashpoint. As Gerwarth and Horne put it: 'violence was most extreme in areas where ideological conflicts interacted both with ethnic tensions and with the attempt to construct new nation states.'[12]

The core countries of the old Central Powers empires – Germany, Austria and its erstwhile twin Hungary – now found themselves diminished territorially and living with the sting of defeat which polarised their internal politics. Banned from union with Germany, the Republic of Austria was, by 1922, an economic disaster zone requiring humanitarian aid to relieve hunger and a League of Nations-led financial rescue effort to stave off state collapse.[13] Politically-inspired violence increased hugely therefore in countries that had been on the defeated side in 1919 though there were notable exceptions to this trend: in Italy military victory was followed by rapid disillusionment with an allegedly 'mutilated victory' at the Versailles peace negotiations, disappointment at which spurred a nationalist and fascist cult of violence. The War of Independence in Ireland, meanwhile, was taking place in what was, from the British point of view, the Irish part of the then-United Kingdom, forming an insurgency within the core territory of a victorious empire.[14]

The Russian civil war – which was rumbling on in the background in the years 1918–22 – loomed large in the political imaginary of 'post-War' Europe, east and west. A multi-sided conflict fought over vast territories, and ultimately won by Leon Trotsky's Red Army in 1922 thereby securing the future of Lenin's regime, this civil war reverberated through the entire continent. Leading what was from 1918 restyled as the Communist party, Lenin had launched the Comintern or Third International from the new Soviet capital of Moscow in 1919 as a body pledged to spreading proletarian revolution throughout Europe and the colonial world. It was an emphatic rejoinder to the blood and treasure victorious capitalist powers like Britain were spending on foreign interventions to help their White Russia opponents, such as that at Murmansk in 1919. The continued existence of the Soviet state 'embodied [for those who feared it] the violence of revolution ... and the attempt to extend it to the rest of the world.'[15] Worried observers in comparatively safe France and Britain observed with horror the turn of events in Hungary in 1919 which seemed to confirm all their worst fears.

The Hungarian 'shatterzone' experience in 1918–20 combined dramatically the impacts of defeat, dislocation and the Russian Revolution. The end of the Habsburg empire meant that suddenly hundreds of thousands of Hungarian speakers were living as minorities in new or enlarged neighbouring states. After a short-lived democratic Hungarian republic, the leader of the Hungarian Communists Bela Kun established a Soviet Republic in Hungary in March 1919. He ruled for 133 days and instituted his own Communist revolution, complete with Leninist-style repression of opponents and of the Catholic Church whilst also leading an unsuccessful bid to regain territory from the Czechoslovaks. The Communist regime in Budapest produced a nationalist anti-Communist reaction; a Hungarian counter-revolutionary army joined forces with Romania to depose Kun in August 1919. Once in power, Admiral Miklos Hórthy's nationalists launched a White Terror in revenge. When the new Hungarian nationalist government signed a peace treaty – the treaty of Trianon – with the Western Powers in June 1920, Hungarian grievances about territory got little sympathy much to the anger of Hungarian nationalists.[16] Whereas Bela Kun failed, Lenin's regime had won the civil war by 1922 when the Soviet Union was formalised; anti-Communism would remain a powerful tool of political rhetoric and mobilisation across Europe. By 1923, Irish Free State propaganda was excusing the recent extra-judicial executions of republican prisoners not alone as a means of shortening the civil war but as 'inevitable if Ireland was to be saved from a descent into Bolshevism.'[17]

Demobilisation(s)?: Ireland in a Europe of ex-soldiers, 1923–24

A final structural factor needs to be borne about European societies around 1923, namely that Europe was full of former combatants (some of whom continued fighting). Belligerent nations of the First World War, as well as the colonies they enlisted and exploited in it, experienced demobilisation and 'exits from war' in a variety of ways in the years 1918–24. Conversely, non-demobilisation – the refusal or inability to demobilise wartime mental categories of friend and enemy – was also a lived reality for many in Europe in 1923: indeed, elements of both cultural demobilisation and non-demobilisation could compete and co-exist within society according to political tastes.[18] Ireland and the eastern European 'successor states' had a much more ambiguous relationship with the demobilisation process than most, of course. How are we to categorise those Irish republican volunteers of the War of Independence who were themselves former British soldiers and officers? More straightforwardly, one obvious part of demobilising from war was that armies reduced in size. Even for 'victorious' national armies in Europe in 1919–24, demobilising a regular army and downsizing it to 'peacetime' size was no mere technocratic exercise but one that involved intensely political choices. As far apart as Ireland and Yugoslavia, the integration of freedom fighters and servants of the past imperial order into single national armies produced tensions.

The Irish 'Army Mutiny' incident of May 1924 is a complicated crisis well beyond the scope of this chapter.[19] However, it reminds us that some pro-treaty War of Independence veterans who had joined the National Army to defend the new Free State in 1922 could end up, by 1924, greatly resenting those ex-British Army men who, having sat out the War of Independence, had served alongside them in the civil war (to fight republicans they consciously delegitimated by calling 'Irregulars'). This resentment of British-trained comrades in the new Irish Army by former IRA men was heightened, it seems, by a perception that the Free State government in some cases was retaining British-trained officers for the shrunken peacetime National Army in preference to those like themselves who had fought for Irish freedom, rather than serving Britain, since 1916.[20] The composite army of the new Kingdom of Yugoslavia had even knottier issues of identity to resolve. John Paul Newman refers to a bumpy integration process in this multi-ethnic – but Serbian-centred – successor state. As in Ireland, salaries and pensions incurred in service to the previous regime had to be regulated and harmonised: 'Many Habsburg officers resented their perceived loss of status in the new army; many Serbian officers [servants of the independent Serbia attacked by the Habsburg *k.u.k armee* in 1914] tended to look upon veterans of the Austro-Hungarian army as soldiers of a defeated enemy.'[21] Like almost everywhere else after the First World War, including in countries forged through independence struggles the War had helped launch, the Irish state faced the tricky issue of how veterans and the dependents of the dead (from the fight for freedom, in the Irish case) were to be compensated – materially and symbolically – for their service to and sacrifices for the nation, as the protracted history of Ireland's Military Service Pensions Board was to show.[22]

A tour of 'democratic' Europe, August 1923: the roadmap

Bearing in mind all the above structural factors of a Europe grappling with unresolved issues of the First World War since 1918, what then can we say about the state of 'democratic' Europe and its hinterland in the late summer of 1923? The complicated picture included large and small countries where democracy was resilient but also others where democracy was under threat in various ways from military pronunciamentos, foreign intervention or from Fascist-led governments that were feeling their way towards full dictatorship. Political developments in Spain and Bulgaria in 1923 showed the willingness of impatient armies to replace with military governments parliamentary institutions they deemed corrupt or inimical to the national interest, as they defined it. National contexts and traditions varied of course – Spain, unlike Bulgaria, had not been a combatant nation in the recent war but even there the Primo de Rivera military dictatorship of the 1920s – much commented upon in Ireland – was in part a response to the dislocation in the Spanish economy consequent to the end of the First World War. We have already encountered the post-war travails of Hungary: the nationalist authoritarian 'regency' there under Admiral Horthy (which would last until World War Two) dated from 1920. In 1924, Greece – still smarting from humiliation at the hands of Turkey in 1922–23 (of which more anon) – experienced a coup d'état albeit one where the military installed a republic, on the military's terms, to replace the monarchy. Instructive and all as these cases of small or less powerful nations were, though, the drastic actors in the story of liberal democracy's fate in Europe in 1923 remained the larger states, particularly Italy, Germany and Turkey. In the following sections we shall examine these three – Italy, Germany and the new Turkish Republic – as case studies whilst also sampling eastern European 'successor states' like Poland and Bulgaria – before concluding with some reflections on how the newly established Irish state fits into this map of democratic Europe of 1923.

Condition critical: Democracy in Italy, 1923

In October 1922, whilst civil war still raged in Ireland, Benito Mussolini and the fascist movement staged the so-called 'March on Rome'. Though Ireland was rent by civil strife there were still plenty in Ireland who found time to marvel at, to worry about or simply show ambivalence about the dramatic turn of events in Italy.[23] Mythologised as a seizure of power, the key fact remained the ostensibly legal appointment of Mussolini as prime minister by the King of Italy under the existing liberal constitution. Impressario of a new mode of politics – 'fascism' – that married socialist and nationalist rhetoric with a cult of violence valorising the role of military veterans, Mussolini had no intention of being just another civilian prime minster. His tactical awareness told him though that his political position in early to mid-1923 was still precarious: what he led was by no means yet a full fascist dictatorship. As Adrian Lyttleton's classic study of the drawn-out fascist takeover in Italy shows, 1923 – Mussolini's first full year as head of government – was instead one of 'normalization,' fascist-style. Mussolini moved carefully to smooth over the live tensions within his unruly movement between relative 'moderates' – content with a share in power and the spoils of office – and more 'revolutionary' fascists and hardcore Blackshirts for whom the March on Rome was not an end in itself but rather a prelude to a 'second-wave' fascist transformation of politics.[24] Mussolini conjured with these competing 'legalist' and revolutionary wings of his own movement, whilst trying not to alienate the king. Many non-fascist Liberals preferred to believe that the simmering crisis within fascism about its future direction would be resolved by Mussolini in favour of constitutionalism. The creation in December 1922 of two new revolutionary institutions gave more thoughtful democrats in Italy pause for thought; the first of these was the Fascist Grand Council – a type of Fascist party-controlled parallel cabinet. The second was a National Militia whose purpose was to contain paramilitary Blackshirt zeal but also to create a national armed force, separate from the Royal Army, loyal to Mussolini himself.[25]

By supreme coincidence, on 1 September 1923, the Emilia-Romagna section of the National Militia put on a shameless display of flattery for Irish pilgrims to Bobbio, site of St Colombanus' famous monastery during that day's celebrations of the foundation's thirteenth century. Fresh from his election victory at home, president of the executive council W. T. Cosgrave was himself in Bobbio, en route to Geneva where the Free State was about to take its place in the League of Nations General Assembly.[26] At Geneva, Irish delegates guardedly joined other small nations in lamenting the League's marginalisation in the ongoing Corfu Crisis during which Mussolini violently and bombastically exploited a dispute with Greece to seize the island of Corfu (which Italy had to subsequently evacuate).[27] In November 1923, the Italian parliament voted for the major electoral reform contained in the Acerbo Law which abolished single-seat districts in favour of a national list system where the party or combined list with a plurality of votes would take up to two-thirds of the seats.[28] The fascists won the April 1924 election, a success followed by a moment of grave danger for Mussolini when loyalists of the fascist leader abducted and murdered the outspoken young socialist leader Giacomo Matteotti in June 1924. The scandal transfixed Italy for six months during 1924 though, remarkably, by January 1925, Mussolini had bounced back, brazenly assuming moral responsibility for such crimes and daring his divided opponents to dislodge him from power. They could not. The ambiguities of Mussolini's premiership during 1923 helped prepare the way for this naked transition from his heading a government to heading a regime.[29]

The Ruhr occupation: Germany in crisis and the French connection, 1923

Simultaneous with the Irish general election and the Corfu Crisis, Franco-German relations were at their post-war low point in August 1923. The treaty of Versailles (signed in June 1919) had of course established the principle that Germany – and her allies – should pay reparations for war damages to those Entente nations such as France and Belgium with major claims against them. This was the background to rounds of diplomatic and financial wrangling about the sums to be paid and the manner and schedule of German payments.[30] When Germany defaulted on a payment in late 1922, a Franco-Belgian invasion of the Ruhr district followed. By August 1923, French and Belgian military forces were some eight months into a fractious military and economic occupation of what was the industrial heartland of north-western Germany.[31] The German government's policy of passive resistance rallied the country but worsened the country's inflationary spiral. 1923 was also, infamously, the year of hyperinflation in Germany: oft-reproduced photographs from that year show Germans bringing wheelbarrows of banknotes to buy bread. The consequent immiseration of the middle class dimmed the attractions of democracy for many in Germany. August 1923 was one of the worst months of the crisis: as the economy reeled, violent uprisings threatened the Weimar Republic's survival just as they had in 1919. In those weeks, the government had to put down an attempted Communist takeover in Thuringia. In this desperate situation, a new German chancellor Gustav Stresemann took office. Stresemann was a centre-right German nationalist, openly committed to the revision of the Versailles treaty but pragmatic enough to wish to revise it through diplomacy, not open confrontation. In the short term he called off the crippling campaign of passive resistance and took measures that gradually stabilised the German currency. Stresemann's short months-long tenure as chancellor was to be followed by a six-year term as foreign minister which lasted until the statesman's unexpected death in 1929. As foreign minister, Stresemann would manoeuvre Germany out of its post-Versailles isolation and engineer better relations with France.

Such brighter prospects lay in the future: in the late autumn of 1923, a febrile political atmosphere still reigned in the Bavarian capital Munich. There, some right-wing nationalists wished to emulate Mussolini's 'March on Rome' of October 1922 and use the takeover of the Bavarian government as a springboard for a change of regime in Berlin. The failed National Socialist putsch, aimed at overthrowing the Bavarian state government in Munich, fell apart almost as soon as it began on 9 November 1923. Though it produced 14 fatalities amongst the insurgents, the putsch's political significance was greater than the anticlimactic attempted coup itself. The drifter and former lance-corporal-turned-rabblerouser Adolf Hitler (who, during the fighting on 9 November, narrowly avoided a fatal bullet which killed a National Socialist companion right next to him) had in fact harboured hopes of police and military complicity in the attempted coup. There were plenty of anti-democratic forces within the German military and forces of order that Hitler hoped might support him: after all, an open co-conspirator of his in Munich was the former (and by now very wayward and disloyal) First World War commander Erich von Ludendorff.[32] As Ian Kershaw points out though, the configuration of anti-democratic forces in Germany in late 1923 was quite different from what it had been in Italy a year before. Pluralist politics, mediated through a parliament elected on universal manhood suffrage for over half a century, meant elections and democratic practice simply had deeper roots in Germany, even allowing for the imbalance in power between crown, chancellor and Reichstag up until 1918. In 1923, the German military were nervous of backing and lending credibility to a right-wing coup like Hitler's Beer Hall Putsch: the potential outcomes at that stage were simply too uncertain.[33] German democracy, unlike Italy's, would survive 1923. Hitler and his comrades' farcical trial and lenient punishment in 1924 meant, however, that, even if the Nazis faded (for now) from the frontline of German politics, a reckoning with the anti-democratic forces that beset the ostensibly model republic of Weimar Germany was merely deferred, not decided.

Meanwhile, the Ruhr occupation itself – the occasion of the great German crisis of 1923 – ended up by rebounding on the French government. By 1924, public opinion in France turned against prime minister Raymond Poincaré's hard-line policy on Germany. For a French public, tired of the warlike 'cultural mobilization' against the Germans, putting faith in 'the other Germany' – the 'good' Germany – of republican democrats and moderate socialists gradually ceased to seem like disloyalty to France.[34] The French elections of May 1924 confirmed the trend with a left-wing government elected on a commitment to end the Ruhr imbroglio. The ensuing London Agreement of August 1924 (negotiated with the Germans, not dictated to them) internationalised France and Germany's reparations dispute, adopting the Dawes Plan for reduced payments over a longer schedule. Hailed in its day as the true peace agreement between the French and German republics, the London accord inaugurated a 'European' moment in Franco-German relations in the mid-1920s symbolised by the co-operation of the countries' foreign ministers Gustav Stresemann and Aristide Briand. This moment of Franco-German détente in 1925–26 was the context for Germany's admission into the League of Nations in September 1926, some three years after the Irish Free State had taken its place there. The mid-1920s was a fleeting but significant season for what John Horne has defined as 'cultural demobilization of wartime mentalities' expressed in 'acts of mutual recognition and reconciliation not only between veterans but also by trade unionists, feminists, intellectuals and others from across the continent'.[35]

Turkey, Greece and the lessons of Lausanne, 1923: toleration or eviction?

For all the cautious hopes and 'critical support' invested in the League of Nations by the Irish delegates to Geneva in September 1923, it was an agreement reached in another Swiss city – Lausanne – nine months earlier, in January 1923, between the Republic of Turkey, successor state of the defunct Ottoman Empire, and its erstwhile Entente adversaries that was the signal diplomatic event of the year 1923. How was it that by 1923 Turkey got to negotiate on equal terms a second peace treaty, largely reversing the humiliating treaty of Sevres of 1920? The opportunistic Greek invasion of Anatolia in 1919 – in pursuit of the Greek nationalist prime minister Venizelos's Great Idea of a revived Greek imperium in the eastern Mediterranean – had, by 1922, backfired but not before producing its own round of atrocities. The Greek invasion also galvanised Turkish nationalists who abolished the irrelevant sultanate in 1922 and revived Turkey's flagging war effort. Led by Mustafa Kemal, Turkish hero of the defence of Gallipoli in the First World War, Turkish forces had the Greeks on the run by September 1922. That same month, Greek forces abandoned the ethnically mixed port of Smyrna (now Izmir). What followed was an orgy of fire and blood as victorious Turks wrought vengeance on the city's Christian Greeks and Armenians killing an estimated 30,000 of them over a two-week period.[36]

The bloody events at Smyrna were but a prelude to the even larger forced 'population exchanges' between Turkey and Greece, conducted – officially without violence – in 1922–23. The treaty of Lausanne gave legal respectability to a brutal and wrenching process already underway on the ground. A total of about 600,000 people of all ages, Orthodox Greek and Turkish Muslims, lost their homes and crossed the Aegean in opposite directions – for good – with no say in the matter. By ratifying this process, the Lausanne treaty confirmed a number of realities, some of them ominous. The drive for ethnic homogeneity could trump respect for minorities and be recognised internationally. It had not been meant to be like this: in the new liberal order embodied by the League of Nations inaugurated in 1920, minorities were meant to be protected not victimised. Treaty revisionists from Germany to Hungary – who traded in the politics of grievance – now took note: the Kemalist diplomatic triumph at Lausanne was a successful example of the strong-armed ethno-nationalist revision of borders in pursuit of a purer nation.[37]

Successor states, minorities and democracy: the ambivalent east

The Lausanne treaty was an extreme response to a wider set of tensions in the new Europe where, as John Horne puts it, '[Like] a set of Russian dolls, one state's nationality turned out to be the minority in someone else's, especially in Central and Eastern Europe'.[38] The sparing use of plebiscites to determine contested borders could not undo the patchwork quilt of nationalities in parts of eastern and central Europe. The peacemakers of 1919 made recourse to such referendums, under League of Nations auspices, for just six mixed-language regions belonging to the defeated German and Austrian empires: the largest and bitterest plebiscite was that held amongst Germans and Poles in Upper Silesia in March 1921. So fraught was a planned plebiscite in the duchy of Teschen (located between the new Polish and Czech states) that it was abandoned.[39] The limited cycle of plebiscites passed; 35 per cent of the population of the new Polish state were non-Poles, including Ukrainians, Belarussians, Lithuanians and Germans. Beginning as early as the Polish Minorities treaty, or 'Little Versailles treaty' signed on the same day as the main treaty in June 1919, no less than eight successor states of the defeated empires were obliged by the Entente powers in these first years of their independence to sign similar agreements as a condition of their international recognition. Collective rights – such as language rights – for national minorities were included in such agreements with possible appeals to the League of Nations if such rights were not respected.[40] The question remained as to whether parliamentary institutions and electoral competition would facilitate a politics of 'give and take' within new states or whether dominant majorities would chafe at such minority protections. The fate of democracy in eastern and central Europe presented, at the time, a very mixed picture: for us, the record is obscured further by an understandable but unhelpful tendency to read the story backwards from the 1930s as if the 'failure' of democracy in eastern and central Europe was inevitable. Ian Kershaw captures better the sense of contingency that surrounded parliamentarianism in eastern and central Europe around 1923; '[in] the successor states, parliamentary democracy was a fragile flower, planted in less than fertile soil…[It] survived the post-war crisis [of 1919–23], even if only Finland [exiting, like Ireland, from civil war] and Czechoslovakia proved durable successes.'[41] The record was one of partial success therefore. Not even the Czechs – lead-partners in the Czechslovak state often touted as the most democratic of the new nations – had a perfect record in the inclusion of minorities such as the Sudeten Germans or even of Slovak aspirations in spite of the equal billing given to both Czechs and Slovaks their new state's very name – Czechoslovakia. In Poland, meanwhile, the democratic constitution of the Polish Second Republic enacted in 1921 still held sway in Poland in 1923, but only just. The fragmented multiparty Sejm or lower house of parliament failed to produce coherent or long-lasting governments as Poland careered towards a hyperinflation crisis in late 1923 that rivalled Germany's. In a nation that had fought no less than six border wars between 1918 and 1921 it was unsurprising that Poles would look towards a military hero of those wars – Marshal Josef Pilsudski – as a saviour. Disillusionment with Polish parliamentary politicians paved the way in these years for the military coup of May 1926 that established Pilsudski's personal dictatorship.[42] That still lay in the future, however.

In 1923, therefore, barring some prominent exceptions, the prospects for democracy in eastern and central Europe looked reasonable. Democratic institutions in successor states could still rely upon the support of idealistic democrats on the liberal left and of non-Communist socialists. These democracies could summon up, for the time being, 'extensive, if unstable, popular backing [for parliamentary democracy], arising from a combination of social and political interests.'[43] The sizeable peasant parties in successor states' parliaments represented a key interest group in states that could, for a while, be placated within parliamentary coalition governments. In Bulgaria, the Agrarian Union leader Stamboliiski served as Bulgaria's prime minister in a flawed but democratically-elected government until army officers deposed him in 1923.[44] Across east and central Europe as a whole, though, anti-democratic forces did not have the means to overthrow pluralist democracy – but they remained sceptical of it. Populist nationalism, bound up with the minorities question, would prove a powerful tool to undermine it in the following decade as slowly but surely eastern European states (with the exception of Czechoslovakia) succumbed to some form of authoritarian government.[45]

Exiting civil war, existing the European post-war crisis, 1923–24.

On 27 August 1923, polling day in the Irish Free State elections, *L'Oeuvre*, a centre-left Paris newspaper friendly to Irish concerns, editorialised on the vote. Leader writer Camille Lemercier wrote knowledgeably of the mixed record of the outgoing Cosgrave government, which had, in his view, rendered the Irish Free State 'the greatest services' in restoring peace and beginning to rebuild 'devastated regions' – a highly resonant phrase in France in 1923. On the other hand, this 'government of public safety' had also pursued republicans with an energy that 'often looked like savagery'. 'After terrible trials,' the editorialist hoped the Free State might now prosper 'gathering the fruits of her bloody sacrifices.'[46] A year later, in 1924, many European commentators considered that the continent itself was exiting the prolonged post-war crisis and cycle of violence and was at last able to breathe again.

This begs the question, how 'European' was the Irish experience in 1923? As was the case in post-civil war Finland in the same period, relatively quickly, civil war divisions were canalized into electoral competition. Neither in Finland nor in Ireland were the defeated side banned from contesting elections but at the same time there were lasting costs for some on the defeated side. As Risto Alapuro explains, Finland's 'Reds' – the Social Democrats – 'could take part in public life' but they also experienced ongoing '[political] and economic second-class citizenship [accompanied by] cultural isolation.'[47] Nor can Republican gains in the Free State's August 1923 poll obscure the visceral cost of being on the 'wrong side' in the new Ireland: consider those then still interned in camps such as 'Tintown' or, more enduringly and most bitterly, immiserated and humiliated anti-treatyites blacklisted from their old jobs, or sometimes any job, in the war's aftermath. However, bad and all as Irish-style victimisation was, the fate of defeated revolutionaries after civil war could be even worse, as victims of the counter-revolutionary White Terror of 1920 in Hungary could have attested, not to mind defeated Spanish republicans marginalised in or exiled from Franco's Spain after 1939. Amongst Irish political representatives, as we know, Republican abstention from the Dáil would be abandoned by a large proportion – but not all – anti-treatyites with the entry into parliament of de Valera's new Fianna Fáil party in 1927. However imperfectly, in comparative European terms, Ireland's 1923 election showed a grudging 'shared space' between opposing political camps that was unthinkable in many other new states – such as Hungary – in 1923. Flawed as the emergent socially conservative consensus in the Irish Free State was, the willingness, even in 1923, to share the electoral space surely helped to make the more benign Irish political outcome – of an eventual peaceful transfer of power later in 1932 between Ireland's civil war victors and vanquished – more likely.

CHAPTER 11

FROM REVOLUTION TO DEMOCRACY: ANALYSING THE 1923 GENERAL ELECTION

Elaine Callinan

The *Belfast Newsletter,* on 23 August 1923, reported optimistically that 'a large poll would be in favour of the Government'.[1] Their belief was that if 70 per cent of the electors turned out and voted in favour of Cumann na nGaedheal they would be safe, but if the percentage fell below 60 the party would be in danger. According to the *Cork Examiner,* 'every forecast gives the outgoing Government a renewal of office with a working majority'.[2] There were 1,788,854 electors on the register, and of these 1,053,668 recorded their votes, and every constituency, with the exception of Dublin University, was contested.[3] The full results of the election are depicted in Figure 2:[4]

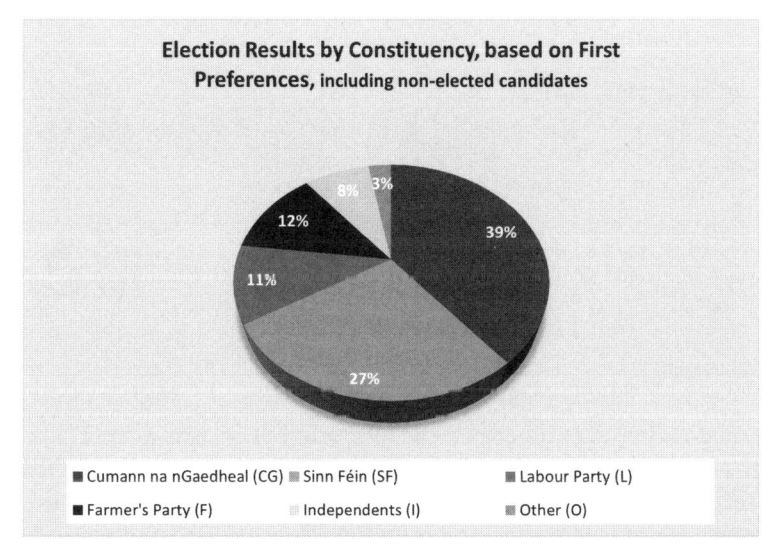

Figure 2

This was a hard-fought election by all parties who campaigned vigorously (as can be seen throughout this volume). However, even though shops and businesses closed for voting in many parts of the country, the numbers demonstrate that there was a large portion of the electorate (just over 41 per cent) that failed to exercise their franchise (the reasons for which will be discussed later).[5] Cumann na nGaedheal, Farmers, and Independents were prepared to take their seats in the Dáil and work with the treaty settlement, whereas Labour's position waivered. Sinn Féin was pledged to abstain.[6] Therefore, on the Anglo-Irish treaty issue the position may, therefore, be broadly summed up as 765,067 for the treaty and 288,610 against. The number of candidates nominated for the 30 constituencies in the Irish Free State was 375, and were divided as follows:

Cumann na nGaedheal	107
Sinn Féin	85
Farmers' Party	64
Labour	49
Independents	70

There were also candidates running under the Businessmen's Party, Cork Progressive Association, National Democratic Party, Dublin Trades Council, Ratepayers' Association and Town Tenants' Association which are referred to in this analysis as 'Other'.[7]

As can be seen from the results, the position of Cumann na nGaedheal was ultimately safe, but it could not claim the sweeping victory that some of its members and supporters had predicted. There were 153 seats in total for the new Dáil Éireann and Cumann na nGaedheal claimed 63 seats, getting 39 per cent of the overall vote;[8] or, out of 1,053,668 votes cast, 410,721 favoured Cumann na nGaedheal.[9] Sinn Féin obtained 44 seats – three fewer than the highest forecast of their organisers – or 288,610 votes which was more than one-fourth of the votes recorded. The total number of seats by party can be seen in table 1:

Party	Third Dáil Seats	Fourth Dáil Seats won	Percentage of Fourth Dáil
Cumann na nGaedheal	58	63	41.2%
Sinn Féin	36	44	28.8%
Farmers' Party	7	15	9.8%
Labour Party	17	14	9.2%
Independent	10	13	8.5%
Other	-	4	2.6%
Total	128	153	

Table 1: Total number of seats by party

Most parties made gains, in part because the total number of seats in the Dáil was increased by 25 – from 128 in 1922 to 153 in 1923. In the election Cumann na nGaedheal won a plurality of seats and a 19-seat lead over Sinn Féin. By comparison to the 1922 'pact' election' Cumann na nGaedheal gained five seats, Sinn Féin gained eight, Farmers eight and Independents seven, while the Labour Party suffered a loss of three seats (the only party that did not substantially improve their position).[10] Clearly, a great many Sinn Féin seats were obtained at the expense of Labour. In Dublin, Labour polled only about six per cent of the first preference votes, and according to the *Irish Independent*, the Dublin workers were so long used to voting on a political ticket that few of them gave their first votes to their own candidates.[11] In the 1922 election the success of some of the Labour and Independent candidates was due largely to the fact that thousands of voters refused to vote for one or other of the 'pact' parties, but in 1923 their votes were cast on party lines. In several instances it was reported that Sinn Féin and Labour voters inter-changed their preferences, and to reinforce their voter preference in Dublin North Sinn Féin sent out sample ballot papers marked with lower preferences being given to the Labour candidates. According to the *Nationalist and Leinster Times*, 'Labour in many districts voted for the Republican candidates, particularly in Offaly'.[12] Some interesting Labour losses were Cathal O'Shannon, who had won a resounding election to the Dáil as Labour candidate in Louth-Meath in 1922, receiving nearly 14,000 first-preference votes (over twice the quota), failed to hold his seat in 1923. Patrick Gaffney, the official Labour candidate for Carlow-Kilkenny, who headed the poll in 1922 with 10,875 votes, ran as an Independent in 1923, with an interest in a Worker's Republic, obtained only a meagre 803 votes. However, another Labour candidate in this constituency, Edward Doyle, an agricultural worker, was successful and secured the fourth seat in this five-seater constituency with 4,783 votes (under the quota).[13] Some strong Labour successes were Richard Corish in Wexford and Hugh Colohan in Kildare, both of whom topped the poll. As the *Offaly Independent* pointed out, 'in the electoral struggle neither the candidates put forward in the interest of the farmers nor of the labourers have done well'. There were some strong victories such as the leader of the party, Denis Gorey, who despite past intimidation still ran and retained his seat in Carlow-Kilkenny.[14] Overall the party lost a seat in Dublin, but won in Clare, Limerick, Kildare, Tipperary, Leix-Offaly, Wicklow and Longford-Westmeath also.

Sinn Féin had some interesting and strong victories. Frank Aiken, chief of staff of the anti-treaty IRA and who was 'on the run', headed the poll in County Louth (three seats) with 6,651 votes. He was the only one elected outright having exceeded the quota. Constance Markievicz, 'one of the wild women' according to the *Belfast Newsletter*, who had topped the poll in 1918 and failed to get elected in 1922 secured the second highest poll in 1923 after Cumann na nGaedheal's Philip Cosgrave.[15] Caitlín Brugha, the widow of Cathal Brugha who was killed in O'Connell Street during the civil war, was elected in Waterford on the first count. In Tipperary Dan Breen, who was then in jail, was elected on the first count, and Mary MacSwiney was elected in Cork City, but only after several counts and eliminations being necessary before she reached the quota in the tenth count. De Valera's success in Clare was as striking as that of the Cumann na nGaedheal leader, W. T. Cosgrave in Carlow-Kilkenny. The total poll in County Clare's five-seater constituency was 39,445 (there were 1,184 spoiled votes) out of an electorate of 58,495. The quota was 6,575 and de Valera attained 17,762 votes (Cosgrave had attained 17,709 votes in his constituency) and was duly elected on the first count.[16] Eoin MacNeill won a seat in this constituency as well as in the National University of Ireland, and he finally decided to take the seat for Clare. The fight for the last seat in the Carlow-Kilkenny constituency was between two Sinn Féin candidates: Michael Skelly, Chairman of Callan Town Commissioners, who had been arrested and interned by the British but was released after the signing of the treaty, won his seat coming in under the quota. The other was Michael Barry, a brother of Kevin Barry who was executed in 1920, who failed to win his seat.[17] There were some surprising losses for Sinn Féin. Robert Barton, a treaty signatory although a chief proponent of de Valera's 'external association' during the treaty negotiations, lost his seat in County Wicklow; Kathleen O'Callaghan, the widow of the Lord Mayor, lost her seat in Limerick. George Gavan Duffy, a former Sinn Féin candidate in 1918 and another treaty negotiator who later offered to resign because he signed, ran as an Independent in 1923 and was reported to have been counted out at the bottom of the poll in County Dublin.[18]

Dublin County (an eight seater) saw an assortment of parties and independents elected, but Cumann na nGaedheal fared well with Kevin O'Higgins topping the poll by a large majority of 20,821 votes followed by Desmond FitzGerald with 3,615 votes and taking third for this party was Michael Derham with 1,986 first preference votes. Labour, Business Party, Sinn Féin and two independents took the rest of the seats. Cumann na nGaedheal attained the highest number of first preference votes in 15 constituencies, Sinn Féin in eight, Labour in three, Independents in two and Farmers in one (excluding universities). Certainly their leader Cosgrave's votes were strong, with the *Kilkenny People* reporting that voters 'thronged the polling booths, young and old, gentle and simple, nearly 18,000 strong, and they one and all put No. 1 before his name'.[19] When the result was announced from the Courthouse balcony a considerable crowd had been waiting outside and they received the news with ringing cheers. Tar barrels had been placed in front of the Courthouse in anticipation of the victory, and they were set alight and 'the flames shot up' with a 'renewed outburst of cheering'.[20]

In parts of the provinces Sinn Féin candidates secured better results, but in only a few constituencies can they claim to have had the support of a majority of the voters, as depicted in figures 3 to 6. In Munster they were nearly on par with Cumann na nGaedheal, but they were weak in Leinster and the three Ulster counties of the Irish Free State. They secured the lowest percentage in the boroughs and they were higher in Connacht.[21] In Dublin only 18.8 per cent of the votes were cast for Sinn Féin as compared with 51.8 per cent for Cumann na nGaedheal. Kerry was the only constituency that returned four Sinn Féin candidates, with Austin Stack getting elected on the first count with 10,333 votes, whereas Cumann na nGaedheal got four seats in five constituencies – Tirconaill, Cork City, Dublin North, Dublin South and Galway.

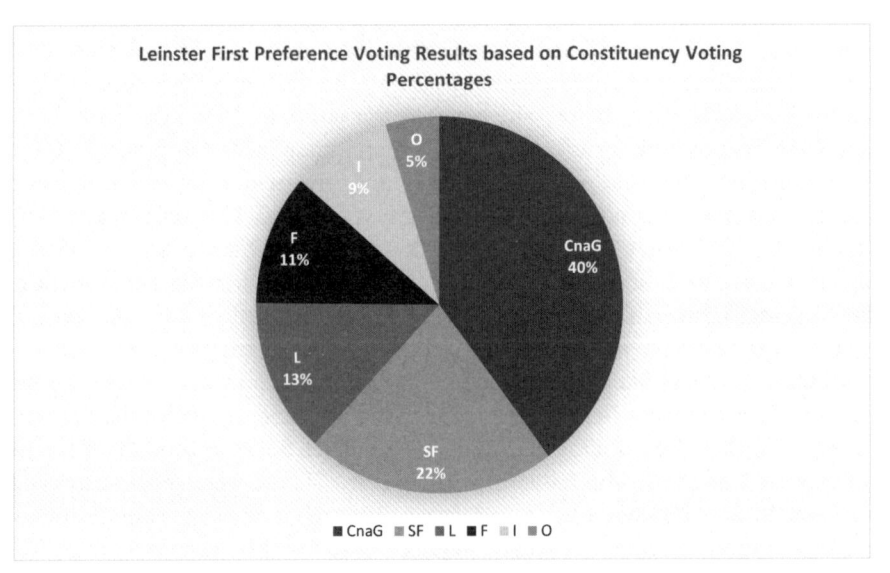

Figure 3[22]

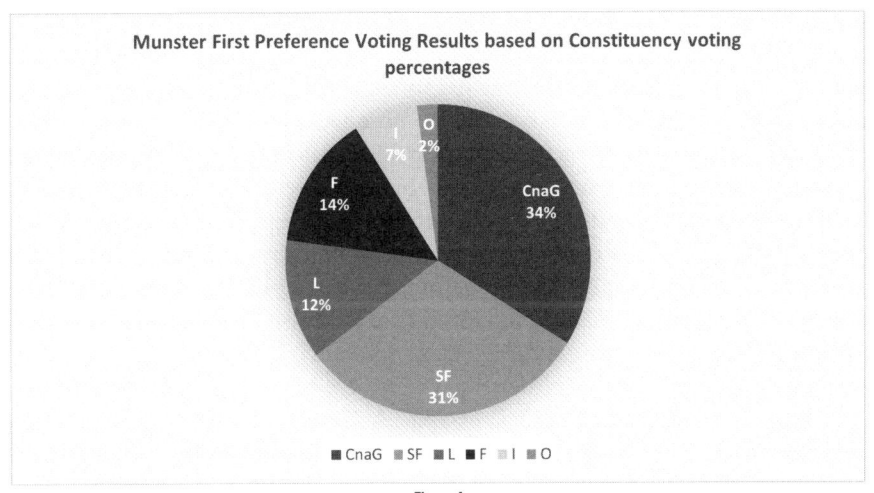

From Revolution to Democracy: Analysing the 1923 General Election

Munster First Preference Voting Results based on Constituency voting percentages

- CnaG 34%
- SF 31%
- L 12%
- F 14%
- I 7%
- O 2%

Figure 4

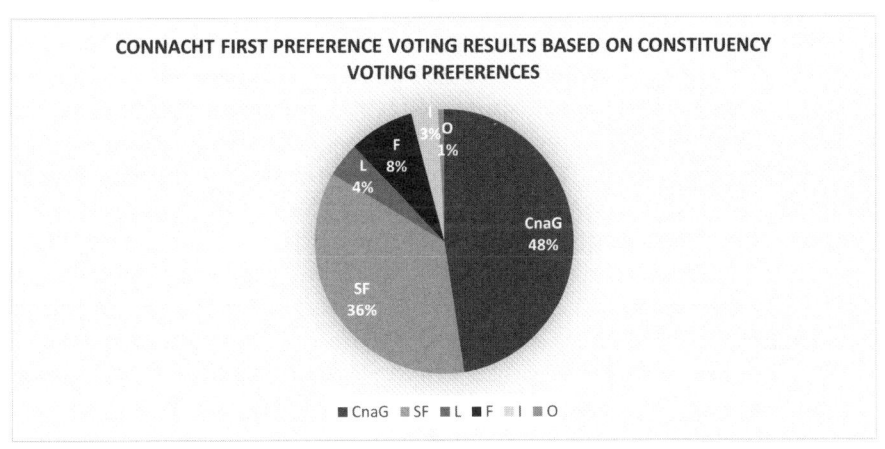

CONNACHT FIRST PREFERENCE VOTING RESULTS BASED ON CONSTITUENCY VOTING PREFERENCES

- CnaG 48%
- SF 36%
- L 4%
- F 8%
- I 3%
- O 1%

Figure 5

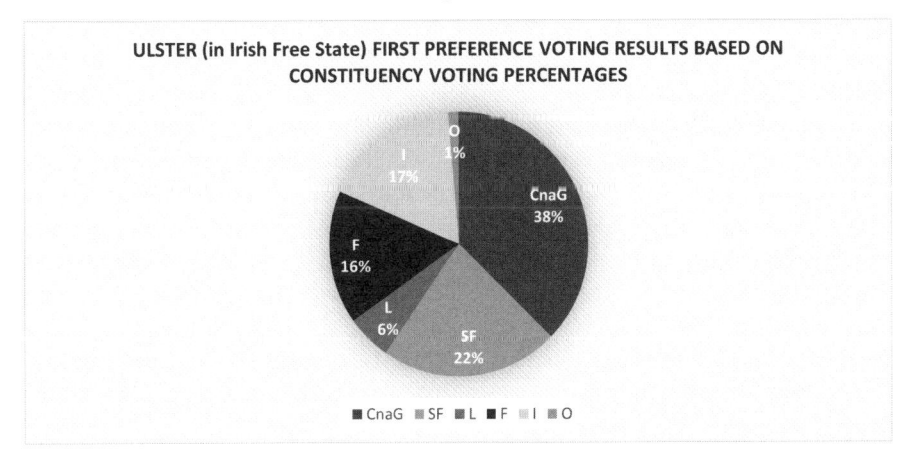

ULSTER (in Irish Free State) FIRST PREFERENCE VOTING RESULTS BASED ON CONSTITUENCY VOTING PERCENTAGES

- CnaG 38%
- SF 22%
- L 6%
- F 16%
- I 17%
- O 1%

Figure 6

The constituencies of Cork North and Waterford provided the worst results of all for the government with Cumann na nGaedheal failing to win a seat in either. Bitter agrarian confrontations with farm labourers from 1921 to 1923, particularly in Waterford, as the Irish Farmers Union battled on wages, land and the broader issues of the economy meant that Cumann na nGaedheal was truly squeezed from all angles in this county (as was Labour).[23] In Cork North of the elected candidates, Sinn Féin's share of the first preference vote was 44 per cent, with Labour obtaining 26 per cent and Farmers 30 per cent. Cork North was 'cow country', an area dominated by large scale dairy farming and this case underlines the extent to which Cumann na nGaedheal was in a fight with the Farmers' Party in the rural constituencies.[24] Conversely, Sinn Féin won no seats in the Kildare, Meath and Wicklow eastern counties where pro-treaty sentiment was strong.

There were a number of constituencies where the battle was between the two main parties of Cumann na nGaedheal and Sinn Féin. As Terence Dooley observed of Cumann na nGaedheal's rural battles with Sinn Féin, the government polled a higher percentage than the anti-treatyites in 18 out of 25 rural constituencies. It performed particularly well in eight of the 11 western constituencies coterminous with the 'congested districts', the very areas that are associated with anti-treaty sentiment during the civil war. They also did well in two-way battles in, for example, Dublin North (Cumann na nGaedheal getting 53.9 per cent to Sinn Féin's 18.6 per cent) and Dublin South (69.8 per cent for Cumann na nGaedheal to Sinn Féin's 21.8 per cent) and Monaghan, where the party defeated the republicans by 69.2 per cent to 30.8 per cent. In Leitrim-Sligo Cumann na nGaedheal came out on top with four seats or 59.6 per cent against Sinn Féin's three seats at 40.4 per cent. The Mayo constituencies also saw two two-way battles. In North Mayo both parties gained two seats but Cumann na nGaedheal scored more votes at 52.8 per cent against Sinn Féin's 47.2 per cent. Here the top two candidates of each party – Sinn Féin's Patrick Rutledge who attained 8,997 votes and Joseph McGrath of Cumann na nGaedheal who attained 8,011 votes had a very close contest. In Mayo South Cumann na nGaedheal came out on top with a stronger victory gaining three seats against Sinn Féin's two seats with a 61.6 per cent high over 38.4 per cent. Louth also saw Cumann na nGaedheal gain two seats with a clear divide between the two main parties at 63.3 per cent against Sinn Féin's 36.7 per cent.[25] This underlines the political expedience, from Cumann na nGaedheal's standpoint, of having the Land Bill enacted ahead of the election – it passed into law on the same day that Cosgrave dissolved the Dáil.[26] Kerry, where the Free State's civil war excesses are well documented, Clare, de Valera's constituency and the aforementioned Cork North, were the exceptions to Cumann na nGaedheal's otherwise strong performance in the west.

In Kerry Sinn Féin came out on top with four seats as compared to Cumann na nGaedheal's three seats, or 60 per cent to 40 per cent of votes. None of the 15 candidates in Kerry were elected on the first count.[27] In Roscommon the Sinn Féin candidate George Noble Plunkett (the father of three sons who took part in the Easter Rising 1916 where one son, Joseph Plunkett, was subsequently executed) scored 5,507 votes against Cumann na nGaedheal's Andrew Lavin who picked up the third seat in this constituency gaining 5,001 votes – so the total constituency divide was a tight one with Sinn Féin beating Cumann na nGaedheal at 51.4 per cent to 48.6 per cent.[28]

Parties performed strongly in constituencies where their leaders and other 'big name' candidates were put forward. In Clare, one of those western outliers, the Sinn

Féin president won 17,762 first preferences, or 59 per cent – more than two quotas and more than double the 8,196 first preferences obtained by Cumann na nGaedheal's Eoin MacNeill.[29] De Valera's vast surplus was enough to elect his party running mate Brian O'Higgins even though he had attained only 114 first preferences, or 0.4 per cent.[30] The *Cork Examiner* reported that 'the remarkable figures by which Éamon de Valera was elected show he was not the representative of a party, but was elected as the representative of the nation'. The overall Sinn Féin party results, however, did not live up to this prospect. Across constituencies large polls were obtained by Cumann na nGaedheal ministers (wherever they went forward). Cosgrave, the Cumann na nGaedheal's leader topped the poll in Carlow-Kilkenny with 17,744 first preference votes. Like de Valera, Cosgrave won more than two quotas and brought in a running mate, Seán Gibbons, who attained 615 first preferences. His deputy, Kevin O'Higgins, as stated, secured 20,821 first preferences in Dublin County while Richard Mulcahy secured 22,205 first preference votes in Dublin North, the highest number of any candidate in the election. Postmaster General J. J. Walsh topped the poll in Cork City with 17,151 first preferences while Ernest Blythe led in Monaghan with 11,290 votes. Éamonn Duggan was favourite in Meath with 8,262 while Joseph McGrath won the second seat on the first count in Mayo North with 8,011. At the end of the first count ten of the 11 ministers had been re-elected, and most of them with many surplus votes.

The results in the four-seat Waterford constituency were also interesting in that Caitlín Brugha topped the poll for Sinn Féin with 8,265 votes, but here the Redmond family held onto a seat coming in second and above quota was William Archer Redmond, the son of John Redmond, the former leader of the Irish Parliamentary Party, who attained 6,441 votes. He was returned on the second count as an Independent. The two other candidates elected in Waterford were John Butler (Labour) on the sixth count and Nicholas Wall (Farmers) on the seventh count. Waterford and Cork North were disastrous results for Cumann na nGaedheal and show the extent to which the minor parties and independents chipped away at its vote. Other ex-Irish Party members were successful in gaining seats. Alfred Byrne ran as an independent in Dublin North and gained 10,518 first preference votes coming second to Richard Mulcahy; James Cosgrave (Ind. Galway) who took the final seat in this constituency and Patrick McKenna (Farmers, Longford-Westmeath) who secured the fifth seat in this constituency but came in under quota (he had lost the famous 1917 by-election to Sinn Féin's Joseph McGuinness, and his brother, Frank, now failed to be elected in this election). However, quite a few were unsuccessful, including Patrick White (Ind. Meath), Hugh Law (Farmers, Donegal), Thomas O'Donnell (Ind. Kerry), Hugh Garahan (Farmers, Longford-Westmeath) and Daniel O'Leary (Ind. Cork West).[31]

A number of ex-Unionists (who had now changed allegiance) also ran in this election and the successful candidates were Major James Sproule Myles who ran as an Independent in Donegal and topped the poll and Major Bryan Cooper (Independent) and John Good (Businessmen's Party) who secured seats in Dublin County. Unsuccessful Unionist candidates were Sir John Harley Scott (Ind., Cork Borough), and Sir Andrew Beattie (Ind., Dublin South).

Even though, as Mary Clancy points out, by the early twentieth century many Irish women had varied experience of political participation, the number of candidates in 1923 was dismally low.[32] Prior to the election the *Cork Examiner* speculated that there was the prospect of 'a number of lady candidates' who would be 'selected to stand purely in the interests of their sex' and that they will be 'named by an organisation which is being organised for the purpose'.[33] The only mention of any such organisation was in a letter to the editor in the *Freeman's Journal* of 30 September 1922 where the author, Patricia Hoey, called for 'an organisation to be formed to provide the expenses of selected women candidates'. This organisation was to be 'non-political and non-sectarian and solely concerned with the running of women as candidates', although it seems that ultimately no such organisation was formed.[34] As Claire McGing pointed out in her chapter, there were only seven women candidates in total in the 1923 election: Mary MacSwiney ran and was declared elected in Cork City after several counts;[35] Margaret Collins O'Driscoll was elected in Dublin North for Cumann na nGaedheal; Constance Markievicz (as mentioned earlier) took a seat in Dublin South for Sinn Féin as did Kathleen Lynn in Dublin County, and Caitlín Brugha (mentioned earlier) topped the poll in Waterford, however Kathleen O'Callaghan, as already stated, contested in Limerick but failed to retain her seat. The other woman candidate was Dr Agnes O'Farrelly who ran as an Independent for the National University of Ireland but failed to gain a seat. The first woman to take up her seat in the new state was Margaret Collins O'Driscoll (the elder sister of Michael Collins), however all those who ran and were elected as Sinn Féin candidates abstained from taking their seats in the Fourth Dáil. The press reported that women across the country turned out to vote in high numbers, for example, in Carlow-Kilkenny it is mentioned that women comprised about 50 per cent of the electorate.[36] However, as McGing points out, it is difficult to ascertain their impact on this election in terms of voting power.[37]

Reaction of Cumann na nGaedheal and Sinn Féin

Cumann na nGaedheal issued a statement on 2 September 1923 claiming that 'the electors have shown that they are still massed behind the 'Treaty', for which 70 per cent of those who voted recorded their votes'.[38] However, while a positive spin was put on the overall results it has to be acknowledged that 40 per cent of the electors were not amassed behind anything because they abstained from voting. All parties and candidates struggled to overcome the apathy identified by Cumann na nGaedheal workers through the summer of 1923.[39] There is also the assumption that all who did not vote for Sinn Féin voted for the treaty and when Labour and Farmers votes are taken into consideration this claim is unwarranted. While a large number of Independents and the Farmers' Party were supporters of the treaty, some Labour members were not. They were opposed to the oath of fidelity and their ambition was for a workers' republic largely on the Bolshevist model.

Cumann na nGaedheal blamed the proportional representation method of voting as the cause for its weak position and argued that if the election had been the First-Past-the-Post method they would have had a substantial majority – of course, this is a claim that is impossible to prove. Certainly, proportional representation encouraged the formation of groups or alliances, and the consequence was that Cumann na nGaedheal had failed to win an outright majority and was able to continue in government with an artificial majority on account of Sinn Féin's abstention.

While Cumann na nGaedheal leaders obtained very large majorities, this does not necessarily mean approval of their policy. It could be a tribute to their personal popularity which was due less to their stern suppression of the civil war rather than to the prominence which they gained as leaders in the war against Britain. As was shown in chapter two, the overall pro-treaty vote in Longford-Westmeath dropped significantly on account of Seán MacEoin's decision not to stand for Cumann na nGaedheal in the 1923 election. The success of Patrick Rutledge, the 'Deputy and Acting President of the Republic', Frank Aiken, the 'Chief of Staff', Caitlín Brugha, the widow of Cathal Brugha, and other Sinn Féin candidates could be set off against those of Kevin O'Higgins, Richard Mulcahy and other Cumann na nGaedheal ministers.

Sinn Féin argued that they could have done much better if 12,000 of their most active men had not been in prison.[40] Cumann na nGaedheal's acerbic retort to this was that if these men had been at liberty there would have been no free election because they would have gone through the constituencies with rifles and revolvers intimidating the electors. Sinn Féin's win of 44 seats was by no means an unsubstantial vote. However, in the aftermath of the election the Sinn Féin Re-organising Committee remarked on the 'awful state of affairs' that rendered the contest 'a farce' mainly because there were '15,000 republicans in jail' and this resulted in almost all the leaders, speakers, writers, organisers and election experts being incapacitated from taking part in the contest. On the other hand, they argued, Cumann na nGaedheal had all its staff of officers and experts complete, and the 'Free State Party used its control of the armed forces to silence the press and their opponent's propaganda'.[41] There were raids on Sinn Féin headquarters, the houses of Mrs Childers, Dr Lynn, O'Hanrahan, O'Connor, Miss Barton and Constance Markievicz. Reaction to this was that Sinn Féin and their supporters had tried to prevent ministers and other treaty speakers obtaining a hearing at public meetings where noisy interrupters endeavoured to create disturbance.[42] The *Sinn Féin* newspaper declared that the election was beneath contempt and charged the Government with outraging every principle of decency and fair play.[43]

Voter apathy

The special correspondent of the Press Association wired that the new Dáil was elected 'without any angry collisions, without any violence' and that it was 'a model election'. There were cases of intimidation in various districts but there seemed to be little personation which had been considerable in past elections.[44] This was probably due to the new Electoral Abuses Act where the penalties were perceived as being too severe to risk being caught trying to pose as someone else.[45] As the correspondent stated, 'one has not, as on other occasions, met respectable citizens who boasted of having voted seventeen times'.[46] Across most of the newspapers there was very little reporting of any personation in this election, but, as seen in chapter two, voter apathy was well documented. According to the *Cork Examiner*, 'the election was the dullest of affairs'. There was no excitement, no life, no laughter, and there appeared to be little interest. There were no queues outside polling stations and, for instance, the only sign of life around some of the Cork polling booths was in the morning 'with the presence of one or two National soldiers nursing rifles and smoking cigarettes'.[47] While the propaganda battles of the election contradict this through the use of strenuous language at some of the political meetings that had good attendance and the tone of some of the election literature, and the mural decorations, the turnout in 1923 for the first election of the Irish Free State was surprisingly low. There were many newspaper reports on voter apathy and low turnout, but this was a strongly contested election and certainly political participation was high, with 19 interests declaring.

Yet, out of a total register of electors at 1,788,154, there were 734,486 who did not cast a vote (41.06 per cent). Cork East (46.55 per cent), Cork West (50.05 per cent), Donegal (45.63 per cent), Dublin South and Dublin County (both at just over 40 per cent), Galway (54.34 per cent), Kildare (47.52 per cent), Mayo North and South (51.17 per cent and 46.17 per cent respectively) all had high levels of absent voters.[48] Explanations for this low turnout include errors in the register (according to the *Irish Independent* and *Cork Examiner*, many registers in the country showed an absence of eight per cent of the voters); the lack of provision of vehicular transport to polling stations for voters (as there was not the same quantity of polling stations as in modern times); and there was also commentary that the election 'was rather rushed' and factors such as the personal canvass, elaborate addresses, and any systematic demonstrations were largely missing. Familiar to the electorate in this era was band playing and flag waving or bunting, and in 1923 these 'were almost negative quantities'.[49] It was also reported that the weather was against the people. There was a genuine fear of disturbances or violence, even though the reality was a quiet election, although Kerry had some outbreaks.[50] Blame was also cast on the lack of organisation by the smaller groups such as the Town Tenants in the Leix-Offaly district. In Galway it was reported that 'not a single voter had appeared at any of the booths until long after breakfast hour, and up to noon voting had been very slow'. Activity improved later in the day, but there was a general spirit of apathy. The length of the ballot paper in this electoral district was also a cause for indifference and led to a delay in recording votes. Roscommon, however, had a 'constant stream of voters' until about midday, but it was reported that 'at the close of poll there were few voters who failed to exercise the franchise, although the absent voters were at 39.88 per cent which is similar to other constituencies.[51]

A few other factors may have led to voter apathy. There had been a large number of general, by-elections and local elections since 1917. Voters had come out in 1918, 1920, 1922 and now again in 1923 (and had been appealed to in 1921 even though no election had taken place in the southern provinces of the country). Election fatigue may have played a strong role in voters abstaining. Given that the two main parties contained many candidates that had run in previous elections, the reality was familiarity.

There were also reports of delayed or lost ballot papers, and spoiled votes. As the *Irish Independent* remarked, 'the only mistake of any consequence was that of declaring Monday [the day of the election] a postal holiday.' The result was the loss of votes by all parties, for example, in the Carlow-Kilkenny constituency over 300 soldiers' votes were delivered late and so were not included in the count. As this newspaper stated, 'since thousands of soldiers were compelled to entrust their ballot papers to the post office' many postal votes must have been lost or delayed. Similarly, some of the National University voters got caught out by delays in the delivery of postal packets.[52] It was also reported that 'over 1,000 votes in Donegal were discarded because the presiding officer failed to stamp the ballot papers'.[53]

In the 1923 General Election Sinn Féin took 27.4 per cent of all the votes cast and while this was largely in areas where there was still a strong IRA presence, it demonstrates the division that still existed in regions of Irish society. Cumann na nGaedheal received nearly 40 per cent of the votes, secured its highest ever share of first preferences for the decade between 1923 and 1933,[54] and returned all its ministers: Cosgrave again became president of the executive council, Richard Mulcahy, minister for defence, Kevin O'Higgins became vice president and minister for home affairs and Ernest Blythe, minister for finance.[55] As previously mentioned, Sinn Féin TDs abstained from taking their seats so no effective opposition existed. Abstention might have been the very reason why they lost out in this election. As Michael Laffan points out, Sinn Féin failed to appreciate that abstention from parliament had been a relatively successful tactic between 1917 and 1921 when it was employed against what was perceived to be an alien British government, but by 1923 with a native Irish administration it had limited appeal.[56] De Valera's establishment of Fianna Fáil in 1926 and Cumann na nGaedheal's electoral success until 1932 certainly lends to this conclusion.

As Mel Farrell points out, 'with more than a quarter of all voters backing a party that denied the authority of the Free State, Cumann na nGaedheal's battle for legitimacy was not yet won'.[57] Having gained electoral success, Cosgrave's party now had to face the task of nation-building to encourage support and confidence at home and abroad. The solution was conservatism through stability, financial restraint and managing the routine matters of state governance.

This Cumann na nGaedheal success had been dependent on the first held peaceful general election of the Irish Free State in 1923. The republican anti-treaty Sinn Féin party had embraced democracy once again but had been bitterly opposed to the pro-treaty Cumann na nGaedheal party. However, as Peter Mair points out, 'in almost no other country in Europe have two sides which were originally, and literally, at war with one another then gone on as fully legitimate parties to continue that contest at the electoral level within a very short space of time'.[58] The 1923 election results demonstrated support for the treaty and the Irish Free State but they also reflect a nuanced and complex political situation among the voting population as the analysis in this book has shown. De Valera soon realised that Sinn Féin's refusal to take the oath and enter Dáil Éireann left them out in the periphery of politics, and in 1926 he, along with talented republicans and their supporters, stepped away and formed the new party Fianna Fáil.[59] For the early decades, as Tom Garvin states, these highly disciplined organisations (Fianna Fáil and Cumann na nGaedheal (subsequently Fine Gael)) controlled the votes of substantial proportions of a newly enfranchised electorate, installed themselves in local councils, took over the Dáil and penetrated the legal and teaching professions, the post office and other public and private organisations.[60] The divide between Fianna Fáil and Fine Gael continued in Irish politics until the 2020 election when a new Sinn Féin, established in the 1970s, set out to challenge the political status quo.

Appendix 1

1923 Election Results by Constituency, based on First Preferences

Percentages based on Constituency Totals, including non-elected candidates

1923 Election Results by Constituency, based on First Preferences

Constituency	Register of Electors	Quota	Cumann na nGaedheal	Sinn Féin	Labour	Farmers	Independents	Other	Constituency Total	Absent Voters
Carlow-Kilkenny	62,937	6,694	19,047 (47.43%)	9,996 (24.89%)	4,783 (11.91%)	5,532 (13.77%)	803 (2.0%)	-	40,161	22,776
Cavan	55,100	6,654	9,567 (28.75%)	6,112 (18.37%)	3,749 (11.27%)	7,551 (22.70%)	6,286 (18.90%)	-	33,265	21,835
Clare	58,495	6,575	11,748 (29.78%)	18,691 (47.38%)	4,223 (10.71%)	4,783 (12.13%)	-	-	39,445	19,050
Cork Borough	66,700	7,102	19,657 (46.13%)	8,440 (19.81%)	5,281 (12.39%)	1,616 (3.79%)	1,029 (2.41%)	6,588 (15.46%)	42,611	24,089
Cork East	56,600	5,059	9,691 (31.93%)	7,131 (23.50%)	-	7,138 (23.52%)	6,391 (21.06%)	-	30,351	26,249
Cork North	37,100	5,121	2,792 (13.63%)	6,290 (30.71%)	3,716 (4.62%)	7,684 (37.52%)	-	-	20,482	16,618
Cork West	59,500	4,954	11,503 (38.70%)	6,218 (20.92%)	3,517 (11.83%)	5,007 (16.85%)	3,478 (11.70%)	-	29,723	29,777
Donegal	96,977	5,859	19,498 (36.98%)	13,067 (24.78%)	2,456 (4.66%)	7,727 (14.65%)	8,550 (16.21%)	1,432 (2.72%)	52,730	44,247
Dublin North	89,800	6,169	26,888 (48.43%)	9,801 (17.65%)	1,653 (2.98%)	-	11,936 (21.50%)	5,242 (9.44%)	55,520	34,280
Dublin South	78,072	5,771	25,478 (55.19%)	9,749 (21.12%)	933 (2.02%)	-	7,525 (16.30%)	2,477 (5.37%)	46,162	31,910
Dublin County	97,167	6,374	27,692 (48.28%)	7,785 (13.51%)	4,721 (8.23%)	2,206 (3.85%)	9,182 (16.01%)	5,777 (10.07%)	57,363	39,804
Dublin University		-	-	-	-	-	-	-	-	-
Galway	106,093	4,845	21,125 (43.61%)	16,225 (33.49%)	2,890 (5.97%)	4,187 (8.64%)	2,719 (5.61%)	1,296 (2.68%)	48,442	57,651
Kerry	90,156	6,856	17,808 (32.47%)	24,732 (45.09%)	4,303 (7.85%)	4,856 (8.85%)	3,146 (5.74%)	-	54,845	35,311

133

Constituency	Register of Electors	Quota	Cumann na nGaedheal	Sinn Féin	Labour	Farmers	Independents	Other	Constituency Total	Absent Voters
Kildare	35,620	4,674	5,056 (27.05%)	3,974 (21.26%)	6,012 (32.16%)	3,650 (19.53%)	–	–	18,692	16,928
Leitrim-Sligo	81,455	5,706	21,881 (47.94%)	16,479 (36.10%)	1,470 (3.22%)	5,081 (11.13%)	735 (1.61%)	–	45,646	35,809
Leix-Offaly	64,211	6,720	10,735 (26.63%)	11,020 (27.33%)	9,040 (22.42%)	5,471 (13.57%)	–	4,051 (10.05%)	40,317	23,894
Limerick	79,840	6,351	21,090 (41.51%)	13,374 (26.32%)	8,901 (17.52%)	5,955 (11.72%)	1,487 (2.93%)	–	50,807	29,033
Longford-Westmeath	58,884	5,811	9,309 (26.70%)	10,860 (31.15%)	2,875 (8.25%)	7,233 (20.75%)	4,452 (12.77%)	136 (0.39%)	34,865	24,019
Louth	38,548	6,127	11,461 (46.77%)	6,651 (27.14%)	2,517 (10.27%)	3,877 (15.82%)	–	–	24,506	14,042
Mayo North	53,719	5,249	14,107 (53.76%)	10,444 (39.80%)	647 (2.47%)	944 (3.60%)	99 (0.38%)	–	26,241	27,487
Mayo South	59,547	5,343	17,276 (53.90%)	11,376 (35.49%)	1,298 (4.05%)	929 (2.90%)	1,175 (3.67%)	–	32,054	27,493
Meath	38,000	5,805	9,895 (42.62%)	3,926 (16.91%)	5,240 (22.57%)	3,974 (17.12%)	183 (0.79%)	–	23,218	14,782
Monaghan	40,170	6,402	12,606 (40.23%)	5,745 (22.44%)	–	2,937 (11.47%)	4,319 (16.87%)	–	25,607	14,563
NUI	1,561	301	829 (69.96%)	237 (19.72%)	–	–	136 (11.31%)	–	1,202	359
Roscommon	51,891	6,240	12,987 (41.63%)	11,394 (36.52%)	1,545 (4.95%)	3,824 (12.26%)	1,447 (4.64%)	–	31,197	20,694
Tipperary	86,703	6,836	21,565 (39.43%)	16,102 (29.44%)	8,535 (15.61%)	6,793 (12.42%)	655 (1.20%)	1,037 (1.90%)	54,687	32,016
Waterford	46,304	6,512	4,794 (14.72%)	8,265 (25.38%)	5,896 (18.11%)	5,422 (16.65%)	8,182 (25.12%)	–	32,559	13,745

1923 Election Results by Constituency, based on First Preferences

Constituency	Register of Electors	Quota	Cumann na nGaedheal	Sinn Féin	Labour	Farmers	Independents	Other	Constituency Total	Absent Voters
Wexford	60,251	5,346	6,704 (17.61%)	10,308 (27.08%)	10,452 (27.45%)	9,152 (24.04%)	1,455 (3.82%)	–	38,071	22,180
Wicklow	36,753	5,725	7,932 (34.64%)	4,218 (18.42%)	5,280 (22.18%)	4,281 (18.70%)	–	1,188 (5.19%)	22,899	13,854
Total	1,788,154		410,721 (38.98%)	288,610 (27.39%)	111,942 (10.62%)	127,810 (12.13%)	85,370 (8.10%)	29,224 (2.77%)	1,053,668	734,486

Sources: Brian M. Walker, *Parliamentary Election Results in Ireland, 1918–92* (Dublin, 1992), pp 108–15; *Irish Independent*, 30 & 31 Aug. and 3 Sept. 1923; *Freeman's Journal*, 29 Aug. 1923; and *Cork Examiner*, 3 Sept., 1923.

APPENDIX 2:

1923 ELECTION RESULTS BY PROVINCE, BASED ON FIRST PREFERENCES

Percentages based on Constituency Totals

1923 Election Results by Province, based on First Preferences

LEINSTER

Constituency	Register of Electors	Quota	Cumann na nGaedheal	Sinn Féin	Labour	Farmers	Independents	Other	Constituency Total	Absent Voters
Carlow-Kilkenny (5)	62,937	5,694	19,047 (47.42%)	9,996 (24.89%)	4,783 (11.91%)	5,532 (13.77%)	803 (2.0%)	-	40,161 (63.81%)	22,776 (36.19%)
Dublin North (8)	89,800	5,169	26,888 (48.42%)	9,801 (17.65%)	1,653 (2.98%)	-	11,936 (21.50%)	5,242 (9.44%)	55,520 (61.83%)	34,280 (38.17%)
Dublin South (7)	78,072	5771	25,478 (55.19%)	9,749 (21.12%)	933 (2.02%)	-	7,525 (16.20%)	2,477 (5.37%)	46,162 (59.13%)	31,910 (40.87%)
Dublin County (8)	97,167	6,374	27,692 (48.28%)	7,785 (13.57%)	4,721 (8.23%)	2,206 (13.85%)	9,182 (16.01%)	5,777 (10.07%)	57,363 (59.04%)	39,804 (40.96%)
Kildare (3)	35,620	4,674	5,056 (27.05%)	3,974 (21.26%)	6,012 (32.16%)	3,650 (19.53%)	-	-	18,692 (52.48%)	16,928 (47.52%)
Leix-Offaly (5)	64,211	6,720	10,735 (26.63%)	11,020 (27.33%)	9,040 (22.42%)	5,471 (13.57%)	-	4,051 (10.05%)	40,317 (62.79%)	23,894 (37.21%)
Longford-Westmeath (5)	58,884	5,811	9,309 (26.70%)	10,860 (31.15%)	2,875 (8.25%)	7,233 (20.75%)	4,452 (12.77%)	136 (0.39%)	34,865 (59.21%)	24,019 (40.79%)
Louth (3)	38,548	6,127	11,461 (46.77%)	6,651 (27.14%)	2,517 (10.27%)	3,877 (15.82%)	-	-	24,506 (63.57%)	14,042 (36.56%)
Meath (3)	38,000	5,805	9,895 (42.62%)	3,926 (16.91%)	5,240 (22.57%)	3,974 (17.12%)	183 (0.79%)	-	23,218 (61.1%)	14,782 (38.9%)
Wexford (5)	60,251	6,346	6,704 (17.61%)	10,308 (27.08%)	10,452 (27.45%)	9,152 (24.04%)	1,455 (2.82%)	-	38,071 (63.19%)	22,180 (36.81%)
Wicklow (3)	36,753	5,725	7,932 (34.64%)	4,218 (18.42%)	5,280 (23.06%)	4,281 (18.70%)	-	1,188 (5.19%)	22,899 (62.31%)	13,854 (37.69%)
Total:	660,243		160,197 (39.87%)	88,288 (21.97%)	53,506 (13.32%)	45,376 (11.29%)	35,536 (8.84%)	18,871 (4.70%)	401,775 (60.85%)	258,469 (39.15%)

137

MUNSTER

Constituency	Register of Electors	Quota	Cumann na nGaedheal	Sinn Féin	Labour	Farmers	Independents	Other	Constituency Total	Absent Voters
Clare (5)	58,495	6,575	11,748 (29.78%)	18,691 (47.38%)	4,223 (10.71%)	4,783 (12.13%)	–	–	39,445 (67.43%)	19,050 (32.57%)
Cork Borough (5)	66,700	7,102	19,657 (46.13%)	8,440 (19.81%)	5,281 (12.39%)	1,616 (3.79%)	1,029 (2.41%)	6,588 (15.46%)	42,611 (63.88%)	24,089 (36.12%)
Cork East (5)	56,600	5,059	9,691 (31.93%)	7,131 (23.50%)	–	7,138 (23.52%)	6,391 (21.06%)	–	30,351 (53.62%)	26,349 (46.55%)
Cork North (3)	37,100	5,121	2,792 (13.63%)	6,290 (30.71%)	3,716 (18.14%)	7,684 (37.52%)	–	–	20,482 (55.21%)	16,618 (44.79%)
Cork West (5)	59,500	4,954	11,503 (38.70%)	6,218 (20.92%)	3,517 (11.83%)	5,007 (16.85%)	3,478 (11.70%)	–	29,723 (49.95%)	29,777 (50.05%)
Kerry (7)	90,156	6,856	17,808 (32.47%)	24,732 (45.09%)	4,303 (7.85%)	4,856 (8.85%)	3,146 (5.75%)	–	54,845 (60.83%)	35,311 (39.17%)
Limerick (7)	79,840	6,351	21,090 (41.51%)	13,374 (26.32%)	8,901 (17.52%)	5,955 (11.72%)	1,487 (2.93%)	–	50,807 (63.64%)	29,033 (36.36%)
Tipperary (7)	86,703	6,836	21,565 (39.43%)	16,102 (29.44%)	8,535 (15.61%)	6,793 (12.42%)	655 (1.20%)	1,037 (1.90%)	54,687 (63.07%)	32,016 (36.93%)
Waterford (4)	46,304	6,512	4,794 (14.72%)	8,265 (25.38%)	5,896 (18.11%)	5,422 (16.65%)	8,182 (25.13%)	–	32,559 (70.32%)	13,745 (29.68%)
Total:	581,398		120,648 (33.94%)	109,243 (30.73%)	44,372 (12.48%)	49,254 (13.85%)	24,368 (6.85%)	7,625 (2.14%)	355,510 (61.15%)	222,988 (38.35%)

1923 Election Results by Province, based on First Preferences

CONNACHT

Constituency	Register of Electors	Quota	Cumann na nGaedheal	Sinn Féin	Labour	Farmers	Independents	Other	Constituency Total	Absent Voters
Galway (9)	106,093	4,845	21,125 (43.60%)	16,225 (33.49%)	2,890 (5.97%)	4,187 (8.64%)	2,719 (5.61%)	1,296 (2.68%)	48,442 (45.66%)	57,651 (54.34%)
Leitrim-Sligo (7)	81,455	5,706	21,881 (47.94%)	16,479 (36.10%)	1,470 (3.22%)	5,081 (11.13%)	735 (1.61%)	–	45,646 (56.04%)	35,809 (43.96%)
Mayo North (4)	53,719	5,249	14,107 (53.76%)	10,444 (39.80%)	647 (2.47%)	944 (3.60%)	99 (0.38%)	–	26,241 (48.85%)	27,487 (51.17%)
Mayo South (5)	59,547	5,343	17,276 (53.90%)	11,376 (35.49%)	1,298 (4.05%)	929 (2.90%)	1,175 (3.67%)	–	32,054 (53.83%)	27,493 (46.17%)
Roscommon (4)	51,891	6,240	12,987 (41.63%)	11,394 (36.52%)	1,545 (4.95%)	3,824 (12.26%)	1,447 (4.64%)	–	31,197 (60.12%)	20,694 (39.88%)
Total:	352,705		87,376 (47.60%)	65,918 (35.91%)	7,850 (4.28%)	14,965 (8.15%)	6,175 (3.36%)	1,296 (0.70%)	183,580 (52.05%)	169,134 (47.95%)

ULSTER (IN IRISH FREE STATE)

Constituency	Register of Electors	Quota	Cumann na nGaedheal	Sinn Féin	Labour	Farmers	Independents	Other	Constituency Total	Absent Voters
Cavan (4)	55,100	6,654	9,567 (28.76%)	6,112 (18.37%)	3,749 (11.27%)	7,551 (22.70%)	6,286 (18.90%)	-	33,265 (60.37%)	21,835 (39.63%)
Donegal (8)	96,977	5,859	19,498 (36.98%)	13,067 (24.78%)	2,456 (4.66%)	7,727 (14.65%)	8,550 (16.21%)	1,432 (2.72%)	52,730 (54.37%)	44,247 (45.63%)
Monaghan (3)	40,170	6,402	12,606 (49.23%)	5,745 (22.44%)	-	2,937 (11.47%)	4,319 (16.87%)	-	25,607 (63.75%)	14,563 (36.25%)
Total:	192,247		41,671 (37.84%)	24,924 (22.33%)	6,205 (5.56%)	18,215 (16.32%)	19,155 (17.16%)	1,432 (1.28%)	111,602 (58.05%)	80,645 (41.94%)

Sources: Brian M. Walker, *Parliamentary Election Results in Ireland, 1918–92* (Dublin, 1992), pp 108–15; *Irish Independent*, 30 & 31 Aug., and 3 Sept., 1923, and a number of provincial newspapers.

Appendix 3

1923 Election Results by Constituency, based on First Preferences (Elected candidates only)

Percentages based on Constituency Totals

Constituency	Register of Electors	Quota	Cumann na nGaedheal	Sinn Féin	Labour	Farmers	Independents	Other	Constituency Total (Elected candidates only)	Total Constituency (including non-elected)
Carlow-Kilkenny (5)	62,937	6,694	18,324 (56.46%)	5,641 (17.38%)	4,783 (14.74%)	3,702 (11.41%)	-	-	32,450	40,161
Cavan (4)	55,100	6,654	5,109 (22.25%)	6,112 (28.80%)	-	6,264 (27.28%)	5,476 (23.85%)	-	22,961	33,265
Clare (5)	58,495	6,575	8,196 (27.26%)	17,876 (59.45%)	2,083 (6.93%)	1,914 (6.37%)	-	-	30,069	39,445
Cork Borough (5)	66,700	7,102	19,657 (60.76%)	6,109 (18.88%)	-	-	-	6,588 (20.36%)	32,354	42,611
Cork East (5)	56,600	5,059	8,175 (34.04%)	5,524 (23.00%)	-	3,927 (16.35%)	6,391 (26.61%)	-	24,017	30,351
Cork North (3)	37,100	5,121	-	6,290 (43.97%)	3,716 (25.98%)	4,299 (30.05%)	-	-	14,305	20,482
Cork West (5)	59,500	4,954	7,687 (45.45%)	3,237 (19.14%)	3,517 (20.79%)	2,473 (14.62%)	-	-	16,914	29,723
Donegal (8)	96,977	5,859	18,009 (50.77%)	6,834 (19.27%)	-	3,673 (10.36%)	6,954 (19.61%)	-	35,470	52,730
Dublin North (8)	89,800	6,169	25,639 (53.88%)	8,835 (18.57%)	-	-	10,518 (22.10%)	2,594 (5.45%)	47,586	55,520
Dublin South (7)	78,072	5,771	24,763 (69.76%)	7,725 (21.76%)	-	-	3,010 (8.48%)	-	35,498	46,162
Dublin County (8)	97,167	6,374	26,422 (60.48%)	3,064 (7.01%)	3,911 (8.95%)	-	7,051 (16.14%)	3,238 (7.41%)	43,686	57,363
Dublin University (3)	-	-	-	-	-	-	(3)	-	-	-

142

1923 Election Results by Constituency, based on First Preferences (Elected candidates only)

Constituency	Register of Electors	Quota	Cumann na nGaedheal	Sinn Féin	Labour	Farmers	Independents	Other	Constituency Total (Elected candidates only)	Total Constituency (including non-elected)
Galway (9)	106,093	4,845	17,712 (49.60%)	14,214 (39.80%)	1,862 (5.21%)	–	1,922 (5.38%)	–	35,710	48,442
Kerry (7)	90,156	6,856	16,500 (40.02%)	24,732 (59.98%)	–	–	–	–	41,232	54,845
Kildare (3)	35,620	4,674	2,186 (21.57%)	–	4,300 (42.42%)	3,650 (36.01%)	–	–	10,136	18,692
Leitrim-Sligo (7)	81,445	5,706	20,579 (59.57%)	13,967 (40.43%)	–	–	–	–	34,546	45,646
Leix-Offaly (5)	64,211	6,720	9,319 (35.89%)	10,323 (39.76%)	6,323 (24.35%)	–	–	–	25,965	40,317
Limerick (7)	78,840	6,351	18,309 (53.99%)	10,758 (31.73%)	3,305 (9.75%)	1,537 (4.53%)	–	–	33,909	50,807
Longford-Westmeath (5)	58,884	5,811	5,147 (24.59%)	8,056 (38.49%)	–	3,274 (15.64%)	4,452 (21.27%)	–	20,929	34,865
Louth (3)	38,548	6,127	11,461 (63.28%)	6,651 (36.72%)	–	–	–	–	18,112	24,506
Mayo North (4)	53,719	5,249	11,008 (52.83%)	9,829 (47.17%)	–	–	–	–	20,837	26,241
Mayo South (5)	59,547	5,343	14,797 (61.59%)	9,228 (38.41%)	–	–	–	–	24,025	32,054
Meath (3)	38,000	5,805	8,262 (53.22%)	–	3,288 (21.18%)	3,974 (25.60%)	–	–	15,524	23,218
Monaghan (3)	40,170	6,402	12,903 (69.19%)	5,745 (30.81%)	–	–	–	–	18,648	25,607

143

Constituency	Register of Electors	Quota	Cumann na nGaedheal	Sinn Féin	Labour	Farmers	Independents	Other	Constituency Total (Elected candidates only)	Total Constituency (including non-elected)
NUI (3)	1,561	301	829	–	–	–	–	–	829	1,202
Roscommon (4)	51,891	6,240	8,828 (48.56%)	9,350 (51.44%)	–	–	–	–	18,178	31,197
Tipperary (7)	86,703	6,836	17,345 (42.73%)	14,533 (35.81%)	5,580 (13.75%)	3,130 (7.71%)	–	–	40,588	54,687
Waterford (4)	46,304	6,512	–	8,265 (40.14%)	2,710 (13.18%)	3,142 (15.28%)	6,441 (31.33%)	–	20,558	32,559
Wexford (5)	60,251	6,346	5,434 (17.72%)	10,308 (33.62%)	7,744 (25.26%)	7,176 (23.40%)	–	–	30,662	38,071
Wicklow (3)	36,753	5,725	7,932 (47.60%)	–	4,450 (26.71%)	4,281 (25.69%)	–	–	16,663	22,899
TOTALS:			350,532 (45.98%)	233,206 (30.59%)	57,572 (7.55%)	56,416 (7.40%)	52,218 (6.85%)	12,420 (1.63%)	762,364	1,053,668

Sources: Brian M. Walker, *Parliamentary Election Results in Ireland, 1918–92* (Dublin, 1992), pp 108–15; *Irish Independent*, 30 & 31 Aug. and 3 Sept. 1923; *Freeman's Journal*, 29 Aug. 1923; and *Cork Examiner*, 3 Sept. 1923

Notes

CHAPTER 1: INTRODUCTION

1. Michael Hopkinson, *Green against Green: The Irish Civil War* (Dublin, 2004 edn), p. 257.
2. Diarmaid Ferriter, *Between Two Hells: The Irish Civil War* (London, 2021), p. 147.
3. Mel Farrell, *Party Politics in a New Democracy: The Irish Free State, 1922–37* (Basingstoke, 2017), pp 75–79; Michael Laffan, *The Resurrection of Ireland: The Sinn Féin Party, 1916–1923* (Cambridge, 1999), pp 422–8; Éamon de Valera to organising committee, 6 June 1923, National Archives of Ireland (NAI), Cumann na Poblachta and Sinn Féin, 1094/1/13.
4. The first anniversary of Collins's death received considerable newspaper attention. See *Irish Independent (II)*, 13 Aug. 1923, 20 Aug. 22 Aug; *Meath Chronicle* 18 Aug. 1923; *Irish Times (IT)*, 18 Aug. 1923.
5. *II*, 30 July 1923.
6. Cosgrave was sentenced to death after the Easter Rising and, like his arch rival Éamon de Valera, had his sentence commuted to imprisonment. Curiously, this never became part of his political identity in the way that it did for de Valera. See Michael Laffan, *Judging W.T. Cosgrave* (Dublin, 2014) p. 106.
7. For example, Dáil Debates, vol. 4, no. 12, 18 July 1923 (Cosgrave), available at: https://www.oireachtas.ie/en/debates/debate/dail/1923-07-18/2/?highlight%5B0%5D=figgis&highlight%5B1%5D=election&highlight%5B2%5D=election
8. *II*, 20 July 1923.
9. Dáil Debates, vol. 4, no. 26, 9 Aug. 1923 (Johnson), available at: https://www.oireachtas.ie/en/debates/debate/dail/1923-08-09/3/
10. David McCullagh, *De Valera Vol. 1 Rise, 1882–1932* (Dublin, 2017), p. 327; Bill Kissane, *Explaining Irish Democracy* (Dublin, 2002), p. 156, p. 170.
11. See Breen Murphy, 'The Government's executions policy during the Irish Civil War', (PhD thesis, National University of Ireland Maynooth, 2010), p.11.
12. Terence Dooley, *The Land for the People: The Land Question in Independent Ireland* (Dublin, 2004).
13. *The Economist*, 2 June 1923; C. J. France to Ernest Blythe, 16 Nov. 1923, UCDA, Ernest Blythe papers, P24/359/13.
14. See Donal P. Corcoran, *The Freedom to Achieve Freedom: The Irish Free State, 1922–32* (Dublin, 2013), pp 141–5; *The Economist*, 28 July 1923.
15. David Fitzpatrick, *Politics and Irish Life, 1913–1921: Provincial Experience of War and Revolution* (Dublin, 1977), p. 72.
16. Martin O'Donoghue, *The Legacy of the Irish Parliamentary Party in Independent Ireland 1922–1949* (Liverpool, 2019), pp 8–9.
17. Alvin Jackson, *Ireland, 1798–1998: War, Peace and Beyond* (Oxford, 2010 edn), p. 332.
18. In June 1922, each wing of Sinn Féin put forward candidates in proportion to their existing Dáil strength. See Ciara Meehan, *The Cosgrave Party: A History of Cumann na nGaedheal, 1923–33* (Dublin, 2010), p. 6.
19. See Mark Mazower, *Dark Continent: Europe's Twentieth Century* (London, 1999 edn) pp 81–2; Philip Morgan, 'The First World War and the challenge of democracy in Europe', in Menno Spiering and Michael J. Wintle (eds), *Ideas of Europe Since 1914: The Legacy of the First World War* (New York, 2002), pp 82–7. See, also, Birgitta Bader-Zaar, 'Controversy: War-related Changes in Gender Relations: The Issue of Women's Citizenship', 1914–1918-online. *International Encyclopedia of the First World War*, ed. by Ute Daniel, Peter Gatrell, Oliver Janz, Heather Jones, Jennifer Keene, Alan Kramer, and Bill Nasson, issued by Freie Universität Berlin, Berlin 2014-10-08. I am grateful to Dr Gearóid Barry for providing this link.
20. Proclamation of Independence: https://www.gov.ie/en/publication/bfa965-proclamation-of-independence/ (accessed 2 June 2023).
21. Electoral Act, 1923, electronic Irish Statute Book: https://www.irishstatutebook.ie/eli/1923/act/12/section/1/enacted/en/html#sec1 (accessed 9 Dec. 2022).

22. *Freeman's Journal (FJ)*, 4 July 1923.
23. Ibid., 8 Aug. 1923.
24. The Prevention of Electoral Abuses Act, 1923, electronic Irish Statute Book: https://www.irishstatutebook.ie/eli/1923/act/38/enacted/en/print#sec26 (accessed 9 Dec. 2022).
25. £100 is worth approximately €3,388 today.
26. *FJ*, 24 Aug. 1923.
27. Linda Connolly (ed.), *Women and the Irish Revolution: Feminism, Activism, Violence* (Newbridge, 2020); Anne Dolan and William Murphy, *Michael Collins: The Man and The Revolution* (Cork, 2018); Gavin Foster, *The Irish Civil War and Society: Politics, Class and Conflict* (London, 2015); Brian Hughes and Conor Morrissey (eds), *Southern Irish Loyalism, 1912–1949* (Liverpool, 2020); Daithí Ó Corráin and Gerard Hanley, *Cathal Brugha: 'An Indomitable Spirit'* (Dublin, 2022); Martin O'Donoghue, *The Legacy of the Irish Parliamentary Party*, pp 25–8 and p. 68; Mícheál Ó Fathartaigh and Liam Weeks (eds), *The Treaty: Debating and Establishing the Irish State* (Newbridge, 2018); Mícheál Ó Fathartaigh and Liam Weeks (eds), *Birth of a State: The Anglo-Irish Treaty* (Newbridge, 2021); Margaret Ward, *Unmanageable Revolutionaries: Women and Irish Nationalism, 1880–1980* (Galway, 2022 edn).
28. Corcoran, *The Freedom to Achieve Freedom*; Mel Farrell, Jason Knirck and Ciara Meehan (eds), *A Formative Decade: Ireland in the 1920s* (Sallins, 2015); Jason Knirck, *Afterimage of the Revolution: Cumann na nGaedheal and Irish Politics, 1922–1932* (Madison, 2014); Kevin Hora, *Propaganda and Nation Building: Selling the Irish Free State* (London and New York, 2017).
29. Joseph M. Curran, *The Birth of the Irish Free State* (Tuscaloosa, 1980); Tom Garvin, *1922: The Birth of Irish Democracy* (Dublin, 2005 edn).
30. Bill Kissane, *The Politics of the Irish Civil War* (Oxford, 2007); John M. Regan, *The Irish Counter-Revolution, 1921–1936: Treatyite Politics and Settlement in Independent Ireland* (Dublin, 2001 edn); John M. Regan, 'Southern Irish nationalism as a historical problem', in *The Historical Journal*, vol. 50, no. 1 (2007) p. 213.
31. Terence Brown, *Ireland: A Social and Cultural History, 1922 to the Present* (Ithaca, 1985); Mary Kotsonouris, *Retreat from Revolution: the Dáil Courts, 1920—24* (Dublin, 1994).
32. Elaine Callinan, *Electioneering and Propaganda in Ireland, 1917–21: Votes, Violence and Victory* (Dublin, 2020).
33. Kissane, *Politics of the Irish Civil War*, p. 90.

CHAPTER 2: 'SAFETY FIRST': CUMANN NA NGAEDHEAL'S ELECTION CAMPAIGN IN AUGUST 1923

1. *Irish Times (IT)*, 27 Aug. 1923.
2. John M. Regan, *The Irish Counter-Revolution, 1921–1936: Treatyite Politics and settlement in independent Ireland* (Dublin, 2001 edn.), p. 143.
3. General and Election Committee, minutes of meeting, 29 Aug. 1922, University College Dublin Archives Department (UCDA), Cumann na nGaedheal papers, P39/min/1.
4. General and Election Committee, minutes of special meeting, 7 Sept. 1922 ibid.
5. See Donal P. Corcoran, *The Freedom to Achieve Freedom: The Irish Free State, 1922–32* (Dublin, 2013), pp 141–5; *The Economist*, 28 July 1923.
6. Quoted in Terence Dooley, *Burning the Big House: The Story of the Irish Country House in a Time of War and Revolution* (London, 2022), p. 245.
7. Jason Knirck, *Afterimage of the Revolution: Cumann na nGaedheal and Irish Politics, 1922–1932* (Madison, 2014), p. 45, p. 51.
8. David Fitzpatrick, *The Two Irelands, 1912–1939* (Oxford, 1998), p. 187.
9. Ferriter, *Between two Hells*, p. 147; Liam de Róiste diary entry, 8 Aug. 1923, Cork City and County Archives (CCCA), Liam de Róiste papers, U271/A/49.
10. The party organisation peaked at 800 branches in 1926. See Meehan, *Cosgrave Party*, pp 4–9; Farrell, *Party Politics in a New Democracy*; Ó Fathartaigh and Weeks (eds) *Birth of a State*, p. 66.
11. Fitzpatrick, *The Two Irelands, 1912–39*, p. 187.
12. Dooley, *The Land for the People*, p. 50.
13. Ferriter, *Transformation*, p. 302; Laffan, *Resurrection*, p. 400.
14. Regan, *Counter-Revolution*, p. 150; Laffan, *Judging W. T. Cosgrave*, pp 166–7; Hopkinson, *Green against Green*, p. 262.

15. Meehan, *Cosgrave Party*, pp 10–13.
16. Regan, *Counter-Revolution*, p. 148; Provisional General Council, minutes of meeting, 2 Feb. 1923, UCDA, Cumann na nGaedheal papers, P39/min/1.
17. In 1931 Captain William Redmond joined Cumann na nGaedheal. See Pat McCarthy, *The Redmonds and Waterford: A Political Dynasty 1891–1952* (Dublin, 2018); Séamus Dolan circular, 3 May 1923, CCCA, Barry Egan papers, U404/2; Provisional General Council, minutes of meeting, 16 Mar. 1923, UCDA, Cumann na nGaedheal papers, P39/min/1.
18. Pat McCarthy, *Waterford: The Irish Revolution, 1912–23* (Dublin, 2015), p. 121.
19. General and Election Committee, minutes of meeting, 5 Jan. 1923 UCDA, Cumann na nGaedheal papers P39/min/1.
20. Chief Organiser Reports, 22 June, 6 July and 13 July 1923, ibid.
21. Instructions to organisers, 21 June 1923, ibid.
22. Meehan, *Cosgrave Party*, p. 26.
23. See Farrell, *Party Politics*, pp 84–5.
24. Coyle was elected, taking the third seat in the constituency. *Western People*, 21 July 1923; See Gerry Coyle, *Henry Coyle: A Forgotten Freedom Fighter* (Ballina, 2022), pp 202–08.
25. Standing Committee, minutes of meeting, 29 June 1923, UCDA, Cumann na nGaedheal papers, P39/min/1.
26. *Southern Star*, 23 June 1923.
27. *Westmeath Examiner (WE)*, 11 Aug. 1923.
28. *Freeman's Journal (FJ)*, 21 July 1923.
29. Chief Organiser's report, 29 June 1923, UCDA, Cumann na nGaedheal papers, P39/min/1.
30. Chief Organiser's report, 6 July 1923, ibid.
31. National Executive, minutes of meeting, 9 July 1923, ibid.
32. Standing Committee, minutes of meeting, 20 July 1923, ibid; £643 is worth approximately, €21,785 today.
33. National Executive, minutes of meeting, 9 July 1923, ibid.
34. *FJ*, 14 July 1923.
35. At its peak Sinn Féin could boast 1,500, a similar number to the United Irish League prior to 1914. See, Peter Pyne, 'The Third Sinn Féin Party: 1923–1926', part one, *Economic and Social Review*, Vol. 1, No. 1 (Oct. 1969), p. 32; National Library of Ireland (NLI) United Irish League, minute book of the National Directory, MS, 700.
36. Chief Organiser's report, 20 July 1923, UCDA, Cumann na nGaedheal papers, P39/min/1.
37. Chief Organiser's report, 26 July 1923, ibid.
38. *FJ*, 25 July 1923.
39. National Executive, minutes of meeting, 9 July 1923, UCDA, Cumann na nGaedheal papers, P39/min/1.
40. *Irish Independent (II)*, 20 July 1923
41. Standing Committee, minutes of meeting, 20 July 1923, UCDA, Cumann na nGaedheal papers, P39/min/1.
42. Standing Committee, minutes of meeting, 26 July 1923, ibid.
43. Provisional General Council, minutes of meeting, 16 Mar. 1923, ibid.
44. *Clare Champion (CC)*, 28 July 1923.
45. Mel Farrell, 'Cumann na nGaedheal: A new "National Party"?', in Farrell et al, *A Formative Decade*, pp 44–5.
46. Callinan, *Electioneering and Propaganda in Ireland, 1917-21*, p. 137.
47. *CC*, 4 Aug. 1923.
48. *FJ*, 1 Aug. 1923.
49. Ibid.
50. *Cork Examiner (CE)*, 6 Aug. 1923.
51. *The Liberator*, 7 Aug. 1923.
52. Newspaper reports mention that slates were ripped from houses, trees were uprooted and there were 'vivid flashes of lightning'. Two teenage lives were tragically lost in separate incidents. *CE*, 7 Aug. 1923; *Nationalist and Leinster Times*, 11 Aug. 1923.
53. *FJ*, 30 July 1923.

54. Standing Committee, minutes of meeting, 20 July 1923, UCDA, Cumann na nGaedheal papers, P39/min/1; *Dublin Evening Mail (DEM)*, 21 July 1923.
55. Standing Committee, minutes of meeting, 3 Aug. 1923, UCDA, Cumann na nGaedheal papers, P39/min/1; *FJ*, 4 Aug. 1923.
56. Liam de Róiste diary entry, 4 Aug. 1923, CCCA, Liam de Róiste papers, U271/A/49.
57. Liam de Róiste diary entry, 25 May 1923, ibid; Aodh Quinlivan, *Dissolved: The Remarkable Story of How Cork Lost its Corporation in 1924* (Cork, 2017), p. 15, p. 31.
58. See Claire McGing's chapter titled '"Without distinction of sex"', pp 87–98; Standing Committee, minutes of meeting, 17 Aug. 1923, UCDA, Cumann na nGaedheal papers, P39/min/1; Laffan, *Judging W.T. Cosgrave*, p. 166.
59. *FJ*, 18 Aug. 1923.
60. Ibid., 20 Aug. 1923.
61. Regan, *Counter-Revolution*, p. 146.
62. Dooley, *The Land for the People*, p. 55.
63. *FJ*, 15 Aug. 1923.
64. *CC*, 11 Aug.; 18 Aug. 1923.
65. *IT*, 16 Aug. 1923; *DEM*, 22 Aug. 1923.
66. Callinan, *Electioneering and Propaganda*, p. 137; *Nationalist and Leinster Times*, 18 Aug. 1923.
67. Warner Moss, *Political Parties in the Irish Free State* (New York, 1933), p. 8.
68. Two days before polling an editorial in the *Westmeath Independent* described Cumann na nGaedheal as 'the only choice' concluding that '"Cosgrave's men" are the men to vote for'. *Westmeath Independent*, 25 Aug. 1923.
69. This mention of Collins prompted an attendee to shout, 'He died by the hand of a traitor', *II*, 13 Aug. 1923.
70. Laffan, *Judging W.T. Cosgrave*, p. 166.
71. *II*, 14 Aug. 1923.
72. Ibid., 13 Aug. 1923.
73. *IT*, 30 July 1923.
74. Ibid., 20. Aug. 1923.
75. *WE*, 25 Aug.1923.
76. *LL*, 25 Aug. 1923.
77. Timothy M. O'Neill, 'Reframing the Republic: Republican socio-economic thought and the road to Fianna Fáil, 1923–26', in Farrell et al., *A Formative Decade*, pp 159–60.
78. *IT*, 22 Aug. 1922.
79. *FJ*, 4 Aug. 1923.
80. Cumann na nGaedheal saw itself as a centre party. Its newspaper, *The Freeman*, boasting 'challenged from the right; challenged from the left; we will keep to the middle of the road', *The Freeman*, 11 Aug. 1927.
81. Sinnott, *Irish Voters Decide: Voting Behaviour in Elections and Referendums since 1918* (Manchester, 1995), p. 98.
82. Quoted in Regan, *Counter-Revolution*, p. 152.
83. O'Donoghue, *The Legacy of the Irish Parliamentary Party in Independent Ireland*, p. 25.
84. *IT*, 6 Aug. 1923.
85. Ibid., 22 Aug. 1923.
86. Lawler was selected for the June 1922 election but had to stand aside under the Collins/de Valera Pact. His efforts in the 'National movement' were also prominent. However, he was not elected in August 1923. *Leinster Leader*, 11 Aug. 1923.
87. *II* 23 Aug. 1923; *IT*, 18 Aug. 1923; Callinan, *Electioneering and Propaganda*, p. 33.
88. *IT*, 6 Aug. 1923.
89. Ibid., 20 Aug. 1923.
90. Ibid.
91. Meehan, *Cosgrave Party*, p. 28.
92. *CC*, 25 Aug. 1923.
93. *CE*, 20 Aug. 1923.
94. Laffan, *Judging W.T. Cosgrave*, p. 166.
95. *FJ*, 20 Aug. 1923; *II*, 20 Aug. 1923; *CE* 21 Aug. 1923.

96. Standing Committee, minutes of meeting, 17 Aug. 1923, UCDA, Cumann na nGaedheal papers, P39/min/1.
97. Meehan, *Cosgrave Party*, p. 27.
98. See 'Introduction' by Mel Farrell and Claire McGing's chapter titled '"Without distinction of sex"' in this volume, pp 1–10, pp 87–98.
99. *FJ*, 23 Aug. 1923.
100. Ibid., 27 Aug. 1923.
101. *CE*, 27 Aug. 1923.
102. *Kilkenny People*, 25 Aug. 1923.
103. Brian M. Walker, *Parliamentary Election Results in Ireland, 1918–92* (Dublin,1992) p. 112.
104. Material from the 1929 by-election, UCDA, Seán Mac Eoin papers, P151/598/838; *Longford Leader*, 30 Jan. 1932.
105. Mel Farrell, '"The tide had definitely turned": The Irish Party, Sinn Féin and the Election Campaigns in Longford, 1917–18', in *New Hibernia Review*, Vol. 21, No. 3 (autumn, 2017), p. 104.
106. £630 is worth approximately €21,345 today.
107. Séamus Hughes to Eoin MacNeill, 28 Apr. 1924, UCDA, Eoin MacNeill papers, LA1/H/64/17; Harry Guinane to Seán Mac Giolla Fhaolain, 3 Nov. 1925, ibid., LA1/H/66/29); McCullagh, *De Valera Vol. 1 Rise*, p. 330.
108. See Ó Corráin and Hanley, *Cathal Brugha: 'An Indomitable Spirit'*, p. 166.
109. Regan, *Counter-Revolution*, p. 149; £4,673 is worth approximately €150,000 today.
110. Standing Committee, minutes of meeting, 31 Aug. 1923, UCDA, Cumann na nGaedheal party minute books, P39/min/1.
111. National Executive, minutes of meeting, 18 Sept. 1923, ibid.
112. *II*, 24 Apr., 9 June, 13 June 1923.
113. Standing Committee, minutes of meeting, 12 Oct. 1923, UCDA, Cumann na nGaedheal party minute books, P39/min/1; £52 is worth approximately €1,760 today.
114. £150 is worth approximately €5,000 today.
115. £200,000 is worth approximately €6,800,000 today.
116. *The Economist*, 8 Sept. 1923; Corcoran, *The Freedom to Achieve Freedom*, p. 145.
117. Farrell, *Party Politics*, p. 88; Laffan, *Judging W.T. Cosgrave*, p. 167; Regan, *Counter-Revolution*, p. 148.
118. Sinnott, *Irish Voters Decide*, p. 98.

Chapter 3: 'Nothing but a bullet will stop me': Éamon de Valera and the 1923 General Election

1. Kathleen Clarke, *Revolutionary Woman: An Autobiography*, Helen Litton (ed.) (Dublin, 1991), p. 194.
2. *Irish Independent*, 18 Mar. 1922.
3. Éamon de Valera to Charles Murphy, 13 Aug. 1922, quoted in Michael Laffan, *The Resurrection of Ireland: The Sinn Fein Party 1916–1923* (Cambridge, 2005), p. 375.
4. Quoted in David Fitzpatrick, *Harry Boland's Irish Revolution* (Cork, 2003), p. 301.
5. Richard Mulcahy note on conversation with Commandant Vincent Byrne, 7 Jan. 1964, University College Dublin Archives Department (UCDA), Richard Mulcahy Papers, P7/3.
6. Éamon de Valera to Miss Ellis, 26 Feb. 1923, ibid., Máire Comerford Papers, LA18/45.
7. Executive Meeting minutes, 17 Oct. 1922, ibid., Moss Twomey Papers, P69/179 (6):
8. Republican members of Standing Committee to de Valera, 25 Oct. 1922, ibid., Éamon de Valera Papers, P150/580:
9. Éamon de Valera to Éamon Donnelly, 25 Oct. 1922, ibid.
10. Éamon de Valera to Éamon Donnelly, 31 Oct. 1922, ibid.
11. Éamon de Valera to Constance Markievicz, 22 Oct. 1922, ibid.; Éamon de Valera to Éamon Donnelly, 25 Oct. 1922, ibid.
12. Éamon de Valera to Mary MacSwiney, 6 Feb. 1923, ibid., P150/657.
13. Report of meeting of Officer Board, 6 Nov. 1922, ibid., P150/580.
14. Bureau of Military History, Witness Statement 1050, Vera McDonnell.
15. Éamon de Valera to P. J. Ruttledge, 16 Nov. 1922, UCDA, Éamon de Valera Papers, P150/1710.

16. Éamon de Valera to P. J. Ruttledge, 11 Apr. 1923, ibid., P150/1710.
17. Éamon de Valera to P. J. Ruttledge, 3 Dec. 1922, ibid.
18. P. J. Ruttledge to President and all ministers, 1st report on Sinn Féin reorganisation, 23 Jan. 1923, ibid., P150/582.
19. Éamon de Valera to P. J. Ruttledge, 6 Jan. 1923, ibid., P150/1710.
20. Count Plunkett to Éamon de Valera, 20 Jan. 1923, ibid., P150/1652.
21. Éamon de Valera to P. J. Ruttledge, 15 Jan. 1923, ibid., quoted in Kissane, Bill, *Explaining Irish Democracy* (Dublin, 2002), p. 169.
22. Éamon de Valera to Mary MacSwiney, 14 Mar. 1923, UCDA, Éamon de Valera Papers, P150/657.
23. Éamon de Valera to Msgr O'Connor, 20 June 1923, ibid., P150/1280.
24. $100,000 is the equivalent of approximately €1.6 million today.
25. Éamon de Valera to Luke Dillon, and to Joseph McGarrity, 6 July 1923, ibid., P150/1191.
26. Éamon de Valera to Cathal Brugha, 6 July 1922, ibid., Mary MacSwiney Papers, P48a/255 (1).
27. Éamon de Valera to Constance Markievicz, 11 July 1923, ibid., Éamon de Valera Papers, P150/1814.
28. Éamon de Valera to P. J. Ruttledge, 26 July 1923, ibid., P150/1710.
29. Éamon de Valera circular letter, 10 Aug. 1923, ibid., P150/184.
30. Éamon de Valera to Frank Aiken, 9 July 1923, ibid., P150/1752.
31. Éamon de Valera to P. J. Ruttledge, 26 July 1923, ibid., P150/1710.
32. C. S. Andrews, *Dublin Made Me* (Dublin, 2001), p. 329.
33. Frank Gallagher diary, 23 Feb. 1923, UCDA, Éamon de Valera Papers, P150/3263.
34. Éamon de Valera to Mary MacSwiney, 6 June 1923, ibid., P150/657
35. Frank Aiken to Éamon de Valera, with de Valera note in margin, 26 June 1923, ibid., P150/1752.
36. Éamon de Valera to Molly Childers, 31 July 1923, ibid., P150/1794.
37. Éamon de Valera to Connolly, 26 Dec. 1922, ibid., P150/1818.
38. Anthony J. Gaughan (ed.), *Memoirs of Senator Joseph Connolly (1885–1961): A Founder of Modern Ireland* (Dublin, 1996), p. 249.
39. Éamon de Valera to A. L., 16 May 1923, UCDA, Éamon de Valera Papers, P150/1825.
40. Peter Pyne, 'The Third Sinn Féin Party: 1923–1926', part one, *Economic and Social Review*, Vol. 1, No. 1 (Oct. 1969), p. 32.
41. Éamon de Valera to Eamon Donnelly, 22 May 1923, quoted in Kissane, *Explaining Irish Democracy*, p. 169.
42. Éamon de Valera to Molly Childers, 31 May 1923, UCDA, Éamon de Valera, P150/1794.
43. A. L. to Éamon de Valera, 26 May 1922, ibid., P150/1825.
44. Ibid.
45. A. L. to de Valera, 30 May 1923, ibid.
46. Comyn to de Valera, 30 May 1923, ibid., P150/1713.
47. Éamon de Valera to organising committee, 31 May 1923, ibid., P150/1818.
48. Comyn to Éamon de Valera, 2 June 1923, ibid., P150/1713.
49. Lynn to de Valera, 6 June 1923, ibid., P150/1828.
50. Éamon de Valera to Hagan, 23 June 1923, ibid., P150/1809.
51. Éamon de Valera to Organising Committee, 6 June 1923, ibid., P150/1710.
52. Judgement by Kingsmill Moore, 26 Oct. 1948, ibid., P150/595.
53. Connolly to de Valera, 10 July 1923, ibid., P150/1818.
54. Éamon de Valera to Connolly, 11 July 1923, ibid.
55. IRA Executive minutes, 11–12 July 1923, ibid., Moss Twomey Papers, P69/179(65).
56. Éamon de Valera to all camps and prisons, 18 July 1923, ibid., Desmond FitzGerald Papers, P80/800.
57. Éamon de Valera memorandum to unidentified recipient, 8 June 1923, ibid. Éamon de Valera Papers, P150/1807.
58. Éamon de Valera to Ruttledge, 21 June 1923, ibid., P150/1710
59. Éamon de Valera to organising committee, 25 July 1923, ibid., P150/1818.
60. Connolly to de Valera, 26 July 1923, ibid.
61. Éamon de Valera to Donnelly, 14 Aug. 1923, Ibid., Desmond FitzGerald Papers, P80/802.
62. Clare Constituency progress report to Director of Elections, 10 Aug. 1923, ibid., Éamon de Valera Papers, P150/1792.
63. Éamon de Valera, election address, 24 July 1923, ibid., P150/1835.

64. Éamon de Valera to Ruttledge, 24 July 1923, ibid., P150/1710.
65. Éamon de Valera to Molly Childers, 31 July 1923, ibid., P150/1794.
66. Éamon de Valera to Organising Committee, 25 July 1923, ibid., MacSwiney Papers, P48a/236(3).
67. Director of Intelligence [Michael Carolan] to de Valera, 4 Aug. 1923 and 10 Aug. 1923, ibid., Éamon de Valera Papers, P150/1849.
68. Éamon de Valera diary, 12 Aug. 1923, ibid., P150/268.
69. O'Connell journal, 14 Aug. 1923. ibid., Kathleen O'Connell Papers, P155/141
70. *Clare Champion*, 22 May 1965: Recollection of Ignatius Barrett, copy in UCDA, Éamon de Valera Papers, P150/1850.
71. Cypher message, GOC to Adjutant, Limerick Command, 13 Aug. 1923, ibid., P150/1849.
72. Report on arrest by Captain T. Power, 15 Aug. 1923, ibid., P150/1849.
73. *Irish Times (IT)*, 16 Aug. 1923.
74. Report on arrest by Captain T. Power, 15 Aug. 1923, UCDA, Éamon de Valera Papers, P150/1849.
75. *IT*, 16 Aug. 1923.
76. Ibid.
77. Detention order signed by Richard Mulcahy, 24 Aug. 1923, UCDA, Éamon de Valera Papers, P150/1849.
78. Quoted in Diarmaid Ferriter, *A Nation and Not a Rabble: The Irish Revolution 1913–23* (London, 2015), p. 291.
79. P. J. Ruttledge statement, UCDA, Ernie O'Malley Papers, P17a/139.
80. J. J. Lee, *Ireland 1912–1985: Politics and Society* (Cambridge, 1989), p. 94.
81. Peadar O'Donnell, quoted in Donal Ó Drisceoil, *Peadar O'Donnell* (Cork, 2001), p. 34.
82. John M. Regan, *The Irish Counter-Revolution, 1921–1936: Treatyite Politics and Settlement in Independent Ireland* (Dublin, 2001 edn), p. 158.
83. Calculated from figures on the website http://electionsireland.org.
84. Eoin to Taddie MacNeill, 14 Aug. 1923; UCDA, Eoin MacNeill Papers, LA1/G/269, for a complete analysis of elections results, see chapter titled 'Results Analysis'.
85. Sinéad de Valera to Adjutant General, 23 Aug. 1923, National Archives of Ireland (NAI), S 1369/15.
86. *Freeman's Journal*, 25 Aug. 1923; also, Sinéad de Valera to Kathleen O'Connell, [u.d.] UCDA, Éamon de Valera Papers, P150/241.
87. Seán T. O'Kelly to Mgr O'Hagan, reporting Ald Tom Kelly conversation with Cosgrave, 13 Feb. 1924, National Library of Ireland, Seán T. O'Kelly Papers, Ms 48,453/1.
88. Secretary to Executive Council to Minister for Defence, 16 Aug. 1923, NAI, S 1369/15
89. Director of Intelligence to Minister for Defence, 23 Aug. 1923, ibid.
90. Secretary, Department of Defence, to Director of Intelligence, 23 Aug. 1923, ibid.
91. Éamon de Valera to Ruttledge, 3 Jan. 1924, UCDA, Kathleen O'Connell Papers, P155/12(2).

CHAPTER 4: SEARCHING FOR THE NORMAL: THE FARMERS' AND LABOUR PARTIES IN THE 1923 ELECTION

1. John Coakley, 'The rise and fall of minor parties in Ireland', in *Irish Political Studies* Vol. 25 No. 4 (Dec. 2010), p. 503.
2. For a positive view, see Paul Daly, 'Labour and the pursuit of power', in *Making the Difference? The Irish Labour Party 1912–2012*, eds, Paul Daly, Rónán O'Brien, and Paul Rouse (Cork, 2012), p. 84.
3. *Irish Independent (II)*, 13 Aug. 1923.
4. Ibid., 24 Aug. 1923.
5. Ibid., 20 Aug.1923.
6. *Voice of Labour*, 21 Apr. 1923.
7. Ibid., 25 Aug. 1923.
8. Ibid., 2 June 1923.
9. *Freeman's Journal (FJ)*, 7 Feb. 1923.
10. Report from Standing Committee to Annual Congress, IFU, 15 Mar. 1923, National Library of Ireland (NLI) MS 43567/1, Farmers' Party papers.
11. *FJ*, 24 Jan. 1923.
12. *II*, 8 Aug. 1923.
13. Ibid., 4 Aug. 1923.

14. Ibid., 13 Aug. 1923.
15. Ibid., 10 May 1923.
16. *FJ*, 7 Feb. 1923.
17. Ibid., 22 June 1923.
18. *II*, 18 Aug. 1923.
19. Ibid., 7 Aug. 1923.
20. *II*, 25 Aug. 1923.
21. Ibid., 10 Aug. 1923.
22. *Cork Examiner (CE)*, 4 July 1923.
23. Ibid., 23 Aug. 1923.
24. *II*, 7 Aug. 1923.
25. Ibid., 14 Aug. 1923.
26. *Voice of Labour*, 6 Jan. 1923.
27. Ibid., 25 Aug. 1923.
28. *II*, 23 Aug. 1923.
29. Ibid., 23 Aug. 1923.
30. Speech by Bart Laffan, 1923, NLI, MS 19021, Farmers' Party papers.
31. *FJ*, 5 May 1923.
32. *II*, 10 Aug. 1923.
33. Ibid., 25 Aug. 1923.
34. Ibid., 22 Aug. 1923.
35. Ibid., 25 Aug. 1923.
36. Ibid., 11 Aug. 1923.
37. Ibid., 10 Aug. 1923.
38. *CE*, 7 Aug. 1923.
39. *II*, 21 Aug. 1923.
40. Ibid., 20 Aug. 1923.
41. *CE*, 7 Aug. 1923.
42. *Voice of Labour*, 4 Aug. 1923.
43. *II*, 23 Aug. 1923.
44. *Voice of Labour*, 25 Aug. 1923.
45. Ibid., 25 Aug. 1923.
46. *II*, 9 Aug. 1923.
47. Ibid., 16 Aug. 1923.
48. Ibid., 22 Aug.1923.
49. Ibid., 18 Aug. 1923.
50. John M. Regan, 'Southern Irish Nationalism as a historical problem', in *The Historical Journal* Vol. 50, No. 1 (Mar. 2007), pp 197–223.
51. See, for example, *Voice of Labour*, 11 Aug. 1923.
52. *II*, 10 Aug.1923.
53. Ibid., 23 Aug. 1923.
54. Ibid., 27 Aug. 1923.
55. See Katie Omans, 'The Belfast Boycott: Consumerism and gender in revolutionary Ireland (1920–1922)', in *Irish Historical Studies* Vol. 46, No. 169 (May 2022), pp 101–18.
56. *Voice of Labour*, 23 Sept. 1922.
57. *II*, 23 Aug.1923.
58. Ibid., 9 Aug. 1923.
59. Ibid., 25 Aug. 1923.
60. Ibid., 16 Aug. 1923.
61. Maurice Moore claimed this. *II*, 21 Aug. 1923.
62. *Voice of Labour*, 1 Sept. 1923.
63. Ibid., 18 Aug. 1923.
64. Testimony of W. H. M. Cobbe, Irish Farmers' Association, 25 July 1923, NLI, Department of Agriculture papers, 2005/68/36.

65. *II*, 21 Aug. 1923. See also Timothy O'Neil, 'Reframing the Republic: Republican socio-economic thought and the road to Fianna Fáil, 1923–26, in Mel Farrell, Jason Knirck, and Ciara Meehan (eds), *A Formative Decade: Ireland in the 1920s* (Sallins, 2015), pp 157–76.
66. *II*, 25 Aug. 1923.
67. *II*, 6 Aug. 1923.
68. Ibid., 6 Aug. 1923.
69. Ibid., 7 Aug. 1923.
70. Ibid., 6 Aug. 1923.
71. Ibid., 11 Aug. 1923.
72. Ibid., 16 Aug. 1923.
73. Ibid., 23 Aug. 1923.
74. Ibid., 25 Aug. 1923.
75. Ibid., 11 Aug. 1923.
76. The number of total seats increased between 1922 and 1923.
77. *Voice of Labour*, 8 Sept. 1923.
78. Micheál Martin, *Freedom to Choose: Cork and Party Politics in Ireland, 1918–1932* (Cork, 2009), p. 109.
79. *Voice of Labour*, 8 Sept. 1923.
80. Ibid., 1 Sept. 1923.

CHAPTER 5: POLITICAL PROPAGANDA IN THE 1923 GENERAL ELECTION: METHODS AND THEMES

1. Kenneth Newton, 'Making news: The mass media in Britain', in *Social Studies Review*, Vol. 6, No. 1 (1990).
2. *Cork Examiner (CE)*, 25 Aug. 1923.
3. *Irish Independent (II)*, 22 Aug. 1923.
4. *CE*, 15 Aug. 1923.
5. *Freeman's Journal (FJ)*, 19 July 1923; *CE*, 15 Aug. 1923.
6. Norman Fairclough, *Language and Power* (Harlow, 2001), pp 19–21.
7. Throughout the 1920s both the anti- and pro-treaty sides used electioneering ploys to attract voters. See W. Moss, *Political Parties in the Irish Free State* (New York, 1933), p. 130.
8. *CE*, 25 Aug. 1923.
9. *FJ*, 21 Aug. 1923.
10. Jason Knirck, 'A regime of squandermania': The Irish Farmers' Party, Agriculture and Democracy 1922–27, in Mel Farrell, Jason Knirck and Ciara Meehan (eds), *A Formative Decade, Ireland in the 1920s* (Sallins, 2015), p. 179.
11. *Evening Herald (EH)*, 22 Aug. 1923. See also '"Safety first"' chapter by Mel Farrell in this volume, pp 11–26.
12. *II*, 13 Aug. 1923.
13. Michael Gallagher, The Pact General Election of 1922, in *Irish Historical Studies*, Vol. 22, No. 84 (Sept., 1979), pp 404–21, p. 412.
14. Basil Chubb, 'The political role of the media in contemporary Ireland', in Brian Farrell (ed.), *Communications and Community in Ireland* (Cork: Mercier Press, 1984), p. 75.
15. Michael Dawson, 'Twentieth Century England. The case of the South West', in *Twentieth Century British History*, Vol. 9, No. 2 (1998), pp 201–18. Evidence of bias in the national newspapers can be seen in the *Irish Times* which was the preserve of Unionist opinion in this era; the *Freeman's Journal* was explicitly Home Rule orientated until its sale in 1919 when the new owners began to express sympathy towards Sinn Féin; however the *Irish Independent* (while anti the Irish Parliamentary Party until its demise in 1918) had set out to be politically neutral. Regional newspapers include, for example, the *Connacht Tribune* which began life as a paper to 'support the Constitutional Party of the Irish people' but became more separatist in tone after the Easter Rising; and the *Galway Express* had been non-political until 1917 but changed hands and subsequently became one of the strongest Sinn Féin papers. See Hugh Oram, *The Newspapers Book: A History of Newspapers in Ireland, 1649–1983* (Dublin, 1983) and Elaine Callinan, *Electioneering and Propaganda in Ireland, 1917–21: Votes, Violence and Victory* (Dublin, 2020), pp 139–46.

16. Notes on the general principles of propaganda: UCDA, Richard Mulcahy Papers, P7/A/42.
17. Louis M. Cullen, 'Establish a communications system: News, post and transport' in Farrell, *Communications and Community*, p. 27.
18. Ibid.; A halfpenny is worth approximately 0.10 euro today. Ref: National Archives UK, Currency converter.
19. Ibid., p. 35.
20. *II*, 23 Aug. 1923.
21. Ibid., 31 Aug. 1923
22. Staff Notice 1922: UCDA, Richard Mulcahy Papers, P7/A/42.
23. Paul H. Neystrom, *Retail Selling and Store Management* (London, 1914), pp 60–1.
24. NLI, Ir 94109/i/8: *Leabhar na hÉireann: The Irish Year Book* (1910), Sinn Féin, pp 309–17. It is unknown who penned the article, but conceivable authors are either Tom Grehan, the advertising manager of the *Irish Independent* since 1909 or Kevin J. Kenny, an Irish advertising pioneer.
25. Edward L. Bernays, *Propaganda* (New York, 1928), p. 28 and p. 100.
26. *Irish Times (IT)*, 30 Dec. 1920. A discount of ten per cent was offered if a series of twelve or more insertions were prepaid. Advertisements not prepaid were charged at a minimum of £3 (approximately €142.60 today) per insertion and publication of these advertisements was not guaranteed on any particular day, which could be problematic during election campaigns if a series of advertisements needed to run before election day.; £1 for twelve words is approximately €47.50 today while 3½d is approximately €0.60 today.
27. *Nationalist and Leinster Times (NLT)*, 25 Aug. 1923: This is approximately €22 in today's money. In the early to mid-1920s this was roughly one day's wages for a skilled tradesman.
28. *CE*, 23 Aug. 1923.
29. Ibid., 20 Aug. 1923.
30. *CE*, 23 Aug. 1923.
31. Bill Kissane, *The Politics of the Irish Civil War* (Oxford, 2005), pp 81–2.
32. *II*, 5 Sept. 1923. For a broader analysis of censorship in Ireland from 1922–39 see Peter Martin, *Censorship in the Two Irelands, 1922–1939* (Dublin, 2006).
33. Calton Younger, *Ireland's Civil War* (London, 1968), p. 333: Image of a wall in Ennis adorned with posters for the 1923 Election.
34. Franklyn S. Haiman, 'A tale of two countries: Media and messages of the 1988 French and American Presidential Campaigns', in Lynda Lee Kaid, Jacques Gerstlé and Keith R. Saunders (eds), *Mediated Politics in Two Cultures: Presidential Campaigning in the United States and France* (New York, 1991), p. 29.
35. Ciara Meehan, 'Politics pictorialised: Free State election posters', in Farrell, Knirck and Meehan (eds), *A Formative Decade*, pp 12–33.
36. Keeping Ireland Down poster, National Library of Ireland (NLI), EPH C200, see Figure 1.
37. *FJ*, 21 Aug. 1923
38. *II*, 5 Sept. 1923. For further information on canvassing in recent past elections see Callinan, *Electioneering and Propaganda*, pp 156–9. As Kissane points out in *Explaining Irish Democracy* (Dublin, 2002), p. 170, quoting Maurice Manning, *Irish Political Parties, An Introduction* (Dublin, 1972), p. 11: '64 of the 85 [Sinn Féin] party's candidates were unable to address their constituents as they were either imprisoned or on the run.'
39. *FJ*, 21 Aug. 1923
40. *Kilkenny People*, 1 Sept. 1923.
41. *II*, 5 Sept. and *CE*, 6 Sept. 1923.
42. *NLT*, 1 Sept. 1923.
43. Irish Statute Book, The Prevention of Electoral Abuses Act 1923, Section 50; See also *CE*, 15 Aug. 1923.
44. *CE*, 20 Aug. 1923. See also Michael Laffan, *Judging W.T. Cosgrave* (Dublin, 2014), p. 166.
45. Harold Lasswell, *Propaganda Techniques in the World War* (New York, 1938). See also Martin Molony, 'Social media and political communication', in Mark O'Brien and Donnacha Ó Beacháin (eds), *Political Communication in the Republic of Ireland* (Liverpool, 2014), pp 18–20 and pp 201–16.
46. *CE*, 23 Aug; *II*, 17 Aug; and, *FJ*, 20 July, 20 and 21 Aug. 1923.
47. See chapter titled 'From Revolution to Democracy' by Callinan in this volume, pp 121–31.
48. *II*, 17 and 18 Aug. and *CE*, 15 and 16 Aug. 1923.

49. Richard Sinnott, *Irish Voters Decide: Voting Behaviour in Elections and Referendums Since 1918* (Manchester, 1995), p. 97.
50. Niamh Puirséil, *The Irish Labour Party, 1922–73* (Dublin, 2007), pp 16–17. See also, Paul Daly, Rónán O'Brien and Paul Rouse, *Making the Difference? The Irish Labour Party 1912–2012*, Chapter 4. For results see Callinan's chapter 'From Revolution to Democracy' and Knirck's chapter 'Searching for the Normal: The Farmers' and Labour Parties in the 1923 Election' in this volume, pp 121–31, pp 38–49.
51. *II*, 23 July 1923.
52. Ibid., 27 July 1923.
53. *FJ*, 13 and 23 Aug; *II*, 13 Aug; *CE*, 16 Aug. 1923
54. *II*, 23 July 1923.
55. Michael Laffan, 'Labour must wait: Ireland's conservative revolution', in Patrick J. Corish (ed.), *Radicals, Rebels and Establishments* (Belfast, 1985), p. 203.
56. *II*, 18 Aug. 1923.
57. Ibid., 24 Aug. 1923.
58. £1,600,000 is the equivalent of approximately €76,032,871 today.
59. *CE*, 25 Aug. 1923; £1.5 million is the equivalent of approximately € 71,279,584 today.
60. *FJ*, 19 July 1923.
61. *CE*, 23 Aug. 1923.
62. £100 is worth approximately €5,752 today, £20,000 is worth €950,624 and £10,000,000 is worth €475,344,806.
63. See Keeping Ireland Down poster: NLI, EPH C200; *II*, 23 July 1923, Figure 1.
64. *IT*, 27 Aug. 1923. See Farrell's chapter entitled '"Safety first"' in this volume, pp 11–26.
65. An example of this as an advertisement can be found in the *FJ*, 25 Aug. 1923, p. 9.
66. *II*, 23 July 1923.
67. *Dundalk Democrat*, 25 Aug. 1923.
68. For further information on violence in recent past elections see Callinan, *Electioneering and Propaganda in Ireland*, pp 159–63.
69. £100 is the equivalent of approximately €5,752 today.
70. *FJ*, 21 Aug. 1923.
71. *EH*, 22 Aug. and *II*, 23 July 1923.
72. *II*, 22 Aug. and 5 Sept. 1923.
73. See 'From Revolution to Democracy' chapter in this volume, pp 121–31, as there was considerable evidence that voter apathy was an issue after the Civil War.
74. For examples see, Ben Novick, *Conceiving Revolution, Irish Nationalist Propaganda During the First World War* (Dublin & Portland, Or, 2001); P. M. Taylor, *Munitions of the Mind: War Propaganda from the Ancient World to the Nuclear Age* (Manchester, 1990); David Welch *Germany, Propaganda and Total War, 1914–1918: The Sins of Omission* (London, 2000); and Francis J. Costello, 'The role of propaganda in the Anglo-Irish War 1919–1921', in *The Canadian Journal of Irish Studies*, Vol. 14, No. 2 (Jan., 1989), pp 5–24 – to name a few. Kevin Hora's *Propaganda and Nation Building: Selling the Irish Free State* (London and New York, 2017) provides an analysis of propaganda in the Free State.
75. Garth S. Jowett and Victoria O'Donnell, *Propaganda and Persuasion* (LA and London, 2012 5th edn), p. 15. See also Farrell, Knirck and Meehan (eds), *A Formative Decade*, pp 14–15.
76. *II*, 23 July 1923.
77. Basil Chubb, 'Political communication and the mass media', in *The Government and Politics of Ireland* (Essex, 1970, 3rd edn), p. 55.

CHAPTER 6: 'THE ONLY HOPE WAS TO WORK THE TREATY': LOCAL NEWSPAPER COVERAGE OF THE 1923 GENERAL ELECTION IN KERRY

1. Gordon Revington, 'Rifles, rivals and revolution: Kerry newspapers report,' in Bridget McAuliffe, Mary McAuliffe and Owen O'Shea (eds), *Kerry 1916: Histories and Legacies of the Easter Rising – A Centenary Record* (Tralee, 2016), p. 183.
2. Alan McCarthy, *Newspapers and Journalism in Cork, 1910–23: Press, Politics and Revolution* (Dublin, 2020), p. 200, 267.

3. Elaine Callinan, *Electioneering and Propaganda in Ireland, 1917–21: Votes, Violence and Victory* (Dublin, 2020), p. 140.
4. Ibid.
5. John Burke, 'Evolving nationalism: Michael McDermott Hayes and the Westmeath Independent, 1900–20' in Ian Kenneally and James T. O'Donnell (eds), *The Irish Regional Press 1892–2018* (Dublin, 2018), p. 29.
6. Alan McCarthy, 'The story behind the storytellers: Cork newspapermen during the Irish revolutionary period, 1914–22' in Kenneally and O'Donnell (ed.), *Irish Regional Press*, p. 77.
7. John Horgan, 'Foreword' in Kenneally and O'Donnell (eds), *Irish Regional Press*, p. 9.
8. McCarthy, *Newspapers and Journalism in Cork*, op. cit.; Christopher Doughan, *The Voice of the Provinces: The Regional Press in Revolutionary Ireland, 1914–1921* (Liverpool, 2019); Callinan, *Electioneering and Propaganda*.
9. Kenneally and O'Donnell (eds), *Irish Regional Press*.
10. For the civil war in Kerry, see Owen O'Shea, *No Middle Path: the Civil War in Kerry* (Newbridge, 2022) and Tom Doyle, *The Civil War in Kerry* (Cork, 2008).
11. Mark O'Brien, 'All the news of interest: the *Kerryman*, 1904–88' in Kenneally and O'Donnell, *Irish Regional Press*, p. 41.
12. Christopher Doughan, 'Censorship and suppression of the Irish provincial press, 1914–1921' in *Media History*, Vol. 24 No. 3–4 (2018), p. 374.
13. Doyle, *Civil War in Kerry*, p. 134.
14. Letter from Maurice P. Ryle, editor of the *Kerry People*, to Piaras Béaslaí, 28 May 1923; National Library of Ireland (NLI), Papers of Piaras Béaslaí MS 33,918 (9).
15. *Cork Examiner (CE)* 25 Mar. 1922; Dónal Ó Drisceoil, 'Irish Newspapers, the Treaty and the Civil War' in John Crowley, Donal Ó Drisceoil, Mike Murphy and John Borgonovo (eds), *Atlas of the Irish Revolution* (Cork, 2017), p. 661.
16. Ó Drisceoil, *Atlas of the Irish Revolution*, p. 664; *The Liberator*, 7 Aug. 1923.
17. Owen O'Shea and Gordon Revington, *A Century of Politics in the Kingdom: A County Kerry Compendium* (Newbridge, 2018), pp 225–6.
18. O'Brien, 'All the news of interest', p. 45; Doughan, *Voice of the Provinces*, p. 202. *The Liberator* re-emerged on 7 Aug. 1923 and *The Kerryman* on 18 Aug.
19. *Irish Times (IT)*, 8 Jan. 1925.
20. O'Shea, *No Middle Path*, pp 236–8.
21. Reproduced in the *Freeman's Journal*, 1 June 1923.
22. *Kerryman*, 18 Aug. 1923.
23. Ibid., 5 Jan. 1924.
24. Dónal Ó Drisceoil, 'Sledge-hammers and blue pencils': censorship, suppression, and the Irish regional press, 1916–23' in Kenneally and O'Donnell (eds), *Irish Regional Press*, p. 151; Ó Drisceoil, 'Irish newspapers', *Atlas of the Irish Revolution*, p. 661.
25. O'Brien, 'All the news of interest' in Kenneally and O'Donnell, *Irish Regional Press*, p. 41; McAuliffe et al, *Kerry 1916*, p. 239; *Centenary of Irish Local Government, 1899–1999, Tralee Urban District Council Results 1899–1994* (Tralee, 1999), p. 21.
26. Christopher Doughan, 'A supplementary nationalism: the emergence of the Irish provincial press before independence,' in Kenneally and O'Donnell, *Irish Regional Press*, p. 109, n. 15.
27. *Kerryman*, 13 May 1916; McCarthy, *Newspapers and Journalism in Cork*, p. 94; Doughan, 'A supplementary nationalism' in Kenneally and O'Donnell, *Irish Regional Press*, p. 109, n. 15.
28. Ó Drisceoil, 'Sledge-hammers and blue pencils' in Kenneally and O'Donnell (eds), *Irish Regional Press*, p. 143.
29. Revington in *Kerry 1916*, p. 184.
30. Ibid; Doughan, *Voice of the Provinces*, p. 201.
31. *Kerryman*, 11 Jan. 1980.
32. *Liberator*, 23 Aug. 1923.
33. Maurice P. Ryle to Piaras Béaslaí TD, 28 May 1923, NLI, Papers of Piaras Béaslaí, MS 33,918 (9); £1,000 is worth approximately €47,747 today.
34. *Liberator*, 18 Aug. 1923.
35. Ibid.
36. Ibid., 9 Oct. 1923.

37. O'Shea, *No Middle Path*, pp 57–69 and pp 162–70.
38. *Liberator*, 16 Jan. 1932.
39. *Kerryman*, 18 Aug. 1923.
40. Ibid., 18 Aug. 1923.
41. *Liberator*, 9 August 1923.
42. Ibid., 23 Aug. 1923; *Kerryman*, 25 Aug. 1923.
43. *Liberator*, 16 Aug. 1923.
44. Ibid., 23 Aug. 1923: 'Notice of Poll'.
45. *Kerryman*, 18 Aug. 1923.
46. Ibid., 25 Aug. 1923.
47. *Liberator*, 9 Aug. 1923.
48. *Kerryman*, 25 Aug. 1923.
49. *Liberator*, 9 Aug. 1923; *Kerryman*, 18 Aug. 1923.
50. *Liberator*, 7 Aug. 1923.
51. Ibid., 23 Aug. 1923.
52. Ibid., 11 Aug. 1923, 16 Aug. 1923, 21 Aug. 1923.
53. Ibid., 18 Aug. 1923.
54. Ibid., 7 Aug. 1923.
55. *Kerry People*, 18 Aug. 1923.
56. *Liberator*, 18 Aug. 1923.
57. Ibid., 21 Aug. 1923.
58. *Liberator*, 1 Sep. 1923.
59. Ibid., 23 Aug. 1923.
60. Radio Report, Kerry Command, 18 Aug. 1923, Military Archives, Civil War Operations and Intelligence Reports Collection, IE/MA/CW/OPS; *CE*, 17 and 20 Aug. 1923 and *Irish Independent (II)*, 20 Aug. 1923.
61. *Liberator*, 16 Aug. 1923.
62. Ibid., 4 Sept. 1923.
63. Callinan, *Electioneering and Propaganda*, p. 146.
64. *Kerryman*, 14 May 1927.
65. *Liberator*, 18 Aug. 1923 and 21 Aug. 1923.
66. *Kerryman*, 18 Aug. and 25 Aug. 1923.
67. *Liberator*, 21 Aug. 1923.
68. O'Shea, *No Middle Path*, p. 236–9.
69. *Liberator*, 23 Aug. 1923.
70. Ibid.
71. Ibid., 7 Aug. 1923.
72. Michael Gallagher, *Irish Elections 1922–44: Results and Analysis* (Limerick, 1993), p. 44; 1922 general election results in Kerry, www.electionsireland.org.
73. *Liberator*, 6 Dec. 1923.
74. Doyle, *Civil War in Kerry*, p. 312; J. J. Lee, 'The Irish Free State' in Crowley et al., *Atlas of the Irish Revolution*, p. 783.
75. Gallagher, *Irish Elections*, p. 45; Basil Chubb, *The Government and Politics of Ireland*, (Oxford, 1970), p. 78.
76. Doyle, *Civil War in Kerry*, p. 314.
77. Gallagher, *Irish Elections 1922–44*, pp 34, 44.
78. O'Shea, *No Middle Path*, pp 57–69.
79. Jeffrey Prager, *Building Democracy in Ireland: Political order and cultural integration in a newly independent Ireland*, (Cambridge, 1986), p. 190.
80. *CE*, 3 Sep. 1923; *Liberator*, 4 Sep. 1923.
81. *Kerryman*, 1 Sept. 1923.
82. Ibid.
83. Ibid., 8 Sept. 1923.
84. *Liberator*, 7 Aug. 1923.
85. Ibid., 18 Aug. 1923.

86. Úna Newell, *The West Must Wait: County Galway and the Irish Free State, 1922–32* (Manchester, 2013), p. 34.
87. *Liberator*, 30 Aug. 1923.
88. Ibid., 8 Sept. 1923.
89. *Kerryman*, 1 Sept. 1923
90. *Liberator*, 15 Nov. 1923, 20 Nov. 1923.
91. Ibid., 20 Sept. 1923.
92. Reproduced in the *II*, 25 Sept. 1923
93. *Liberator*, 15 Nov. 1923; £37,000 is worth approximately €1,766,653 today.
94. Ibid.
95. *Liberator*, 10 Nov. 1923.
96. *Kerryman*, 5 Jan. 1923.
97. Letter from John Fisher, Listowel to *Liberator*, 11 Oct. 1923.
98. Ó Drisceoil, 'Irish Newspapers' in *Atlas of the Irish Revolution*, pp 661–4.
99. MA Busteed, *Voting Behaviour in the Republic of Ireland: A Geographical* Perspective (Oxford, 1990), pp 21–2; Tom Garvin, *Judging Lemass* (Dublin, 2009), p. 94; John M. Regan, *The Irish Counter-Revolution 1921–1936: Treatyite politics and settlement in independent Ireland* (Dublin 1999), p. 133; Stephen Collins, *The Power Game: Ireland under Fianna Fáil*, (Dublin, 2001), p. 17; Michael Gallagher, *Political Parties in the Republic of Ireland* (Manchester, 1985), p. 41.
100. Newell, *The West Must Wait*, pp 131, 141.
101. *Liberator*, 23 Apr. 1925 and 11 Nov. 1926.
102. Callinan, *Electioneering and Propaganda*, p. 141.
103. Owen O'Shea, 'Party organisation, political engagement and electioneering in Kerry, 1927–1966' in Maurice Bric (ed.) *Kerry: History and Society* (Dublin, 2020), p. 564.

CHAPTER 7: 'RETURN THEM TO POWER WITH SUFFICIENT STRENGTH TO COMPLETE THEIR WORK': THE ROMAN CATHOLIC CHURCH AND THE 1923 GENERAL ELECTION

1. Archbishop Thomas Gilmartin's advice to voters, *Tuam Herald*, 25 Aug. 1923.
2. Cornelius O'Leary, *Irish Elections, 1918–1977: Parties, Voters and Proportional Representation* (Dublin, 1979), p. 17.
3. Michael Laffan, *Judging W.T. Cosgrave* (Dublin, 2014), p. 165. On this see Mel Farrell's chapter titled '"Safety first"' in this volume, pp 11–26.
4. Bill Kissane, *The Politics of the Irish Civil War* (Oxford, 2007), p. 163.
5. *Freeman's Journal (FJ)*, 20 Aug. 1923.
6. Patrick Murray, *Oracles of God: The Roman Catholic Church and Irish Politics, 1922–37* (Dublin, 2000), pp 34–136.
7. The pastoral was published in the press on 11 October but a more refined version in pamphlet form was read in all churches on 22 October 1922. On the pastoral, see Daithí Ó Corráin, 'Weaponising the sacraments: the Roman Catholic Church and civil war' in Darragh Gannon and Fearghal McGarry (eds), *Ireland 1922: Independence, Partition, Civil War* (Dublin, 2022), pp 277–81.
8. M. P. McCabe, *For God and Ireland: The Fight for Moral Superiority in Ireland, 1922–1932* (Dublin, 2013), p. 148.
9. See Patrick Murray, 'The Anglo-Irish Treaty: the Catholic Appeal Committee to Pope Pius XI, 10 December 1922', *Analecta Hibernia*, 51 (2020), pp 207–27.
10. *Connacht Telegraph*, 17 Feb. 1923.
11. *Tipperary Star*, 17 Feb. 1923.
12. *Derry Journal*, 11 May 1923.
13. On this see Mel Farrell, *Party Politics in a New Democracy: The Irish Free State, 1922–37* (Basingstoke, 2017), p. 87.
14. W.T. Cosgrave, *To the People of Ireland* (Dublin, 1923).
15. *FJ*, 23 July 1923.
16. Ibid., 20 Aug. 1923.
17. Ibid., 6 Aug. 1923.
18. *Irish Catholic Directory 1924*, pp 586–7.

19. Laffan, *Judging W.T. Cosgrave*, p. 127.
20. *Irish Independent (II)*, 13, 14 and 15 Feb. 1923.
21. *FJ*, 6 Aug. 1923.
22. *Irish Catholic Directory 1924*, p. 585.
23. Ibid.
24. Public Safety (Emergency Powers) Act, 1923, electronic Irish Statute Book: https://www.irishstatutebook.ie/eli/1923/sro/950/made/en/print?q=Public+Safety (accessed 7 Nov. 2022).
25. *FJ*, 9 July 1923.
26. Ibid.
27. *FJ*, 30 July 1923.
28. *Belfast Telegraph (BT)*, 11 Aug. 1923.
29. *II*, 23 Aug. 1923.
30. O'Leary, *Irish Elections*, p. 17.
31. *BT*, 11 Aug. 1923.
32. Pauric J. Dempsey, 'Barry, Ralph Brereton', *Dictionary of Irish Biography*, DOI: https://doi.org/10.3318/dib.000457.v1 .
33. Ralph Brereton Barry to the editor of the *FJ*, 12 Aug. 1923 published on 15 Aug. 1923.
34. Ibid.
35. *FJ*, 23 July 1923.
36. Ibid., 20 Aug. 1923.
37. John M. Regan, *The Irish Counter-Revolution, 1921–1936: Treatyite Politics and Settlement in Independent Ireland* (Dublin, 1999), p. 135.
38. Ibid., p. 146.
39. *FJ*, 6 Aug. 1923.
40. Farrell, *Party Politics*, p. 83
41. *FJ*, 23 July 1923.
42. *II*, 23 Aug. 1923.
43. On this see David McCullagh, *De Valera: Rise, 1882–1932* (Dublin, 2017), pp 329-30.
44. *FJ*, 20 Aug. 1923.
45. *Irish Catholic Directory 1918*, p. 538.
46. Kieran Sheehy, *The Clare Elections* (Dublin, 1993), p. 356; Farrell, *Party Politics*, p. 89; McCullagh, *De Valera*, p. 331.
47. *Nationalist and Leinster Times*, 25 Aug. 1923.
48. *FJ*, 20 Aug. 1923.
49. On the establishment of Cumann na nGaedheal, see Ciara Meehan, *The Cosgrave Party: A History of Cumann na nGaedheal, 1923–33* (Dublin, 2010), p. 7; Regan, *Irish Counter-Revolution*, p. 143.
50. *Weekly Irish Times*, 5 May 1923.
51. *Irish Times (IT)*, 3 May 1923.
52. *Anglo-Celt*, 14 July 1923.
53. *FJ*, 1 Aug. 1923; on elections in Clare see Sheehy, *The Clare Elections*, p. 352.
54. *IT*, 20 Aug. 1923.
55. Ibid.
56. *Northern Standard*, 24 Aug. 1923.
57. *Cork Examiner (CE)*, 20 Aug. 1923.
58. *Limerick Leader*, 22 Aug. 1923.
59. Ibid.
60. *Connacht Tribune*, 25 Aug. 1923.
61. Ibid.
62. *CE*, 20 Aug. 1923.
63. Ibid.
64. *Mayo News*, 7 July 1923.
65. *FJ*, 23 July 1923.
66. Daniel Gallogly, *The Diocese of Kilmore, 1800–1950* (Cavan, 1999), p. 292.
67. *FJ*, 9 July 1923.
68. *IT*, 13 Aug. 1923.
69. *FJ*, 17 Aug. 1923.

70. Ibid.
71. Fr Patrick Daly (St Michael's Castlepollard) to Patrick Shaw, 22 Aug. 1923, published in *FJ*, 27 Aug. 1923.
72. Regan, *Irish Counter Revolution*, p. 148.
73. Laffan, *Judging W.T. Cosgrave*, p. 167.
74. Liam Weeks, 'We don't like (to) party. A typology of Independents in Irish Political Life, 1922–2007', *Irish Political Studies* vol. 24, no. 1 (2009), p. 27 Appendix 2 Table 6 'Numbers and shares of votes and seats for Independents'.
75. *IT*, 4 Oct. 1923; Thomas J. Morrissey, *Edward J. Byrne, 1872–1941: The Forgotten Archbishop of Dublin* (Dublin, 2010), p. 116.
76. Bill Kissane, 'Electing not to fight: Elections as a mechanism of deradicalisation after the Irish Civil War, 1922–1938', *International Journal of Conflict and Violence*, vol. 6, no. 1 (2012), p. 42.
77. Byrne to W.T. Cosgrave, 28 Oct. 1923 cited in McCabe, *For God and Ireland*, p. 178.
78. *Ulster Herald*, 24 Nov. 1923.
79. Kissane, *Politics of the Irish Civil War*, p. 166.
80. M. J. Browne, *The Synod of Maynooth 1927. Decrees which affect the Catholic Laity* (Dublin, 1930), pp 2–3. National synods were held at Thurles in 1850 and at Maynooth in 1875 and 1900.
81. Ibid, pp 3–4.
82. *Pastoral Address issued by the Archbishops and Bishops of Ireland to their Flocks on the Occasion of the Plenary Synod held in Maynooth* (Dublin, 1927), p. 7
83. Ibid., p. 31.
84. Murray, *Oracles of God*, p. 26; Canon 139, *The 1917 or Pio-Benedictine Code of Canon Law in English Translation*, curated by Edward N. Peters (San Francisco, 2001).
85. Murray, *Oracles of God*, p. 417.
86. *FJ*, 27 Aug. 1923.
87. Tom Garvin, *1922: The Birth of Irish Democracy* (Dublin, 1996), p. 180.
88. Cosgrave to Fogarty, 12 Dec. 1923, Killaloe Diocesan Archives (KDA), Fogarty MSS 33, 1-23/l, cited in Laffan, *Judging W.T. Cosgrave*, p. 166.

CHAPTER 8: 'WITHOUT DISTINCTION OF SEX': THE ROLES OF WOMEN IN THE 1923 GENERAL ELECTION

1. Karen Beckwith, 'A Common language of gender?' in *Politics and Gender*, vol.1 no. 1 (Mar. 2005), pp 128–137.
2. Caitriona Beaumont, 'After the vote: Women, citizenship and the campaign for gender equality in the Irish Free State (1922–1943)' in Louise Ryan and Margaret Ward (eds), *Irish women and the vote: Becoming citizens* (Dublin, 2018), p. 231.
3. Claire McGing, 'Women's political representation in Dáil Éireann in revolutionary and post-revolutionary Ireland, in Linda Connolly (ed.), *Women and the Irish revolution* (Newbridge, 2020), pp 85–6.
4. Mari Takayanagi, 'Women and the vote: The parliamentary path to equal franchise, 1918–28' in *Parliamentary History* vol. 37, no. 1 (Feb. 2018), p. 1.
5. Ibid., '"One of the most revolutionary proposals that has ever been put before the House": The Passage of the Parliament (Qualification of Women) Act 1918', in Lucy Bland and Richard Carr (eds), *Labour, British radicalism and the First World War* (Manchester, 2018), p. 174.
6. Sarah Childs, 'Votes for women… and seats, parliaments, and politics for women', n.d. available at: http://blogs.bbk.ac.uk/bbkcomments/2018/02/06/votes-for-women-and-seats-parliaments-and-politics-for-women/) accessed, 9 Sept. 2022.
7. Margaret Ward, *Unmanageable revolutionaries: Women and Irish nationalism, 1880–1980* (Dublin, 2021), pp 225–6.
8. Ibid., p. 239.
9. Helen Litton (ed.) *Kathleen Clarke: Revolutionary Woman* (Dublin, 1991), p. 170.
10. In June 1921, the parliament in Southern Ireland met, but only the four Independent Unionist members attended. It was dissolved in 1922.
11. McGing, 'Women's political representation in Dáil Éireann', p. 88.
12. *Cork Examiner (CE)*, 21 Apr. 1921.

13. Maedhbh McNamara and Paschal Mooney, *Women in parliament – Ireland: 1918–2000* (Dublin, 2000), p. 75.
14. Jason Knirck, '"Ghosts and realities": Female TDs and the Treaty debate' in *Éire-Ireland*, vol. 32, no. 4, (Winter/Spring 1997–98), p. 171.
15. Sinéad McCoole, 'Debating not negotiating: The female TDs of the Second Dail' in Liam Weeks and Mícheál Ó Fathartaigh (eds), *The Treaty: Debating and establishing the Irish State* (Newbridge, 2018), pp 136–59. See also: McGing, 'Women's political representation in Dáil Éireann', p. 89–94.
16. Dáil Debates, vol. T, no. 7, 20 Dec. 1921 (O'Callaghan), available at https://www.oireachtas.ie/en/debates/debate/dail/1921-12-20/2/ ; Margaret Ward, *In their own voice: Women and Irish nationalism* (Dublin, 2001), p.124.
17. McGing, 'Women's political representation in Dáil Éireann', p. 94.
18. *Irish Independent (II)*, 25 Feb. 1922.
19. Knirck, 'Ghosts and realities', p. 177.
20. Dáil Debates, vol. T, no. 8, 21 Dec. 1921, available at https://www.oireachtas.ie/en/debates/debate/dail/1921-12-21/.
21. Ibid., no. 7, 20 Dec. 1921, available at https://www.oireachtas.ie/en/debates/debate/dail/1921-12-20/.
22. Ibid., no. 9, 22 Dec. 1921 (O'Ceallaigh), available at: https://www.oireachtas.ie/en/debates/debate/dail/1921-12-22/2/ .
23. Ibid., no. 7, 20 Dec. 1921 (O'Callaghan) available at: https://www.oireachtas.ie/en/debates/debate/dail/1921-12-20/
24. Ibid., no. 11, 4 Jan. 1921 (English), available at: https://www.oireachtas.ie/en/debates/debate/dail/1922-01-04/2/
25. Litton, *Revolutionary woman*, p. 196.
26. *II*, 11 Nov. 1922.
27. P. S. O'Hegarty, *The Victory of Sinn Féin* (Dublin, 1924), p. 104.
28. Ward, *Unmanageable Revolutionaries*, p. 288.
29. Jason Knirck, *Women of the Dáil: Gender, Republicanism and the Anglo-Irish Treaty* (Dublin, 2006), p. 171.
30. Ward, *Unmanageable revolutionaries*, pp 289–290.
31. Ibid, p. 290.
32. Mary McAuliffe, '"An idea has gone around that all women were against the Treaty": Cumann na Saoirse and pro-Treaty women in 1922–3' in Liam Weeks and Mícheál Ó Fathartaigh (eds), *The Treaty: Debating and establishing the Irish State* (Kildare, 2018), p. 171.
33. *Irish Times (IT)*, 12 Feb. 1922.
34. McAuliffe, 'Cumann na Saoirse and pro-Treaty women in 1922–3', p. 179.
35. McNamara and Mooney, *Women in parliament*, pp 18–19.
36. Dáil Debates, S2, no. 1, 28 Feb. 1922 available at: https://www.oireachtas.ie/en/debates/debate/dail/1922-02-28/9/ .
37. Ibid.
38. Margaret Ward, *Hannah Sheehy-Skeffington – Suffragette and Sinn Féiner: Her memoirs and political writings* (Dublin, 2017), p. 192.
39. Dáil Debates, S2, no. 1, 28 Feb. 1922 (O'Callaghan), available at: https://www.oireachtas.ie/en/debates/debate/dail/1922-02-28/9/ .
40. Ibid.
41. Ibid.
42. Ibid.
43. Mel Farrell, *Party Politics in a New Democracy: The Irish Free State, 1922–37* (Basingstoke, 2017), p. 64.
44. *CE*, 17 Nov. 1922.
45. NAI, Constitution Committee, T2, undated memorandum on 'Exercise of the Franchise' by P. A. O'Toole.
46. National Coalition Panel Joint Statement, 20 May 1922.
47. Thomas Mohr, 'The rights of women under the constitution of the Irish Free State' in *Irish Jurist*, vol. 41, p. 3.

48. Dáil Debates, vol. 1, no. 7, 19 Sept. 1922 (Blythe), available at: https://www.oireachtas.ie/en/debates/debate/dail/1922-09-19/4/
49. Ward, *Unmanageable revolutionaries*, pp 289–290.
50. Mohr, 'The rights of women under the constitution of the Irish Free State', p. 56.
51. *II*, 28 Sept. 1922 and 30 Sept. 1922.
52. Farrell, *Party Politics*, p. 81.
53. Ibid, p.87.
54. *CE*, 8 Aug. 1923.
55. *Belfast Newsletter*, 20 Aug. 1923.
56. *Freemans Journal*, 8 Aug. 1923.
57. *CE*, 22 Aug. 1923.
58. Farrell, *Party politics*, p. 81.
59. *IT*, 27 Aug. 1923.
60. Figures calculated by the author based on the above article.
61. *The Nationalist (Tipperary)*, 11 Aug. 1923.
62. *IT*, 25 Aug. 1923.
63. *IT*, Aug.1923.
64. *II*, 28 Aug.1923.
65. Ibid; *IT*, 28 Aug. 1923.
66. *IT*, 1 Sept. 1923.
67. McGing, 'Women's political representation in Dáil Éireann', p. 79.
68. Mary McAulife, 'Remembering Caitlín Brugha, TD for Waterford, 1923–1927', n.d. available at: https://marymcauliffe.blog/2018/12/04/remembering-caitlin-brugha-td-for-waterford-1923-1927, accessed 10 Oct. 2022.
69. Farrell, *Party Politics*, p. 90.
70. Marie Coleman, 'Compensation claims and women's experiences of violence and loss in revolutionary Ireland' in Linda Connolly (ed.), *Women and the Irish revolution*, p. 130.
71. For example, Rose Anne Martin, MSP34REF21118.
72. For example, Bridget Culligan, MSP34REF33301.
73. For example, Helen Clune, MSP34REF59350.
74. For example, Angela Collins, MSP34REF18308.
75. For example, Delia McArdle, MSP34REF34181.
76. For example, Annie M. P. Smithson, MSP34REF8969.
77. For example, Mary Agnes Burke, MSP34REF40894.
78. For example, Bridget Forde, MSP34REF56936.
79. For example, Nora McMahon, MSP34REF11892.
80. For example, Annie Maria McGoldrick, MSP34REF56387.
81. For example, Margaret Joyce, MSP34REF18767.
82. For example, Florence Brennan, MSP34REF22742.
83. Margaret Gallery, MSP34REF40092.
84. Nora McMahon, MSP34REF11892.
85. Ward, *Unmanageable revolutionaries*, p. 352.
86. Delia McArdle, MSP34REF34181.
87. Lily O'Brennan, MSP34REF2229.
88. May Casey, MSP34REF60958.
89. Mary Agnes Byrne, MSP34REF40894.
90. Ibid.
91. Maire Comerford, MSP34REF60668.
92. Marie Coleman, 'O'Driscoll, Margaret Collins' in *Dictionary of Irish Biography* (Dublin, 2009). Available at: https://www.dib.ie/biography/odriscoll-margaret-collins-a6725, accessed 7 Sept. 2022).
93. Knirck, 'Ghosts and realities', p. 177.
94. McNamara and Mooney, *Women in parliament*, p. 91.
95. Maria Hegarty and Martina Murray, *Power to Serve: The Voices of the Women of Cumann na nGaedheal and Fine Gael* (Dublin, 2021), p. 27.
96. Standing Committee, minutes of meeting, 7 July 1925, UCDA, Cumann na nGaedheal papers, P39/min/1.

97. Figure calculated by the author based on the Dáil record.
98. McNamara and Mooney, *Women in Parliament*, p. 85.
99. Hegarty and Murray, *Power to Serve*, p. 27.
100. McNamara and Mooney, *Women in Parliament*, p. 85.
101. Ibid., p. 157.
102. Hegarty and Murray, *Power to Serve*, p. 14.
103. Dáil Debates, vol. 13, no. 6, 18 Nov. 1925, (Collins-O'Driscoll), available at: https://www.oireachtas.ie/en/debates/debate/dail/1925-11-18/24/
104. Marie Coleman, 'O'Driscoll, Margaret Collins'.
105. Ibid.
106. Dáil Debates, vol. 42, no. 5, 7 June 1932, (Collins-O'Driscoll), available at: https://www.oireachtas.ie/en/debates/debate/dail/1932-06-07/20/
107. Ibid., vol. 11, no. 2, 23 Apr. 1925 (Collins-O'Driscoll) Available at: https://www.oireachtas.ie/en/debates/debate/dail/1925-04-23/9/
108. Ibid., vol. 23, no. 3, 20 Apr. 1928 (Collins-O'Driscoll) available at: https://www.oireachtas.ie/en/debates/debate/dail/1928-04-20/11/
109. Ibid., vol. 26, no. 6, 19 Oct. 1928, (Collins-O'Driscoll) available at: https://www.oireachtas.ie/en/debates/debate/dail/1928-10-19/2/
110. Ibid., vol. 13, no. 6, 18 Nov. 1925 (Collins-O'Driscoll), available at: https://www.oireachtas.ie/en/debates/debate/dail/1925-11-18/24/
111. Ibid., vol. 9, no. 27, 19 Dec. 1924 (Collins-O'Driscoll), available at: https://www.oireachtas.ie/en/debates/debate/dail/1924-12-19/40/#spk_165
112. Maryann Gialanella Valiulis, 'The politics of gender in the Irish Free State, 1922–1937' in *Women's History Review*, vol. 20, no. 4 (2011), p. 1.
113. McGing, 'Women's political representation in Dáil Éireann', p. 98.
114. Maurice Manning, 'Women in Irish National and Local Politics, 1922–1977' in Margaret MacCurtain and Donnacha O'Corrain (eds), *Women in Irish Society: The Historical Dimension* (Dublin, 1978), p. 96.

Chapter 9: The AARIR and the 1923 General Election in the United States

1. The author would like to acknowledge the staff at the University of Michigan Special Collections Department, Ann Arbor, for their assistance in accessing and sourcing AARIR correspondence for this research.
2. For more on the evolution of Irish-American nationalism during the late 19th and early 20th centuries see: Bruce Nelson, *Irish Nationalists and the Making of the Irish Race* (Princeton, 2012); Patrick Steward and Bryan P. McGovern, *The Fenians: Irish Rebellion in the North Atlantic World* (Knoxville, 2013); Regina Donlon, 'John O'Keeffe and the Fenian Brotherhood in the American west and Midwest, 1866–1890' in *New Hibernia Review*, xxi (2017), pp 86–103; Francis M. Carroll, *America and the Making of an Independent Ireland: A History* (New York, 2021), Chapter 6; Alan J. Ward, *Ireland and Anglo-American Relations, 1899–1921* (Toronto, 1969), pp 214–55; Michael Doorley, *Irish-American Diaspora Nationalism: The Friends of Irish freedom* (Dublin, 2005), pp 36–137; Timothy G. Lynch, '"A Kindred and Congenial element": Irish-American nationalism's embrace of Republican rhetoric' in *New Hibernia Review*, xiii (2009), pp 77–91 and Howard Lune, *Transnational Nationalism and Collective Identity Among the American Irish* (Philadelphia, 2020).
3. For more on Doheny and the AARIR in California see: Timothy J. Sarbaugh, 'American recognition and Éamon De Valera: The heyday of Irish Republicanism in California, 1920–1922', in *Southern California Quarterly*, lxix (1987), pp 133–50 and Timothy J. Sarbaugh, 'The AARIR of California and the De Valera connection, 1923–1936' in *Southern California Quarterly*, lxix (1987), pp 223–40.
4. Kevin Kenny, 'American-Irish nationalism' in J. J. Lee and Marion Casey, *Making the Irish American: History and Heritage of the Irish in the United States* (New York, 2006), pp 209–302; p. 295.
5. For extended discussion see Michael Doorley, *Irish-American Diaspora Nationalism: The Friends of Irish freedom* (Dublin, 2005), pp 36–137. For contrast see also: Tony King, *Home Rule from a transnational perspective: the Irish Parliamentary Party and the United Irish League of America, 1901–1918* (Wilmington, DE, 2021), pp 151–94.

6. Ibid.
7. *Cordova Daily Times*, 17 Nov. 1920.
8. *New York Tribune*, 13 Dec. 1920.
9. *Sheffield Evening Telegraph*, 18 Nov. 1920.
10. *Freeman's Journal*, 19 Nov. 1920.
11. David Brundage, *Irish Nationalists in America: The Politics of Exile, 1798–1998* (Oxford, 2016), p. 162.
12. Brundage, *Irish Nationalists in America*, p. 161; Kevin Kenny, 'American-Irish nationalism', p. 296.
13. Brundage, *Irish Nationalists in America*, p. 162.
14. Ibid., p. 169.
15. Circular from AARIR National Executive to all AARIR members, 4 January 1923, University of Michigan Library – Special collections, John F. Finerty Irish Papers, 1921–1906, AARIR series, Box 4, folder 1, hereafter referred to as UMich, Finerty Papers.
16. Ibid.
17. For more on the experience of hyphenated Americans in this period see: Michael Nieberg, *The Path to War: How the First World War Created Modern America* (Oxford, 2016), pp 179–205.
18. Letter from Adelia Christy, Cleveland to John Finerty, Washington, 31 Jan. 1923, UMich, Finerty Papers, AARIR series, Box 4, folder 1.
19. Letter from Frank Horgan to John Finerty, 10 Jan. 1923, UMich, Finerty Papers, AARIR series, Box 4, folder 1.
20. Letter from Jeremiah O'Leary to John Finerty, 4 Mar. 1923, ibid, folder 3.
21. Circular to National Executive members of the AARIR, 20 Mar. 1923, ibid.
22. Telegram from Thomas W. Lyons to John Finerty, 23 Mar. 1923, ibid.
23. Minutes of AARIR national executive meeting, 7 Apr. 1923, ibid.
24. John Larkin Hughes to John Finerty, 6 Apr. 1923, ibid.
25. Circular to AARIR members, 9 Jan. 1923, ibid., folder 1.
26. $200 is worth approximately €3,278.45 today, $1 is worth approximately €16.40.
27. Circular to AARIR officers, 21 May 1923, ibid., folder 4.
28. Circular to AARIR membership, 25 May 1923, ibid.
29. Statement of John Finerty to AARIR membership, 22 Jun. 1923, ibid.
30. Circular to AARIR membership, 4 Jan. 1923, ibid., folder 1.
31. Letter from John Finerty to Margaret Walsh, Ohio, 27 Jan. 1923, ibid.
32. Letter from John Finerty to Joseph Burtchall, Philadelphia, 23 Jan. 1923, ibid.
33. $22.41 is worth approximately €367.35 today, $154.16 is worth €2,527.04.
34. $5.54 is worth approximately €90.82 today, $48.88 is worth €801.25.
35. Letter from J. J. Castellini, Ohio to J. J. O'Kelly, New York, for the attn. of John Finerty, 16 Jan. 1923, ibid.; $100,000 is worth approximately €61,639,227.77 today.
36. Letter from Frank Horgan to John Finerty, 16 Jan. 1923, ibid.
37. Letter from Patrick D. Morgan, Minneapolis to John Finerty, 19 Jan. 1923, ibid.
38. Telegram from Kevin Barry Council to John Finerty, 19 Jun. 1923, ibid., folder 4.
39. *Cork Examiner*, 12 Feb. 1923.
40. Statement of John Finerty, AARIR, 16 Feb. 1923, UMich, Finerty Papers, AARIR series, Box 4, folder 2.
41. Minutes of the national executive meeting, 16 Jun. 1923 Washington DC, ibid., folder 4.
42. Ibid.; $600 is worth approximately €9,835.37 today, $11.06 is worth €181.30.
43. $1,706.08 is worth approximately €27,966.23.
44. Statement of John Finerty to AARIR membership, 25 February 1923, ibid., folder 2.
45. Statement of John Finerty to AARIR membership, 22 Jun. 1923, ibid., folder 4.
46. Letter from Thomas D. O'Connor to John Finerty, 30 Jun. 1923, ibid., folder 5; $1,500 is worth approximately €24,588.42 today, $200,000 is worth €3,278,455.53 and $300,000 is worth €4,917,683.29.
47. Telegram from John Finerty to Thomas Lyons, 17 Aug. 1923, ibid.
48. £500 is worth approximately €16,925.49 today.
49. Letter from Tom Connaughton, Cleveland to John Finerty, 21 Aug. 1923, ibid.
50. Francis M. Carroll 'AARIR' in Michael Funchion (ed.), *Irish American Voluntary Organisations* (Westport, CT, 1983), pp 11–12.

51. Letter from Joseph Burtchall to John Finerty, 10 Sept. 1923, UMich, Finerty Papers, AARIR series, Box 4, folder 5.

Chapter 10: Ireland and the 'End of the European Crisis,' 1923–24

1. BNF Gallica, Press photograph, 'Dublin, revue de troupes, général Mulcahy et général Mac Mahon [juin 1923],' credited to Agence Rol. https://gallica.bnf.fr/ark:/12148/btv1b531093339 [accessed 1 September 2022].
2. Alvin Jackson, 'The Two Irelands' in Robert Gerwarth (ed.), *Twisted Paths. Europe, 1914–1945* (Oxford, 2007), pp 60–83.
3. Mel Farrell, *Party Politics in a New Democracy: The Irish Free State, 1922–37* (Basingstoke, 2017).
4. Mícheál Ó Fathartaigh and Liam Weeks (eds), *Birth of a State: The Anglo-Irish Treaty* (Newbridge, 2021); Bill Kissane, '"A Nation Once Again"? Electoral Competition and the Reconstruction of National Identity After the Irish Civil War, 1922–1923' in Bill Kissane (ed.), *After Civil War: Division, Reconstruction and Reconciliation in Contemporary Europe* (Philadelphia, 2014), pp 43–69. Examples of the 'global' turn in studies of the revolutionary period in Ireland include Enrico Dal Lago, Róisín Healy and Gearóid Barry, 'Globalising the Easter Rising. 1916 and the Challenge to Empires' in Enrico Dal Lago, Róisín Healy and Gearóid Barry (eds), *1916 in Global Perspective: An Anti-Imperial Moment* (London, 2018), pp 3–17; Enda Delaney and Fearghal McGarry, 'Introduction: A global history of the Irish Revolution' in *Irish Historical Studies*, xliv (2020), pp 1–10; Darragh Gannon, 'Revolution Before Colour: The Irish Republic and the Ukrainian National Republic' in Stephen Velychenko, Joseph Ruane and Liudmyla Hrynevych (eds), *Ireland and Ukraine: Studies in Comparative Imperial and National History* (Stuttgart, 2022), pp 419–42.
5. Peter Gattrell, 'The wars after the War' in John Horne (ed.), *A Companion to World War One* (Chichester, 2010), pp 669–89.
6. Robert Gerwarth and Erez Manela, 'Introduction' in Robert Gerwarth and Erez Manela (eds), *Empires at War, 1911–1923* (Oxford, 2014), pp 1–16, p. 4.
7. Ibid., p. 4. On the concept of the shatterzone, see also Omer Bartov and Eric D Weitz (eds), *Shatterzone of Empires: Coexistence and Violence in the German, Habsburg, Russian, and Ottoman Borderlands* (Bloomington, 2013).
8. Robert Gerwarth, *The Vanquished: Why the First World War Failed to End, 1917–1923* (London, 2016), p. 5.
9. Ibid., p. 9.
10. Robert Gerwarth and John Horne, 'Paramilitarism in Europe after the Great War' in Robert Gerwarth and John Horne (eds), *War in Peace: Paramilitary Violence in Europe after the Great War* (Oxford, 2012), p. 1.
11. Julia Eichenberg, 'Soldiers to Civilians, Civilians to Soldiers: Poland and Ireland after the First World War' in Gerwarth and Horne (eds), *War in Peace*, pp 184–99.
12. Robert Gerwarth and John Horne, 'The Great War and Paramilitarism in Europe, 1917–23' in *Contemporary European History*, xix (2010), pp 267–73, p. 270.
13. Patricia Clavin, *Securing the World Economy: The Reinvention of the League of Nations, 1920–1946* (Oxford, 2013), pp 26–32.
14. Gerwarth, *The Vanquished*, p. 14.
15. Robert Gerwarth and John Horne, 'Bolshevism as Fantasy: Fear of Revolution and Counter-Revolutionary Violence, 1917–1923' in Gerwarth and Horne (eds), *War in Peace*, pp 40–51, p. 41.
16. Gerwarth, *The Vanquished*, pp 132–135.
17. Diarmaid Ferriter, *Between Two Hells. The Irish Civil War* (London, 2022), p. 94.
18. For a comparative treatment with a particular emphasis on issues of 'cultural' demobilisation, see John Horne, 'Demobilizations' in Martin Conway, Pieter Lagrou and Henri Rousso (eds), *Europe's Postwar Periods – 1989, 1945, 1918* (London, 2019), pp 9–30. For a survey of demobilisation after World War One in major belligerent nations, some successor states and in the victorious powers' colonial empires, see Gearóid Barry: 'Demobilization, in: 1914–1918' – online. *International Encyclopedia of the First World War*, ed. by Ute Daniel, Peter Gatrell, Oliver Janz, Heather Jones, Jennifer Keene, Alan Kramer, and Bill Nasson, issued by Freie Universität Berlin, Berlin 2018-12-04. DOI: 10.15463/ie1418.11323.

19. On this incident, see Ferriter, *Between Two Hells*, pp 161–70.
20. Ibid., pp 161–70.
21. John Paul Newman, 'Serbian and Habsburg Military institutional legacies in Yugoslavia after 1918' in *First World War Studies*, v (2014), pp 319–35, p. 329.
22. Ferriter, *Between Two Hells*, pp 136–42, 188–95.
23. Mark Phelan, 'Irish responses to Fascist Italy, 1919–1932' (Ph.D. thesis, NUI Galway, 2013). Thesis available at http://hdl.handle.net/10379/3401
24. Adrian Lyttleton, *The Seizure of Power: Fascism in Italy, 1919–1929* (3rd edn, London & New York, 2003), pp 100–11.
25. Ibid., p. 86.
26. Phelan, 'Irish responses', pp 20–21.
27. Mark Phelan, 'Ireland and the Corfu Crisis, 1923' in *History Ireland*, xxv (2017), pp 28–30.
28. R. J. B. Bosworth, *Mussolini's Italy. Life under the dictatorship* (London, 2006), p. 191.
29. Mauro Canali, 'The Matteotti murder and the origins of Mussolini's totalitarian Fascist regime in Italy' in *Journal of Modern Italian Studies*, xiv (2009), pp 143–167.
30. For a detailed discussion of the reparations settlement, including the findings of the Reparations Commission which reported in April 1921, see Alan Sharp, *The Versailles Settlement: Peacemaking After The First World War, 1919–1923* (Basingstoke, 2008), pp 98–108.
31. The best single study in English of this episode is Conan Fischer, *The Ruhr Crisis, 1923–1924* (Oxford, 2003).
32. Conan Fischer, *Europe between Democracy and Dictatorship, 1900–1945* (Chichester, 2011), pp 211–12.
33. Ian Kershaw, *To Hell and Back: Europe, 1914–1949* (London, 2016), pp 145–47.
34. On the role of French Christian Democrats and socialists in turning French public opinion in favour of cautious engagement with republican Germany, see Gearóid Barry, 'Marc Sangnier and the "Other Germany": The Freiburg International Democratic Peace Congress and the Ruhr Invasion, 1923' in *European History Quarterly*, xli (2011), pp 25–49.
35. Horne, 'Demobilizations', p. 53. On the place of Franco-German Catholic youth groups in this reconciliation project, see Gearóid Barry, *The Disarmament of Hatred. Marc Sangnier, French Catholicism and the Legacy of the First World War* (Basingstoke, 2012).
36. Gerwarth, *The Vanquished*, p. 3.
37. Ibid., p. 247.
38. Horne, 'Demobilizations', p. 55.
39. Marcus M. Payk and Roberta Pergher (eds), *Beyond Versailles. Sovereignty, Legitimacy, and the Formation of New Polities after the Great War* (Bloomington, IND., 2019). For the German-Polish controversy, see also Róisín Healy, *Poland in the Irish Nationalist Imagination, 1772–1922. Anti-Colonialism within Europe* (Basingstoke, 2017), pp 261–2.
40. Gerwarth, *The Vanquished*, p. 217.
41. Kershaw, *To Hell and Back*, p. 127.
42. Ibid., pp 129–31.
43. Ibid., p. 133.
44. Ibid., p. 125.
45. Konrad Jarausch, *Out of Ashes: A New History of Europe in the Twentieth Century* (Princeton, 2016), p. 141.
46. *L'Oeuvre*, 27 Aug. 1923.
47. Risto Alapuro, 'The legacy of the Civil War of 1918 in Finland' in Bill Kissane (ed.), *After Civil War: Division, Reconstruction and Reconciliation in Contemporary Europe* (Philadelphia, 2014), pp 17–42, p. 30.

CHAPTER 11: FROM REVOLUTION TO DEMOCRACY: ANALYSING THE 1923 GENERAL ELECTION

1. Newspaper references to the 'government' meant Cumann na nGaedheal.
2. *Cork Examiner (CE)*, 21 Aug. 1923.
3. The figures provided by Department of Local Government and Health Memorandum on the Conduct of the General Election to Dáil Éireann (Dublin, Messrs Alex Thom and Co. Ltd, July 1924),

state that the total number of ballot papers (including NUI) was 1,093,996 and the total number of papers rejected as invalid and not counted was 40,047 (3.66 per cent). Some of the calculations in this analysis excludes the university seats and were based on the results in Walker, *Parliamentary Election Results*, pp 18–115 and results published in contemporary newspapers.
4. See appendix 1 for full breakdown of parties and votes.
5. See appendix 1 for absent voters.
6. Note, the anti-treaty Republicans will be referred to by the party name Sinn Féin in this analysis. However, they are often referred to in newspapers as anti-treatyites or Republicans.
7. *Irish Independent (II)*, 21 Aug. 1923; all these additional parties have been grouped together under 'other' (see appendices also). In this instance the Labour total includes candidates of the official Labour Party, the four Dublin Trades Council nominees, and the Larkinite candidate in Tipperary, but does not include Independent candidates that stood in Labour interests. The Farmers' total is that of the official Farmers' Party.
8. See appendix 1 for figures in column titled 'constituency votes'.
9. See appendices 1,2 and 3 for full results.
10. *II*, 3 Sept. 1923
11. *II*, 30 Aug. 1923
12. *Nationalist and Leinster Times (NLT)*, 8 Sept. 1923
13. *Freeman's Journal (FJ)*, 21 Aug. 1923.
14. *Offaly Independent*, 23 Sept. 1923; *Kilkenny Journal*, 10 June 1922.
15. *Belfast Newsletter (BN)*, 29 Aug. 1923.
16. *II*, 30 Aug. 1923.
17. *FJ*, 21 Aug. 1923
18. *BN*, 30 Aug. 1923
19. *Kilkenny People*, 1 Sept.1923
20. Ibid.
21. See appendix 2 for full breakdown of first preference results by province.
22. Figures are calculated for all provinces, but do not include universities. See Appendix 1 for calculated results; and Brian Walker, *Parliamentary Election Results in Ireland 1918–92* (Dublin and Belfast, 1992), pp 108–15 for election results list. In diagrams: Cumann na nGaedheal (CnaG), Sinn Féin (SF), Labour (L), Farmers (F), Independents (I) and Others (O).
23. Pat McCarthy, *Waterford: The Irish Revolution, 1912–23* (Dublin, 2015), p. 121.; Emmet O'Connor, 'Agrarian Unrest and the Labour Movement in County Waterford 1917–1923', *Saothar*, Vol. 6 (1980), pp 40–58.
24. Dooley, *'The Land for the People'*, p. 55. Note: Figures based on appendix 3.
25. Note: Figures based on appendix 3.
26. Ibid., pp 54–56.
27. *BN*, 31 Aug. 1923.
28. See appendix 3, Elected Candidates Only.
29. David McCullagh, *De Valera vol.1 Rise, 1882–1932* (Dublin, 2017), p. 331.
30. See appendix 3, Elected Candidates Only.
31. *II*, 3 Sept. 1923.
32. Mary Clancy, 'Women in the Free State Parliament, 1923–1937' in *Contesting Politics, Women in Ireland, North and South*, ed. by Yvonne Galligan, Eilis Ward and Rick Wilford (Colorado and Oxford, 1999), pp 204–05.
33. *CE*, 8 Aug. 1923.
34. Information and reference kindly provided by Claire McGing.
35. *BN*, 31 Aug. 1923.
36. *FJ*, 21 Aug. 1923.
37. See chapter by Claire McGing titled '"Without distinction of sex"', pp 87–97.
38. *BN*, 3 Sept. 1923.
39. See chapter titled '"Safety first"' in this volume by Mel Farrell, pp 11–26.
40. *BN*, 3 Sept. 1923.
41. See chapter by Elaine Callinan on political propaganda.
42. *II*, 5 Sept. 1923 and *CE*, 6 Sept. 1923.
43. Report in *BN*, 3 Sept. 1923.

44. See Elaine Callinan, *Electioneering and Propaganda in Ireland, 1917–21, Votes, Violence and Victory* (Dublin, 2020), p. 63.
45. See introduction chapter.
46. *CE*, 28 Aug. 1923.
47. Ibid.
48. See appendix 1.
49. See 1918 General Election for comparison in Callinan, *Electioneering and Propaganda 1917–1921*, pp 163–9.
50. See Owen O'Shea's chapter titled '"The only hope was to work the Treaty"' in this volume, pp 63–76.
51. *NLT*, 1 and 8 Sept. 1923; *FJ*, 28 Aug. 1923; *Offaly Independent*, 23 Sept. 1923.
52. *II*, 30 Aug. 1923.
53. *II*, 5 Sept. 1923 and *CE*, 6 Sept. 1923.
54. Ciara Meehan, *The Cosgrave Party: A History of Cumann na nGaedheal, 1923–33* (Dublin, 2010), p. 28.
55. Dorothy Macardle, *The Irish Republic* (Dublin, 1999 edn), p. 863.
56. Michael Laffan, *The Resurrection of Ireland, The Sinn Féin Party 1916–1923* (Cambridge, 2005), p. 438.
57. Mel Farrell, *Party Politics in a New Democracy: The Irish Free State, 1922–37* (Basingstoke, 2017), p. 90.
58. Peter Mair, 'Party competition and the changing party system' in John Coakley and Michael Gallagher (eds), *Politics in the Republic of Ireland* (London and New York, 1999, 3rd edn), p. 132.
59. Laffan, *The Resurrection*, p. 442.
60. Tom Garvin, 'Democratic politics in Ireland' in *Politics in the Republic of Ireland*, p. 355.

Select Bibliography

Bowman, John, *De Valera and The Ulster Question, 1917–1973* (Oxford, 1989).
Cahillane, Laura, *Drafting the Irish Free State Constitution* (Manchester, 2016).
Callinan, Elaine, *Electioneering and Propaganda in Ireland, 1917–21: Votes, Violence and Victory* (Dublin, 2020).
Campbell, Fergus, *Land and Revolution: Nationalist Politics in The West Of Ireland* (Oxford, 2005).
Carty, R. K., *Party and Parish Pump: Electoral Politics in Ireland* (Ontario, 1981).
Chubb, Basil, *The Government and Politics of Ireland* (London, 1982).
Coakley, John, 'The rise and fall of minor parties in Ireland', in *Irish Political Studies*, vol. 25, no. 4 (Dec. 2010), pp 503–39.
— 'The Significance of Names: The evolution of Irish Party labels', in Études *Irlandaises*, vol. 5 (1980), pp171–81.
Coakley, John and Michael Gallagher (eds), *Politics in The Republic of Ireland* (London, 2010).
Connolly, Linda (ed.), *Women and the Irish Revolution: Feminism, Activism, Violence* (Newbridge, 2020).
Corcoran, Donal P., *Freedom to Achieve Freedom: The Irish Free State, 1922–1932* (Dublin, 2013).
Cronin, Mike and John M. Regan (eds), *Ireland: The Politics of Independence, 1922–49* (London and New York, 2000).
Dolan, Anne, *Commemorating the Irish Civil War: History and Memory, 1923–2000* (Cambridge, 2003).
Dooley, Terence, *'The Land for the People': The Land Question in Independent Ireland* (Dublin, 2004).
Dunphy, Richard, *The Making of Fianna Fáil Power in Ireland, 1923–1948* (New York, 1995).
Farrell, Mel, Jason Knirck and Ciara Meehan (eds), *A Formative Decade: Ireland in the 1920s* (Sallins, 2015).
Farrell, Mel, *Party Politics in a New Democracy: The Irish Free State, 1922–37* (Basingstoke, 2017).
Ferriter, Diarmaid, *Between Two Hells: The Irish Civil War* (London, 2021).
Fitzpatrick, David, *The Two Irelands, 1912–1939* (Oxford, 1998).
Foster, Gavin, *The Irish Civil War and Society: Politics, Class and Conflict* (Basingstoke, 2015).
Gallagher, Michael, 'The Pact General Election of 1922', in *IHS*, vol. xxi, no. 84 (Sept. 1979).
Garvin, Tom, *1922: The Birth of Irish Democracy* (Dublin, 2005 edn).
Gerwarth, Robert (ed.), *Twisted Paths: Europe, 1914–45* (Oxford, 2008).
Girvin, Brian, *Between Two Worlds: Politics and Economy in Independent Ireland* (Dublin, 1989).
Hughes, Brian, and Conor Morrissey (eds), *Southern Irish Loyalism, 1912–1949* (Liverpool, 2020).
Kissane, Bill, *The Politics of the Irish Civil War* (Oxford, 2005).
— *Explaining Irish Democracy* (Dublin, 2002).
Knirck, Jason, *Afterimage of the Revolution: Cumann na nGaedheal and Irish Politics, 1922–1932* (Madison, 2014).
— *Democracy and Dissent in the Irish Free State Opposition, Decolonization, and Majority Rights* (Manchester, 2023).
Laffan, Michael, *Judging W. T. Cosgrave* (Dublin, 2014).
— *The Resurrection of Ireland: The Sinn Féin Party, 1916–1923* (Cambridge, 1999).
Mair, Peter, *The Changing Irish Party System* (London, 1997 edn).
Martin, Micheál, *Freedom to Choose: Cork and Party Politics in Ireland, 1918–1932* (Cork, 2009).
Mazower, Mark, *Dark Continent: Europe's Twentieth Century* (Bath, 1998).
McCullagh, David, *De Valera Vol. 1 Rise, 1882–1932* (Dublin, 2017).
Meehan, Ciara, *The Cosgrave Party: A History of Cumann na nGaedheal, 1923–33* (Dublin, 2010).
Newell, Úna, *The West Must Wait: County Galway and the Irish Free State, 1922–32* (Manchester, 2015).

O'Donoghue, Martin, *The Legacy of the Irish Parliamentary Party in Independent Ireland 1922–1949* (Liverpool, 2019),

Ó Fathartaigh, Micheál and Liam Weeks (eds), *The Treaty: Debating and Establishing the Irish State* (Newbridge, 2018).

O'Leary, Cornelius, *Irish Elections, 1918–77: Parties, Voters and Proportional Representation* (Dublin, 1979).

Prager, Jeffrey, *Building Democracy in Ireland: Political Order and Cultural Integration in a Newly Independent Nation* (Cambridge, 1986).

Puirséil, Niamh, *The Irish Labour Party, 1922–73* (Dublin, 2007).

Regan, John M., *The Irish Counter-Revolution, 1921–1936: Treatyite Politics and Settlement in Independent Ireland* (Dublin, 2001 edn).

Sheedy, Kieran, *The Clare Elections* (Dún Laoghaire, Dublin, 1993).

Sinnott, Richard, *Irish Voters Decide: Voting Behaviour in Elections and Referendums Since 1918* (Manchester, 1995).

Gialanella Valiulis, Maryann, *Portrait of a Revolutionary: General Richard Mulcahy and the Founding of the Irish Free State* (Dublin, 1992).

Varley, Tony, 'On the road to extinction: Agrarian parties in twentieth-century Ireland', in *Irish Political Studies*, vol. 25, no. 4 (Dec. 2010), pp 584–7.

Walker, Brian M. (ed.), *Parliamentary Election Results in Ireland: 1918–92* (Dublin, 1992).

Index

advertising
    costs/cost-sharing 53, 54
    in newspapers 22–4, 48, 53–4, 59, 70–1
'Advertising Problem, The' (Sinn Féin) 53
agricultural industry 40–1, 47, 60, 74
Aiken, Frank 1, 31, 32, 35, 79, 123, 129
Air Corps 22, 56
Alapuro, Risto 120
American Association for the Recognition of the Irish Republic (AARIR) 9, 99–109
    boycott of English goods and services 102, 103
    Cosgrave criticised by 106, 107–8
    de Valera and 100, 101, 102, 107–8
    decline of 102, 104, 108–9
    formation 100–1
    fundraising 101, 103, 105, 106–7
    General Election (1923) and 107
    internal disputes 103–4, 105, 106, 108
    Irish Republican Bonds 101, 102, 103, 104
    Irish Republican Defence Fund 103, 106–7
    membership 101
    National Executive 102–3, 105, 106–7
    objective 101
    President Harding petitioned by 106
    press coverage 100–1
    reorganisation 103, 108
    republican leaders' criticism of 106
Anglo-Irish relations 43, 45, 49
Anglo-Irish Treaty
    anti-treaty women TDs 89, 90
    Catholic hierarchy and 77
    Collins and 26, 101
    Cumann na mBan's opposition to 90
    Cumann na nGaedheal's support for 3, 11, 12
    Dáil debates 6, 87, 89
    de Valera and 22, 27, 28
    General Election (1923) and 58, 59, 69, 72, 77, 94–5, 122, 128
    Irish Americans' perception of 101–2
    negotiations 22, 27, 47, 123–4
    ratification 1, 6, 27, 78, 91
    voters' support for 62
    women, Dáil debates and 89
    see also anti-treaty IRA; anti-treatyites; pro-treatyites
anti-treaty IRA 77–8, 79
    Kerry People suppressed by 64

anti-treatyites 6, 81
    abstentionist policy 2
    attacks on 62
    Catholic clergy and 9, 83
    Cumann na mBan 90
    General Election (1922) 4, 52, 58
    General Election (1923) 3, 7, 34, 42, 55, 58
    imprisonment 33
    newspapers and 9, 54, 64
    victimisation of 120
Arbour Hill Prison, Dublin 36
Arnott, Lady 48
Ashe, Thomas 81
Associated Press of America 58
Austria 4, 112
Austro-Hungarian Army 114

Baldwin, Stanley 38
Barrett, Dick 11
Barry, Kevin 123
Barry, Michael 123
Barton, Miss 62, 129
Barton, Robert 123
Baxter, P.F. 41
Beamish, Richard 17, 24
Béaslaí, Piaras 16, 66
Beattie, Sir Andrew 127
Belfast Boycott 45
Belfast Newsletter 93, 121, 123
Belfast Women's Advisory Council 5
Bermingham, Patrick J. 43, 82
Bernays, Edward L. 53
Bibliothèque Nationale de France (BNF) 110
Black and Tans 64
Blythe, Ernest 21, 61, 79, 82, 92, 127, 131
Bobbio, Italy 116
Bolger, Tom 82
Bolsheviks/Bolshevism 4, 111, 112, 128
Borris, County Carlow 16, 18
Boundary Commission 21, 45
Boylan, A.H. 21
Brady, Revd Bernard 83
Breathnach, Cormac 57
Breen, Dan 123
Breen, William 14
Brennan, Michael 20
Brennan, Revd P.J. 83
Brereton Barry, Ralph 80
Briand, Aristide 117

Brodrick, Albinia 70
Brown, Terence 7
Brugha, Caitlín 93, 94, 98, 123, 128, 129
    General Election (1923) results 25, 127
Brugha, Cathal 6, 25, 27, 37, 123, 129
Brundage, David 101
Bulfin, Francis 84
Bulgaria 114–15, 119
Burke, Seamus 47–8
Burke, Revd Thomas 83
Burtchall, Joseph 105, 109
Businessmen's Party 5, 45, 122, 124, 127
Butler, John 127
by-elections
    East Clare (1917) 27, 36, 81
    Leitrim-Sligo (1929) 24
    South Longford (1917) 24, 127
Byrne, Alfred 127
Byrne, Conor 84
Byrne, Edward, Archbishop of Dublin 85
Byrne, Mary Agnes 95

Cahersiveen, County Kerry 68, 70
Cahill, Francis 24
Cahill, Patrick (Paddy) 64, 68, 72
Callinan, Elaine, *Electioneering and Propaganda in Ireland, 1917–21: Votes, Violence and Victory* 7
Canada 4, 99, 100, 111
canvassing 18, 55–6, 62, 68
capitalism 39, 41, 46
Carlow-Kilkenny
    candidate nominations, Bishop Foley and 82
    Cosgrave's first preference votes 24, 124, 127
    Cosgrave's tour of the constituency 50, 52
    Cumann na nGaedheal selection convention 16
    election campaign, Cosgrave and 20, 24
    Labour Party 123
    public speeches 55
    Sinn Féin and 123
    women voters 128
Carney, Winifred 88
Carolan, Michael 35
Carroll, Francis M. 108
Casey, May 95
Castellini, John 105–6
Castlebar, County Mayo 79
Castlerea, County Roscommon 57
Catholic Church 1
    electoral process, disengagement from 86
    influence of 7, 8, 9, 84–5
    see also Catholic clergy; Catholic hierarchy
Catholic clergy
    anti-treaty candidates proposed by 83
    anti-treatyites, opposition to 9
    candidates proposed by 82–3
    Cumann na nGaedheal and 14, 16, 51, 77, 82–3
    election campaign/meetings and 82, 83–4
    Farmers' Party and 82, 83
    letters in support of candidates 84
    pro-government partisanship 83–4
    republican candidates and 83
Catholic hierarchy
    Anglo-Irish Treaty and 77
    anti-treaty IRA, condemnation of 77–8
    boundary with Northern Ireland 81
    candidates, nomination/recommendation of 82
    Civil War and 78
    Cosgrave and 77, 82, 86
    Cosgrave government and 78–9, 80, 81, 82
    Cumann na nGaedheal and 9, 16, 51, 77
    Cumann na nGaedheal manifesto 78, 81
    election meetings, letters addressed to 78–80, 81
    faith and morals, dangers to 85
    General Election (1923) 79, 85, 86
    Independent candidates, views on 80, 84
    land issues 81
    law and order 78
    Maynooth plenary synod (1927) 85–6
    pastorals 77–8
    political fragmentation, fear of 78, 80–1
    stable government, need for 78, 80
    Treaty, endorsement of 9
Cavan 13, 21, 47, 79, 81, 82, 83
Ceannt, Áine 33
censorship of the media 54
Censorship of Publications Bill (1928) 97
Childers, Erskine 33
Childers, Molly 33, 35, 62, 129
Christy, Adelia 102
Chubb, Basil 52, 62
Civic Guard 62, 68–9, 70
Civil Service Regulation (Amendment) Bill (1925) 97
Civil War (1922–3) 1, 3
    aftermath 3, 9–10, 12–13
    anti-treaty IRA 77–8, 79, 90
    anti-treaty women and 90
    atrocities in Kerry 67
    Catholic hierarchy and 78
    censorship during 54
    Cosgrave's views on 20–22
    Cumann na mBan 90
    de Valera and 8, 29, 29–30
    economic impact of 3, 71
    ending of 1, 31, 33, 79
    European context 110
    executions, state-sanctioned 3, 11, 78
    extra-judicial murders in Kerry 67
    Four Courts, shelling of 29
    IRA destruction/disruption in Kerry 66–7

Index

in Kerry 9, 63, 66–7
Kerry Command and 64, 67
Kerry newspapers and 64–5, 66–7
Lynch, death of 31
perception of 2, 20–22
politicians and 43–4
pro-treaty TDs attacked 11
'civil war politics' 1, 43–4, 49
Clan na Gael 99, 100
Clancy, Mary 127
Clann na Poblachta 89
Clare
    by-election East Clare (1917) 27, 81
    candidate selection 18
    Catholic clergy, candidates proposed by 83
    Cumann na nGaedheal and 16, 18, 20, 21, 22, 25
    de Valera and 35–6, 81
    de Valera's success (1923) 25, 36, 81–2, 123
    election rally, Cosgrave and 22
    election results (1923) 25, 82
    Farmers' Party and 82
    General Election (1923) 126–7
    Labour Party and 82, 123
    MacNeill and 16, 18, 82, 83
    National Army troops, shots fired by 35–6
    Sinn Féin and 35, 126–7
Clare Champion 16
Clarke, Kathleen 30, 58, 89
Clarke, Tom 58
Coakley, John 39
Cobbe, W.H.M. 47
Cohalan, Daniel, Bishop of Cork 79–80, 86
Cohalan, Daniel F., Judge 19, 20, 81, 100
Colbert, Con 83
Colbert, James 83
Coleman, Marie 97
Collins, Michael 1, 2, 6, 11, 19, 21
    death of 29, 35, 71, 96
    pact with de Valera 7, 28, 44, 92
    sisters 9, 17, 93, 96, 128
    'stepping stones to freedom' 26, 101
Collins O'Driscoll, Margaret
    Committee on Registration and Electoral Reform (1925) 96
    Cumann na nGaedheal vice-president 96
    Dáil attendance 96
    Fourth Dáil, only woman in 87, 94, 95
    gender politics and 96, 97
    General Election (1923) 9, 17, 24, 93, 94, 128
    letter to the editor 48
    parliamentary role 96–8
    re-election (1927 and 1932) 96
    retirement (1933) 96
    teaching post 96
Collins Powell, Mary 17, 93
colonialism/colonial world 38, 39, 46, 48, 111, 112, 113

Columbanus, St 116
Comerford, Maire 95–6
Comey, Revd Martin 82, 83
Commission on Agriculture (1923) 47
communism 111, 113, 116
Comyn, Michael 33, 83
Connacht 79, 124, 125
Connaughton, Tom 108
Connolly, Joseph 32–3, 34
Connolly, Linda, *Women and The Irish Revolution* 6
Constitution Committee 91–2
Constitution of the Irish Free State (1922) 9, 18, 37
    Article (3) 92, 98
    Article (14) 91, 92
    universal adult suffrage 18, 25, 87, 88, 91, 92
Cooper, Major Bryan 45, 46, 127
Corcoran, Donal P., *Freedom to Achieve Freedom* 6
Corcoran, Timothy 54
Cordova Daily Times 100
Corfu Crisis 116
Corish, Richard 123
Cork City
    Cumann na nGaedheal and 17, 54, 79, 124, 127
    Farmers' Party and 54
    MacSwiney, Mary 89, 93, 94, 123
Cork County, newspapers, influence of 63
Cork Examiner
    absent voters 130
    advertisement, Cumann na nGaedheal 59
    Constitution of the Irish Free State 91
    Cosgrave, aeroplane used by 56
    Cosgrave manifesto 22–3
    electioneering activity 55
    Farmers' Party election results 49
    General Election (1923) 121, 129
    Labour campaign 51
    lady candidates 127–8
    partition, Kathleen Clarke and 58
Cork North, election results (1923) 25, 126, 127
Cork Progressive Association (CPA) 5, 11, 13, 122
    General Election (1923) 17, 24, 44
    pact with Cumann na nGaedheal 17, 24
Cosgrave government 1–2, 12–13, 41, 90
    Catholic clergy and 83
    Catholic hierarchy and 78–9, 80, 81, 82
    criticism of 36, 40, 59
    enactment of the Constitution 18
    universal adult suffrage 18, 87
Cosgrave, Philip 123
Cosgrave, William T. 2, 5, 17, 38
    AARIR's criticism of 106, 107–8
    air corps aeroplanes, use of 22
    Bobbio, visit to 116

Catholic hierarchy and 77, 82, 86
Civil War and 20–22
Cumann na nGaedheal party leader 51
Daily Mail interview 106
de Valera criticised by 22
de Valera's arrest 36, 37
death of uncle 79
dissolution of the third Dáil 2
election campaign 19–22, 51, 59
election rallies and 19–22, 51
Executive Council, President of 131
family home, burning of 79
General Election (1923) 24, 25, 124
Kerry newspapers' support for 65
manifesto 'To the people of Ireland' 22–3
polling day, announcement of 2
pro-treaty stance 52
'Safety first' (1923) 11
stable government, focus on 51
universal adult suffrage 92
see also Carlow-Kilkenny; Cosgrave government
Costello, Eileen 90
Coyle, Henry 14
Crowley, James 16, 68, 72
Cullen, L.M. 52
Culligan, Revd Charles 16, 82
Cumann na mBan 37, 56, 58, 90, 95
Cumann na nGaedheal 1, 2, 6
advertising 22, 23–4, 48, 54, 59, 70–1
branches, formation of 13, 14
business classes and 41
Catholic clergy and 14, 16, 51, 77, 82–3
Catholic hierarchy and 9, 51, 77–82
Committee on Registration and Electoral Reform 96
constituency committees 18, 25
Cork Progressive Association, pact with 17, 24
debts (1923) 25, 26
Director of Elections (1923) 16, 82
Election Committee (1922) 15
election committees 14, 15
election debts in Clare 25
election manifesto 22–3, 78, 81
formation of 11
General Council 82
General Election (1922) 13, 94
General and Election Committee 11
Griffith, party named as a tribute to 11
Kerry newspapers and 65, 66, 67, 68, 69, 73, 75–6
leaders, large majorities (1923) 128–9
leaflets **22, 23**
National Executive 14, 15
newspaper coverage 9, 65, 66
non-class national party 14, 15, 18, 42
official launch (April 1923) 1, 11, 82
organisation, building of 13–15

organisers 13–14, 22, 25
pro-treaty stance 3, 11, 12, 20, 21, 58, 59
propaganda **22, 23**, 55, 58, 59–60, 62
selection convention 16
Sinn Féin movement and 12
Standing Committee 13, 14, 15, 16, 22, 25
supporters, middle and upper class 75
women TDs 9, 96–8
women voters 23–4, 48, 93
women's rights, legislation undermining 98
see also Cosgrave government; Cosgrave, William T.; election campaign (1923); General Election (1923)
Cumann na nGaedheal government (1923–32) 74
Cumann na Poblachta 29, 33, 107
Cumann na Saoirse, pro-treaty stance 90
Cumann Sugradh an Airm 25
Cummins, Canon T. 83–4
Curran, Joseph, *Birth of The Irish Free State 1921–23, The* 6
Czechoslovakia 4, 119, 120

Dáil Éireann
abstention of republicans, effects of 45, 85, 87, 89–90, 92, 95
Anglo-Irish Treaty debates 87, 89
Anglo-Irish Treaty, ratification of 27
anti-treaty boycott 89–90
Constitution debates 92
Fourth Dáil 5, 74, 85, 87, 92, 94, 129
Fourth Dáil, seats by party **122**
Sixth Dáil 96
Markievicz as first female TD 88
republican women TDs 87, 95
Second Dáil 4, 88
Sixth Dáil 96
Third Dáil, dissolution of 2, 15, 18
Third Dail, seats by party **122**
women elected to (1923) 7, 87, 94, 95
women TDs 87, 95, 96
Daily Mail, Cosgrave's interview 106
Dawes Plan 117
de Rivera, Primo 115
de Róiste, Liam 17
de Valera, Éamon 6, 26, 38
AARIR and 100, 101, 102, 107–8
abstentionist stance 3
Anglo-Irish Treaty and 22, 27, 28
anti-treaty stance 30, 52, 58, 81
arrest 22, 25, 36, 81, 107–8
by-election East Clare (1917) 27, 81
Civil War and 8, 29
condemnation by Bishop Fogarty 81
Cosgrave's criticism of 22
Cumann na Poblachta established by 29, 33
election campaign 31, 35–6, 58–9, 95
external association, promotion of 27, 123

174

Index

Fianna Fáil and 120, 131
General Election (1922) 28–9
General Election (1923) 8, 25, 27, 36, 81–2, 123
General Election (1923) and 8, 25, 27, 36
historical theme, focus on 51–2
imprisonment 36–7
IRA and 32
Irish Americans and 100, 106
Irish politics, dominance of 8
newspaper, establishment of 31–2
oath of allegiance and 35, 58
pact with Collins 7, 28, 44, 92
perception of 32
political comeback 30–1, 34, 35–6, 37
politics, loss of faith in 28
Presidential Election (1966) 27
proposed as candidate 83
republican 'government' 29, 32
republican hardliners and 27, 28, 30
risk to his life 35
rumours about 35
St Patrick's Day speech (1922) 28, 37
Sinn Féin and 1, 28, 29–31, 32, 33–4, 51
Sinn Féin election manifesto 58
speeches 28, 37, 58–9
tour of his constituency 52
unity of Sinn Féin and 27
USA, tour of 19, 31, 81, 100
de Valera, Sinéad 36–7
Decade of Centenaries 7
democracy
    Europe and 10, 114–15
    General Election (1923) and 4, 7, 39, 85
    Sinn Féin and 8
    transition from revolution 5, 7, 10, 121–31
Denmark 46–7
Department of Local Government 93
Derham, Michael 124
Despard, Charlotte 69, 70
Devoy, John 100
dictatorships 7
Dingle, County Kerry 70
Doheny, Edward L. 100
Dolan, Anne and Murphy, William, *Michael Collins* 6
Dolan, Séamus 13
Dooley, Terence 18, 126
Doughan, Christopher 63
Doyle, Edward 123
Doyle, Michael 41, 59, 83
Doyle, Revd Patrick 82
Doyle, Revd P.J. 82
Dublin
    Cumann na nGaedheal and 13
    Cumann na nGaedheal election rallies 19, **19**
    Pro Cathedral 85
    women voters 94

Dublin Castle 74
Dublin County 24, 124
Dublin North 94, 96
    Cumann na nGaedheal 17, 24, 36, 126, 127, 128
    Independent 127
    Sinn Féin 126
Dublin South 94, 124, 126, 127, 128
Dublin Trades Council 122
Dublin University 4, 121
Duchy of Teschen 119
Duggan, Éamonn 30, 34, 127
Dundalk Democrat 61
Dunne, Revd Peter 82

Easter Rising (1916) 26, 65–6, 99, 126
economic issues 62, 74–5
    Farmers' Party and 42–3
    Independents and 44–5
    Labour Party and 42
Economist, The 3, 12, 25
Egan, Patrick 84
Eichenberg, Julia 112
election campaign (1923) 78
    Cumann na nGaedheal 3–4, 8, 11, 12, 18–24, 26, 47–8, 61, 70, 77
    Farmers' Party 18, 21, 39–41, 42, 51, 57, 61, 69
    Independents 21, 44–6
    Labour Party 18, 21, 39, 40, 42, 46, 51, 57–8, 69
    Sinn Féin 18, 34–5, 50, 68–9, 70
    violence, outbreaks of 61–2, 69, 70
    women as activists 95–6
    see also advertising; propaganda; propaganda methods; propaganda themes
election meetings/rallies
    Catholic clergy and 83–4
    Catholic hierarchy's letters to 78–80, 81
    Cumann na nGaedheal 18–20, **19**, 21–2
    Farmers' Party 18
    Labour Party 18
    Sinn Féin 18
Electoral Act (1923) 4–5, 56
electoral politics 4, 6, 7, 30
electorate
    total register (1923) 93, 121, 130
    votes recorded (1923) 121
English, Ada 89
Europe
    demobilisation 9, 110, 113–14
    democracy (1923) 10, 114–15
    empires, fall of 111, 112, 113
    fatalities (1918–23) 111
    military dictatorship 115
    nation-states 112
    national armies 114
    national minorities 119

plebiscites 118–19
populist nationalism 120
post-war (1918–23) 9, 110–11
'shatterzones of empire' 112, 113
'successor states' 4, 111, 114, 115
'wars after the War' (1918–23) 9, 110, 111–13
ex-Unionists 127
Executive Council 2, 14, 37, 67, 131

Fahy, Frank 83
farm labourers' strikes 13, 126
Farmers' Party 3, 15, 21, 26, 38, 53
    advertisement 54
    agricultural industry 40–1, 56–7
    attack on 61
    Catholic clergy and 82, 83
    Denmark, perception of 47
    economic issues 42–3
    flag 57
    General Election (1922) 8
    modernisation of Ireland 39
    National Executive 57
    'no pact' idea 57
    public speeches 62
    see also election campaign (1923); General Election (1923)
Farrell, Mel, *Party Politics in a New Democracy: The Irish Free State, 1922–37* 7
Farrell, Mel et al., *Formative Decade, A. Ireland in the 1920s* 6
fascism 115–16
Fenian Brotherhood 99, 100
Fianna Fáil 26, 49, 64, 131
    de Valera and 120, 131
    Irish Press and 32
    Kerry Champion and 64, 76
    Kerry constituency and 76
    women's rights, legislation undermining 98
Figgis, Darrell 2, 44
Findlater, William 41, 45
Fine Gael 8, 24, 25–6, 131
Finegan, Patrick, Bishop of Kilmore 79, 81
Finerty, John F. 100, 103, 104–5, 106, 107–8
Finland 111, 119, 120
Finnish Civil War (1918) 112
Firearms Act (1925) 79
First World War (1914–18)
    demobilisation 9, 110, 113–14
    Gallipoli 118
    legacy of 110–11
    post-war period 4, 38
    'war of empires' 111
    'wars after the War' (1918–23) 9, 110, 111–13
fishing industry 57, 60, 74
FitzGerald, Desmond 19, 35, 124
Fitzpatrick, David, *Politics and Irish Life* 6

Fitzsimons, J.J. 43–4
Fogarty, Michael, Bishop of Killaloe 77, 79, 80, 81, 84, 86
Foley, Patrick, Bishop of Kildare and Leighlin 82
Forrestal, Revd A. 83
Foster, Gavin, *Irish Civil War and Society, The* 6
Foster, Roy, *Vivid Faces* 6
Franco, Francisco 120
Franco-Belgian occupation of the Ruhr 110, 116–17
Franco-German relations 116, 117–18
Free State forces *see* National Army
Free State Seanad 90
Freeman's Journal 52
    AARIR 101
    Cosgrave manifesto 22, 23
    election campaign 55
    equal franchise 18
    Farmers' Party campaign 51
    letter in support of candidate 84
    women candidates 128
Friends of Irish Freedom (FOIF) 99, 100, 101

Gaffney, Patrick 123
Gallagher, Frank 32
Gallagher, Michael 52
    Irish Elections, 1922–44: Results and Analysis 6
    'Pact General Election of 1922, The' 6
Gallery, Margaret 95
Galway Farmers' Association 40
Garahan, Hugh 127
Garvin, Tom 86, 131
    1922: The Birth of Irish Democracy 6
Gaughran, Laurence, Bishop of Meath 80, 81
Gavan Duffy, George 123–4
Gaynor, Revd P. 84
gender politics 9, 96–7
    Collins O'Driscoll and 96, 97
    General Election (1918) and 88
    General Election (1923), impact of 87
    Irish Free State and 98
    legislative reforms 96–7
gender roles, revolutionary period and 98
General Election (1910) 4
General Election (1918) 4, 7, 8, 43, 88, 123
General Election (1921) 4, 88, 89
General Election (1922) 3, 6–7, 12, 21, 40, 71
    anti-treatyites 28–9, 58
    Collins-de Valera pact 4, 5, 7, 28, 44, 92
    Cumann na nGaedheal 13, 24
    de Valera and 28–9
    Farmers' Party 8
    General and Election Committee 11
    Independents 122
    Labour Party and 4, 8, 39, 58, 89, 122, 123
    pro-treaty candidates 89–90
    pro-treatyites 28–9, 58

Index

republican share of vote 84
results in Kerry 71
Sinn Féin and 4, 5, 28
women TDs 89
women voters 90–1
General Election (1923) 1, 4, 5, 39
   AARIR and 107
   aftermath, economic issues 74–5
   analysis of 121–31
   Anglo-Irish Treaty and 58, 59, 69, 72, 77, 94–5, 122, 128
   announcement of date 2
   anti-treatyites 3, 7, 34, 42, 55, 58
   candidates, number of 4, 122
   Catholic Church, influence of 7, 8, 9
   centenary of 98
   Connacht voting percentages **125**
   Cumann na nGaedheal and 3–4, 5, 24–6
   Cumann na nGaedheal candidates 15–18, 20, 68, 82–4
   Cumann na nGaedheal candidates, number of 122
   Cumann na nGaedheal women candidates 41, 48
   Cumann na nGaedheal's percentage of the vote 130–1
   Cumann na nGaedheal's results 7, 8, 24–6, 36, 72, 82, 94, **121, 122, 124, 125**, 126
   Cumann na nGaedheal's statement on 128
   democracy and 4, 7, 39, 85
   electors on the register 93, 121
   European context 110
   Farmers' Party and 8, 24, 25, 36, 39–41, 42
   Farmers' Party candidates 42, 43–4, 54, 68, 69
   Farmers' Party candidates, number of 122
   Farmers' Party results 5, 49, 72, 82, **121, 122, 124, 125**, 126, 127
   gender politics, impact on 9, 87
   Independent candidates, number of 122
   Independents and 5, 26, 43, 44–5, 49, 84
   Independents' results **121, 122, 124, 125**, 127
   Irish diaspora and 9, 99
   Kerry newspapers and 65, 67–8
   Labour Party and 39, 42, 50
   Labour Party candidates 68, 69
   Labour Party candidates, number of 122
   Labour Party's results 5, 25, 36, 49, 58, 59, 72, 82, 84, **121, 122, 124, 125**, 127
   Leinster voting percentages **124**
   Munster voting percentages **125**
   newspapers and 9, 63, 65, 67–8, 120
   Other (O) results **121, 122, 124, 125**
   polling day 8, 14, 17, 23–4, 36, 62, 67–8, 81, 84
   polling day designated a public holiday 2, 50, 92
   postal votes 130
   pro-Treatyites 3
   results 7, 24–6, 36, 49, 71, 72, 73, 81–2, 84, 94–5, **121**
   Sinn Féin and 5, 8, 24, 25, 34–5, 72, 73, 123
   Sinn Féin candidates 34–5, 36, 68–9, 129
   Sinn Féin candidates, number of 3, 36, 122
   Sinn Féin women candidates 93, 94
   Sinn Féin's percentage of the vote 130
   Sinn Féin's results 36, 72, 81–2, **121, 122, 124, 125**, 126
   Sinn Féin's views on 129
   threats/violence during campaign 61–2, 129
   Ulster (in Free State) voting percentages 124, **125**
   women candidates 9, 41, 92–3, 128
   women elected to the Dáil 7, 9, 87
   women's roles in 87
   see also propaganda; propaganda methods; propaganda themes; universal adult suffrage; voter turnout; voters
General Election (June 1927) 96
General Election (September 1927) 23, 96
General Election (1932) 7, 96
General Election (1933) 84, 96
General Election (1977) 89
General Election (1982) 8, 26
Germany
   Franco-Belgian occupation of the Ruhr (1923) 110, 116–17
   hyperinflation (1923) 116
   League of Nations 117–18
   National Socialist putsch 117
   Nazis 38, 117
   post-war 4, 38, 112
   Sudeten Germans 119
   war reparations 116, 117
   Weimar Republic 110, 116, 117
   women's emancipation 4, 38
Gerwarth, Robert 112
   Vanquished, The 112
Gerwarth, Robert and Horne, John 112
Gerwarth, Robert and Manela, Erez 111–12
Gibbons, Seán 20, 24, 127
Gilmartin, Thomas, Archbishop of Tuam 78, 79
Ginnell, Laurence, Special Envoy 102, 103, 106
Glin, County Limerick 57, 59
Gonne-MacBride, Maud 19
Good, John 127
Goresbridge, County Kilkenny 61
Gorey, Denis 123
Gorman, Revd John 82
Gormanstown prison camp 32
Gort, County Galway 59
Government of Ireland Act (1920) 4, 88
Government Publicity Department 61
Governor General's office, cost of 74
Grange, County Louth 62
Grangegorman Mental Hospital 97–8
Grattan Bellew, Sir Henry 40

Grattan Esmonde, Osmond 83
Great War 54, 62
    see also First World War
Greco-Turkish War (1919–22) 112
Greece 115, 116
    invasion of Anatolia 118
    population exchanges (1922–23) 118
    Smyrna (now Izmir) 118
Griffin, Maurice 65, 66
Griffith, Arthur 1, 2, 11, 19, 21, 83
    suffrage issue and 91, 92
Grimes, Canon Christopher 82
Guinane, Harry 25

Habsburg empire 111, 113, 114
Hagan, Revd John 34
Haiman, Franklyn S. 54
Hales, Seán 11, 71
Hanley, Gerard, *Cathal Brugha* 6
Harding, Warren 38, 106
Harrigan, John 103
Hart, Peter, *IRA and its Enemies, The* 6
Harty, John, Archbishop of Cashel 78, 80
Hayes, Richard 83
Hearn, J.J. 102, 105, 106, 108
Hehir, Michael 20
Hickey, Revd Joseph 82
Hitler, Adolf 117
Hoey, Patricia 128
Hogan, Conor 36, 51
Hogan, Patrick 36, 39, 83
Home Rule 17, 38
Home Rule Parliaments 88
Home Rule Party 6, 12, 16
Hora, Kevin, *Propaganda and National Building* 6
Horgan, Frank 106
Horne, John 118
Hórthy, Admiral Miklos 113, 115
Houlihan, Revd Joseph 84
Hughes, Brian and Morissey, Conor, *Southern Irish Loyalism* 6
Hughes, John Larkin 104
Hungarian Soviet Republic (1919) 113
Hungary 111, 112, 113, 115
    White Terror (1920) 113, 120
hunger strikes (1923) 85, 95

Independent Unionists 88
Independents 2, 3, 44
    advertising 70, 71
    Catholic hierarchy's views on 80, 84
    criticism of 48
    economic issues and 44–5
    General Election (1922) 122
    in Kerry 68
    partition and 45
    see also election campaign (1923); General Election (1923)

internment 84, 85, 120
Irish Americans 99
    Anglo-Irish Treaty, perception of 101–2
    de Valera and 100, 106
    Irish Republic, interpretation of 99, 101, 108
    republican organisations and 99–100
    self-determination for Ireland 100
Irish diaspora 9, 99
Irish Farmers' Union (IFU) 39–40, 42, 47
Irish Free State 1, 3, 6, 7
    Electoral Act (1923) 4–5
    emergence of 111
    execution of IRA prisoners 11
    gender politics in 98
    infrastructure, post-Civil War 3
    League of Nations and 12, 110, 116, 118
    National Loan 3, 12, 25
    party system, formation of 111
    perception of 6–7
    Provisional Government 87, 90
    republicanism, marginalisation of 9
    universal adult suffrage 2, 4–5, 18, 67, 80, 87, 90–2, 98
    see also Constitution of the Irish Free State; Cosgrave government; Executive Council
Irish Independent
    absent voters 130
    anti-treaty stance, de Valera and 58
    attacks on anti-treatyites 62
    Boundary Commission 45
    circulation figures 52
    Cohalan's praise for Cosgrave 20
    Cosgrave manifesto 22
    Dublin workers 122
    election rally in Dublin 19, 20
    electioneering activity 55
    Farmers' Party, letter of support for 53
    Figgis's letter 2
    General Election (1923) 39
    independent or business candidates 43
    partition 45
    Sinn Féin election campaign 50
    women voters 94
Irish nationalism 12, 14, 15, 46, 62
Irish Parliamentary Party (IPP) 4, 38, 42, 43, 66, 68, 127
Irish Press 32, 64
Irish Race Convention (1916) 100
Irish Republic
    Irish Americans and 99, 100, 101, 108
    Sinn Féin and 20
Irish Republican Army (IRA)
    AARIR criticised by 106
    Aiken's 'dump arms' order 1, 31, 79
    de Valera and 29, 32
    Director of Intelligence 35
    economic impact of campaign 71

Index

executions, state-sanctioned 11
Executive 29, 32, 33, 34
Irregulars 114
Kerry, destruction and disruption in 66–7
Sinn Féin and 30, 33, 34, 130
Southern Division 106
see also anti-treaty IRA
Irish Republican Bonds 101, 102, 103, 104
Irish Republican Brotherhood (IRB) 99
Irish Republican Defence Fund 103, 106–7
Irish Times 52, 53
    Cosgrave 11, 22
    election campaign 21
    total electorate (1923) 93
    women voters (1923) 94
Irish Transport and General Workers' Union (ITGWU) 58
Irish Women's Franchise League (IWFL) 88
Irish-America 99, 100, 101
Irregulars 114
Italy 110, 115–16
    Acerbo Law 116
    Blackshirts 116
    Bobbio, Irish pilgrims and 116
    Fascist Grand Council 115
    National Militia 115, 116

Jackson, Alvin 111
Johnson, Thomas 2, 39, 40
Johnston, James 82
Jordan, Michael 83
Juries Bills (1924 and 1927) 97

Keating, J. 16, 17
Kelly, Revd James 83
Kelly, Michael A. 103, 104
Kelly, Seán 82, 84
Kemal, Mustafa 118
Kenmare, County Kerry 16, 62, 69, 70
Kenneally, Ian and O'Donnell, James T. 63
Kennedy, Hugh, Attorney General 37
Kenny, Kevin 100, 101
Kenny, Kevin J. 45–6
Kenny, Patrick 21
Keran, Revd Patrick 83
Kerry Champion 64, 76
Kerry constituency
    anti-treaty vote 72
    anti-treatyites 68–9
    candidates in prison 68
    constitutional issue 65, 67, 69, 71, 73, 74
    Cumann na nGaedheal candidates 69, 72
    electoral register, concerns about 72
    Farmers' Party candidates 68, 69, 72
    Fianna Fáil and 76
    General Election (1923) results 72, 73
    Labour Party candidates 68, 69, 72
    number of eligible electors 71
    polling stations 71
    Republican candidates 68, 69, 72
    Sinn Féin 68–9, 72
    violence, outbreaks of 69, 70
    voter abstentions 72
Kerry County
    atrocities 67
    Black and Tans 64
    Civil War in 9, 63, 66–7
    Cumann na nGaedheal 16–17
    extra-judicial murders 67
    General Election (1923) 67–9, 124, 126
    Sinn Féin and 124, 126
    Town Tenants groups 71
    see also Kerry newspapers
Kerry Leader 64
Kerry News 64
Kerry newspapers 63–70
    advertisements 70–1
    anti-treaty combatants, condemnation of 65
    anti-treatyites, lack of coverage for 68, 76
    Cumann na nGaedheal, support for 65, 66, 67, 69, 73, 75–6
    economic issues 74–5
    Farmers' Party and 69
    General Election (1923) and 65, 73
    influence of 75–6
    Kerry Command, lack of commentary on 67
    Labour Party and 69
    post-civil war 64–5
    readership 75
    Sinn Féin and 68–9
Kerry People
    economic issues 74
    editorial, post-civil war 65
    pro-treaty stance 66
    re-emergence of 64
    suppression by anti-treaty forces 64, 66
    violence, outbreaks of 69
Kerry Weekly Reporter 64
Kerry-Limerick West 71
Kerryman, The
    agricultural industry 74
    Civil War, views on 66
    Cosgrave government 67
    cost of 75
    Cumann na nGaedheal and 66, 67, 68, 71
    Easter Rising (1916) 65–6
    editorial, post-civil war 65
    General Election (1923) 67, 73
    'Notes' columnists 65
    ownership 65, 66
    pro-treaty stance 65, 66
    re-emergence 64–5
    readership 65
    sales figures 64–5
Kershaw, Ian 117, 119
Keyes, Michael 51, 57–8

Kildare 17, 123
Kilkee, County Clare 16, 18, 82
Kilkenny People 55, 124
Kilmainham Gaol 95
Kingsmill Moore, Theodore Conyngham 34
Kissane, Bill 54, 85, 111
    Explaining Irish Democracy 6
    Politics of the Irish Civil War, the 6
Knirck, Jason, *Afterimage of the Revolution* 6
Knirck, Jason et al., *Formative Decade, A: Ireland in the 1920s* 6
Kotsonouris, Mary 7
Kun, Bela 113

Labour Party 2, 3, 15, 21, 26, 38
    advertising 70, 71
    Anglo-Irish Treaty and 59
    civil war politics and 44
    Denmark, perception of 46–7
    economic issues 42
    fishing industry and 57
    General Election (1918) 8
    General Election (1922) 4, 8, 39, 58, 89, 122, 123
    internal divisions 58
    militarism, condemnation of 44
    modernisation of Ireland 39, 46
    oath of allegiance and 57
    partition and 45
    propaganda 57–8
    Sinn Féin and 57, 59, 123
    workers, plight of 42
    see also election campaign (1923); General Election (1923)
Laffan, Batt 42
Laffan, Michael 58, 77
    Resurrection of Ireland, The 6
Land Act (1923) 18, 81
Land Bill 3, 126
Land Purchase and Arrears Conference 12
Larkin, Jim 58
Lasswell, Harold 56
Lavin, Andrew 126
Law, Hugh 127
Lawler, Thomas 17, 21
League of Nations
    Austria and 112
    Germany and 117–18
    Irish Free State and 12, 110, 116, 118
    plebiscites 118–19
Ledden, James 83
Leinster 13, 124, **124**
Leitrim-Sligo 96, 126
    by-election (1929) 24
Leix-Offaly 43, 82, 123, 130
Lemass, Noel 37
Lemercier, Camille 120
Lenin, Vladimir, Comintern 111, 113

Liberator, The
    advertising 71
    anti-treaty meeting, Civic Guard and 68–9
    'Auspicious Start, An' 74
    Civil War, views on 66
    Cumann na nGaedheal meeting 70
    destruction of 64
    'Dose of their own medicine, A' 70
    Easter Rising (1916) 66
    editorial (August 1923) 66
    electoral register, concerns about 72
    Fourth Dáil 74
    General Election (1923) 67–8
    Kerryman editorials, replication of 66
    'Notes' columnists 65
    'Tralee Topics' columnist 69
Limerick 40, 89, 94, 123
    Cumann na nGaedheal candidates 83
    Farmers' Party candidate 42
    Labour Party meeting 51
    republican candidates 83
Limerick City 89, 93, 123, 128
Limerick East 89
Listowel, County Kerry 57, 58
Little, P.J. 30
Little Treaty of Versailles (1919) 119
Lloyd George, David 47
L'Oeuvre (newspaper) 120
Logue, Michael, Cardinal 48, 78, 80, 84, 85
London Agreement (1924) 117
Longford South, by-election (1917) 24, 127
Longford-Westmeath
    anti-treatyite vote (1923) 24
    Cumann na nGaedheal 14, 15, 17, 24, 84
    election rally, Cumann na nGaedheal 20
    Farmers' Party 84, 127
    General Election (1922) results 84
    General Election (1923) results 84
    Labour Party 84, 123
    pro-treaty vote, drop in 129
Louth-Meath 123
Lynch, Fionán 16, 67, 68, 72, 73
Lynch, Liam 28, 31, 32
Lynch, Revd Peter 83
Lyne, Revd T.J. 83
Lynn, Kathleen 30, 33–4, 62, 93, 94, 128, 129
Lyons, Marian and Ó Corráin, Daithí, *Irish Revolution* series 6
Lyons, Thomas W. 102, 104, 105, 107–8
Lyttleton, Adrian 115

McAndrew, P.J. 17–18
McArdle, Delia 95
McCabe, Michael 78
McCabe, William 45
McCarthy, Alan 63
McCarthy, Thomas 83
McCullagh, David, *De Valera Rise and Rule* 6

McDermott, Revd John 82
McDonnell, Vera 30
McEllistrim, Thomas 68, 72
MacEoin, General Seán 17, 24, 129
McGarrity, Joseph 100
McGarry, Seán 24
McGrath, Joseph 17, 82, 126
McGrath, Michael 14
McGuinness, Frank 20, 24, 127
McGuinness, Joseph 24, 127
McInerney, Revd John 83
McKelvey, Joe 11
Macken, Revd 14
Macken, Thomas F., Dean 83
McKenna, Patrick (Paddy) 24, 43, 127
Mackinnon, Major John 64
McMahon Coffey, Brian 70
McMahon, Nora 95
McNamara, Maedhbh and Mooney, Paschal 96
MacNeill, Eoin 13, 21, 47, 79
    General Election (1923) 25, 36, 82, 123
    Minister for Education 16, 82
    selected as candidate (1923) 16, 18, 83
McSweeney, Jeremiah 71
MacSwiney, Mary 31, 32
    General Election (1923) 89, 93, 94, 123, 128
    speech in Tralee 69–70
Maguire, Hugh 82
Mair, Peter 131
Malone, Simon 17
Mangan, John 103
Mansfield, Edward 59
Mansion House, Dublin
    conference of women 41
    Cumann na nGaedheal's public launch 1, 11, 82
Markievicz, Constance, Countess 31, 62, 88, 93, 94
    first-ever female MP (and TD) 88
    General Election (1918) 123
    General Election (1922) 89, 123
    General Election (1923) 94, 123, 128
    house raid 62, 129
    as Minister for Labour 88
Matteotti, Giacomo 116
Maynooth
    plenary synod (1900) 85
    plenary synod (1927) 85–6
Mayo
    anti-treaty IRA and 79
    Cumann na nGaedheal 13, 14, 17, 82
Mayo North 14, 18, 82, 126, 127
Mayo South 20, 126
Meath 21, 127
Meath Farmers' Union 39–40
Meehan, Ciara 23
    Cosgrave Party, The 6

Meehan, Ciara et al., *Formative Decade, A. Ireland in the 1920s* 6
Mellows, Barney 83
Mellows, Liam 11, 28, 37
Military Service Pensions Collection (MSPC) 95, 114
modernisation of Ireland 38, 39, 46, 47, 49
Mohr, Thomas 92
Monaghan 21, 82, 94, 126, 127
Moran, Canon Patrick 83
Morrisroe, Patrick, Bishop of Achonry 79
Mortished, Ronald 44
Moss, Warner 18
Moylan, Sean 106
Moynihan, Seán 64
Mulcahy, Richard 17, 24, 36, 37
    General Election (1923) 94, 127
    Kerry Command and 64
    Minister for Defence 110
    newspapers, views on 52, 53
Mulligan, Revd Philip 82
Mullingar, County Westmeath 14
Munster 72, 124, **125**
Murphy, Monsignor J. 82
Murphy, Matthew 57, 59
Murphy, N.J. 61
Murphy, William Martin 52
Murray, Patrick 77
Mussolini, Benito 110, 115–16
    'March on Rome' (1922) 115, 117
Myles, Major James Sproule 127

National Army 22, 129
    British-trained officers 114
    Civil War and 78
    de Valera arrested by 36
    demobilisation 74
    Kerry Command 64, 67, 71
    Kerry Leader, suppression of 64
    Mulcahy and 110
    pro-treaty IRA veterans and 114
National Democratic Party 5, 122
National Loan 3, 6, 25
National University of Ireland (NUI) 16, 89, 123, 128, 130
Nationalist and Leinster Times 53, 55, 123
Naughton, James, Bishop of Killala 82
Nesbitt, George 13
New York Tribune 100–1
Newell, Úna 73
Newman, John Paul 114
newspapers
    advertising revenue 75
    Catholic clergy's letters in support of candidates 84
    constituency election messages 52
    Cork County, influence in 63
    Cosgrave manifesto 22–3

de Valera and 31–2
electioneering activity 55
General Election (1923) 9, 63
influence of 2, 9, 52, 53, 63, 75
'Letters to the Editor' section 48, 53
local newspapers 63
morning dailies, total sales of 52
national newspapers 52, 55, 63
partition and 45
political status quo, support for 75
pro-treatyites, support for 18, 31, 54, 65–6
provincial newspapers 52, 55
public meetings/rallies 18, 51, 52
readership 75
regional newspapers 63
revolutionary period and 63
see also advertising; Kerry newspapers
Neystrom, Paul H. 53
Nolan, Daniel 65, 66
Nolan, John 83
Nolan, Thomas 65, 66

oath of allegiance 59
de Valera and 35, 58
Labour Party and 57, 128
Sinn Féin and 20, 42, 131
O'Brennan, Lily 95
O'Brien, William 42
O'Callaghan, Donal, Special Envoy 107, 108
O'Callaghan, Kathleen 89, 90–1, 93, 94, 123, 128
Ó Gaora, Colm 83
O'Carroll, Eamonn 44
O'Connell, Daniel 85
O'Connell, Kathleen 35
O'Connor, Batt 13
O'Connor, Eamon 64
O'Connor, R.H. 62
O'Connor, Rory 11, 28, 29, 37
O'Connor, Thomas D. 107
O'Dea, Louis 83
O'Donnell, Thomas 68, 127
O'Donoghue, Martin, *Legacy of the Irish Parliamentary Party, The* 6
O'Donoghue, Thomas (Tomás) 68, 72
Ó Drisceoil, Dónal, *Atlas of the Irish Revolution* 75
O'Farrelly, Agnes 128
Ó Fathartaigh, Mícheál and Weeks, Liam 111
Birth of a State: The Anglo-Irish Treaty 6
Treaty, The: Debating and Establishing the Irish State 6
Offaly Independent 123
O'Hanrahan, Henry 62, 129
O'Hara, Michael 14, 15
O'Hegarty, Diarmuid 35
O'Higgins, Brian 36, 82, 83
O'Higgins, Kevin 19, 48, 80, 83

death of his father 79
Executive Council 14, 79
General Election (1923) 24, 82, 124, 127
Minister for Home Affairs 79, 131
Oxford Union and 85
O'Higgins, Thomas F. 79
O'Higgins, Tom 27
O'Kennedy, Canon William 16, 82, 83
Old Age Pension (OAP) 74
O'Leary, Daniel 127
O'Leary, Revd David, Dean of Kerry 83
O'Leary, Jeremiah 103
Ó Máille, Pádraic 11
Omeath, County Louth 62
O'Neill, Eugene 70
O'Rahilly, Alfred 17, 24, 93
O'Reilly, Revd John 83
Ó Ríobhirdan, M. 70
O'Rourke, Bernard 82
O'Shannon, Cathal 123
O'Shaughnessy, Andrew 24
O'Sullivan, Charles, Bishop of Kerry 78–9, 80, 81
O'Sullivan, Revd Cornelius 83
O'Sullivan, John Marcus 68, 72
O'Sullivan, Revd P.J. 82

'pact election' see General Election (1922)
Parliament (Qualification of Women) Act (1918) 88
Parnell, Charles Stewart 21, 38, 69
partition of Ireland 1, 45
Catholic hierarchy and 81
Cosgrave and 21
General Election (1923) and 58
Labour Party and 45
newspaper coverage in Kerry 66
as a political issue 21, 45, 58
Pearse, Margaret 89
Pearse, Padraig 58
Pilsudski, Marshal Josef 119
Plunkett, George Noble, Count 30, 57, 126
Plunkett, Joseph 126
Poincaré, Raymond 117
Poland 4, 112, 115
Constitution of the Polish Second Republic 119
hyperinflation crisis (1923) 119
Polish Minority Treaty (1919) 119
politics
British two-party system 38, 42, 43
nationalist-dominated system 47, 48
perception of 41–2
postcolonial Irish politics 49
posters, Great War 54
posters, political 54, 55, 60–1
'Keeping Ireland Down' 55, 60, **60**
PR-STV system, effects on posters 54–5

Prager, Jeffrey 72
Presidential Election (1966) 27
Press Association 129
Prevention of Electoral Abuses Act (1923) 5, 61
prisoners
    anti-treatyite 33
    demand for release of 71
    extra-judicial executions 67, 113
    political prisoners 57, 85
    release from internment 85
Pro Cathedral, Dublin 85
pro-treatyites
    censorship of the media 54
    Cumann na Saoirse 90
    General Election (1923) 7, 58
    newspapers and 18, 31, 54, 65–6
    perception of 6
propaganda 1, 2, 8–9, 56, 129
    General Election (1923) 8–9
    impact of 62
    object/purpose of 53, 62
    symbols and iconography of identity 51, 57
propaganda methods
    booklets 52, 53, 55
    canvassing 18, 55–6, 62, 68
    circulars 54
    'free propaganda' in newspapers 70
    handbills 54, 55, 56
    leaflets **22, 23**
    newspapers 52–3, 54, 55, 70–1
    pamphlets 52, 53, 55
    political speeches 50–2, 53, 61, 62
    postal system 56
    posters **23**, 54–5, 58–9, 60–1, **60**
    see also advertising
propaganda themes 56–62
    agriculture 40–1, 56–7, 60
    anarchy 18, 20, 24, 35, 61
    Anglo-Irish Treaty 58, 59, 69, 72, 122
    constitutional issue 58, 59, 65, 67, 69, 71, 73, 74
    economic issues 42–3, 44–5, 57, 62
    educational reform 60
    everyday issues 59, 69
    finances of the state 59
    fishing industry 57, 60
    history/historical figures 58
    housing 60
    Irish language 60
    partition 58, 59
    pension payments 59
    public expenditure 59
    republicanism 57
    'Safety first' motto 3–4, 8, 11, 12, 26, 61, 77
    social reform 60
proportional representation (PR-STV system) 54–5, 71
Provisional Government 87, 90, 92
Public Safety Act (1923) 79

public speeches/meetings
    Cumann na nGaedheal and 18, **19**, 51
    Farmers' Party and 18, 51, 62
    interruptions/heckling 19, 21, 61, 70, 92, 129
    Labour Party and 51
    Sinn Féin and 18, 35–6, 70
Puirséil, Niamh 58
Purcell, R.J. 13

Queen's Hotel, Ennis 18
Quigley, Revd J. 83
Quinnell family 64

Ramsgrange, County Wexford 61
Ratepayers' Association 5, 122
Rathvilly, County Carlow 16, 51
Redmond dynasty 13
Redmond, John Edward 21, 127
Redmond, William Archer 21, 25, 59, 127
Regan, John M. 6–7, 81
    Irish Counter-Revolution, The 6
Representation of the People Act (1918) 88
republican 'government', de Valera and 29, 32
republican women
    abstention of women TDs 87, 95
    election campaign (1923) 95–6
    hunger strike 95
    imprisonment 95, 96
republicanism, Irish Free State and 9
Republicans
    abstention from the Dáil, effects of 45, 85
    Catholic clergy and 83
    constitutional politics and 85
    hunger strike (1923) 85
    Kerry candidates 68, 69, 72
revolutionary period
    gender roles in 98
    local studies 6
    scholarly publications 6
    transition to democracy 5, 7, 10, 121–31
Reynolds, Mary 96
Romania 113
Rooney, John 40–1, 82
Roscommon 57, 83–4, 126
Rower, County Kilkenny 61
Royal Irish Constabulary (RIC) 59
Ruhr, Franco-Belgian occupation (1923) 110, 116–17
Russia
    Communist regime 111, 113
    post-revolutionary 4
    White Russia 113
Russian Civil War (1917–22) 111, 113
    Red Army 113
Russian Revolution (1917) 9, 110, 111, 112, 113
Ruttledge, Patrick J. 35, 36, 126, 129
Ryan, Revd Innocent, Dean of Cashel 83

Ryan, P.J. 13, 14, 15
Ryan, P.L. 43
Ryle, Maurice P. 64, 66

St Flannan's College, Ennis, County Clare 82
Saorstát Éireann *see* Irish Free State
Scandinavian countries 46–7
Scanlon, Seán 14
Scott, Sir John Harley 127
Seanad Éireann 59
Sears, William 20
Serbia 114
Shaw, Patrick W. 20, 84
Sheffield Evening Telegraph 101
Silesia 112, 119
Sinn Féin
    abstentionist policy 2, 3, 5, 24, 85, 128, 131
    advertising methods 54
    'Advertising Problem, The' 53
    aims of 34
    anti-treaty stance 20, 21, 24, 42, 58, 62
    anti-treaty wing, support for 72
    Ard Comhairle 30
    Belfast Boycott 45
    cumainn, number of (1923) 36
    de Valera and 1, 28, 29–31, 32, 33–4, 51
    Director of Elections 35
    election campaign 18, 34–5, 50, 68–9, 70
    Election Committee 55
    election manifesto 58, 60
    General Election (1918) 4, 8, 88
    General Election (1921) 4, 88, 88–9
    General Election (1922) 4, 5, 8, 28
    headquarters, raids on 30, 61, 129
    intimidation of candidates 61–2
    IRA and 30, 33, 34, 130
    Kerry constituency and 68–72, 126
    Labour Party and 57, 59, 123
    modernisation of Ireland 39
    National Council of Sinn Féin 53
    nationalism 38
    newspaper coverage 68–9
    oath of allegiance and 20, 42, 131
    objections to the name 33
    Officer Board 30
    Organising Committee 33, 34, 35, 129
    party leader, promotion of 51
    perception of 30, 45, 46
    political posters 55, 60, **60**
    politics, views on 42
    pre-truce members 16
    propaganda 55, 58–9, 60, **60**, 62
    reorganisation 33–4
    republic, idea of 20
    split 1, 5, 12, 15, 27, 44, 90
    Standing Committee 29, 30
    status of the state and 42
    Treaty, opposition to 3

women candidates 41, 48
women candidates (1918) 88
women candidates (1921) 88–9
women candidates (1923) 93, 94
    see also General Election (1923)
Sinn Féin (newspaper) 129
Sinn Féin Party (1948) 34
Skelly, Michael 123
Smyth, John A. 83
southern unionism 4, 12, 17
Soviet Republic in Hungary 113
Soviet Union 113
Soviet-Polish War (1920) 112
Spain 114–15, 120
Stack, Austin 27, 30, 68, 72, 81, 124
Stamboliiski, Aleksandar 119
Stopford Green, Alice 90
Strandhill, County Sligo 62
Stresemann, Gustav 116–17
suffrage societies 88, 91
    see also universal adult suffrage
Switzerland 4

Takayanagi, Mari 88
Tipperary 43, 80, 123
Town Tenants' Association 5, 71, 122, 130
Townshend, Charles
    Easter 1916 6
    Republic, The 6
Tralee Board of Guardians 71
Tralee, County Kerry 61, 69, 70, 83
Tralee Urban District Council 65
Tramore, County Waterford 62
Trant, Revd Timothy 83
Traynor, Oscar 32
Treaty of Lausanne (1923) 118
Treaty of Trianon (1920) 113
Treaty of Versailles (1919) 100, 112, 113, 116
Trotsky, Leon 113
Tullow, County Carlow 16, 51
Turkey 111, 115
    Greco-Turkish War (1919–22) 112
    Greece and 118
    population exchanges (1922–23) 118
    Republic of Turkey 115, 118

Ulster 45, 106
Ulster (in Irish Free State) 124, **125**
Ulster Unionists 4
Unionism/unionists 53, 88
    ex-unionists 127
    southern unionism 4, 12, 17
United Kingdom (UK) 5, 87, 113
United States of America (USA)
    de Valera's tour of 19, 31, 81, 100
    Irish immigrants 99, 101
    republican organisations 99–100
    women's political rights 4

see also Irish Americans
universal adult suffrage
    Constitution of the Irish Free State and 18, 25, 87, 88, 91
    Europe and 4, 87, 91, 98
    General Election (1923) and 4, 7, 80, 93
    implementation 90–2
    Irish Free State and 2, 4–5, 18, 67, 80, 87, 90–2, 98
    Provisional Government and 87, 92
    United Kingdom and 5, 87

Venizelos, Eleftherios 118
Voice of Labour 42, 45, 46
    'Denmark: The Land of Co-Operative Democracy' 46–7
    editorial, General Election (1923) 49
    'Labour Confident about Elections' 42
Volunteers 16, 28, 34, 56
von Ludendorff, Erich 117
voter turnout, General Election (1923) 72, 93–4, 129–30
    encouragement of 50
    reasons for low turnout 72, 130
    women voters 93–4
voters
    abstentions 62, 72, 130
    apathy 12, 13, 14, 23, 49, 57, 72, 94, 128, 129

Wall, Nicholas 127
Wall, Revd Thomas 83
Walsh, Revd Daniel F. 83
Walsh, J.J. 17, 24, 25, 127
Walsh, Margaret 105
Walsh, Patrick 83
War of Independence (1919–21) 2, 13, 62, 81, 113
    Irish-American organisations and 100
    Kerry and 64
    MacEoin and 24
    veterans 14, 20, 114
Ward, Margaret, *Unmanageable Revolutionaries* 6
Waterford
    Cumann na nGaedheal and 13, 20, 21, 126
    election results (1923) 25
    farm labourers' strikes 13, 126
    Farmers' Party 127
    Labour Party 127

see also Brugha, Caitlín; Redmond, William Archer
Weimar Republic 110, 116, 117
Westmeath 14, 21
Westminster Parliament 88
Wexford 14, 25, 59, 61, 82, 83, 123
White, Patrick 127
White, Vincent 20
Wicklow 13, 25, 123
Wolfe, George 17
Wolfe Tone, Theobald 38, 58
women
    bereaved women, politics and 89, 93, 94, 98
    election candidates (1918) 88
    election candidates (1921) 88–9
    election candidates (1922) 89, 123
    election candidates (1923) 92–3, 127, 128
    emancipation 4, 38
    enfranchisement of younger women 87
    equal rights 88, 92
    female candidates, need for 41
    General Elections (1918–22) 88–90
    jury service restrictions 97
    Markievicz as first female TD 88
    national office and 88
    partial voting rights (1918) 88
    political rights 4
    universal adult suffrage and 4, 87, 98
    voting rights 88, 91, 94
    see also universal adult suffrage
women TDs
    Fourth Dáil (1923) 7, 9, 87
    political dynasties, reliance on 98
    republican women, abstentionist policy and 87, 95
    Third Dáil (1922) 89
women voters 9, 23, 87, 128
    Cumann na nGaedheal and 23–4, 48
    electorate, percentage of 93
    General Election (1923) 93–5
    partisan appeals to 93
women's rights 91
    Article (3) of the Constitution 92, 98
    legislative reforms restricting 96, 97, 98
Wyse Power, Jennie 13, 19, 30, 34, 90, 96–7

Yeats, W.B., *Nineteen Hundred and Nineteen* 112
Yugoslavia 114